Resolving Conflict
with Justice and Peace

Resolving Conflict
with Justice and Peace

Charles R. McCollough

The Pilgrim Press
New York

Scripture quotations are form the New Revised Standard Version Bible, copyright 1989, Division of Christian Education of the National Council of the Churches of Christ in the United States of American, and are used by permission.

Cover and interior design by Cindy Dolan. The relief sculpture on the cover is a photograph of the Just Peace Award given to outstanding activists at the General Synod of the United Church of Christ. It was sculpted by Charles R. McCollough.

Library of Congress Cataloging-in-Publication-Data
McCollough, Charles R., 1934–
    Resolving conflict with justice and peace / Charles R. McCollough ; commissioned by Office for Church in Society, United Church of Christ.
        p. cm.
    Includes bibliographical references.
    ISBN 0-8298-0870-1 : $14.95
    1. Church controversies. 2. Conflict management—Religious aspects—Christianity. I. United Church of Christ. Office for Church in Society. II. Title.
BV652.9.M35   1990
253—dc20   90-7869

Printed in the United States of America.
10 9 8 7 6 5 4 3 2 1

The Pilgrim Press, 475 Riverside Drive, New York, NY 10115.

Contents

Foreword

Conflict is inevitable in a world where people are different. But conflict does not have to become violent, nor result in a court battle or a split church. Rather conflict is an inevitable part of life that enables new ideas, creativity and all the richness of a diverse society. The issue is how to keep conflict creative rather than destructive.

As President of the United Church of Christ, I am concerned that our church and religious institutions teach us how to deal with conflict constructively and help us overcome the fear of conflict. It seems obvious to me that religious groups would be on the forefront of such peacemaking programs.

This book, *Resolving Conflict with Justice and Peace*, tells us why and shows how believers can manage conflict creatively. Although it is full of humorous stories of church conflicts over social issues, it also gives a no-nonsense analysis of the barriers to conflict management with a careful study of power and of conflict resolution in other cultures.

It also presents a step-by-step course on how to help all of us keep conflict constructive. It helps us overcome our fear of conflict as we move toward shaping a society of peace with justice. I enthusiastically support the use of this book because it helps to make the constructive resolution of conflict a part of everyday experience in the church and in society.

PAUL H. SHERRY

Preface

- "Why can't I handle conflict better?"
- "Can't we avoid a church fight?"
- "Won't the peace issue split the church?"
- "Why is it so hard to get the church to talk about and be active in peace and justice issues?"

Church people asked this author such questions often because my ministry has been about such conflictive issues. I was supposed to have good answers to them. I came up with what I thought were many biblically sound and theologically profound answers. Yet many people found my wisdom resistible. The questions persist.

Church folk usually rate spiritual peace at the top of the church's agenda and social action near the bottom like an unwanted cousin or even a foreign enemy. One reason for this ranking is the fear of conflict in the church. Another, deeper reason is that some people do not like conflict in the church or anywhere else in their lives. I know, I'm one of them. I avoid conflict. I like quiet and harmony. I am one of those introverts who would rather endure an obnoxious person than cause a ruckus.

We introverts may like to compete at work, in debate, or in sports. That is conflict, but it is conflict with clear, accepted rules, and with referees to enforce the rules. Everything is in order. Our attitude is: avoid fights whenever possible. If it is not possible to avoid a fight, then win it; at all costs, win. This avoid-or-win approach to fights has its rewards. We may stay out of trouble for a while by avoidance or we may savor a righteous victory or defeat for a while, but the avoid-or-win approach to fights is only fun for a while. And the cost is high in the long run. Avoidance or suppression is really an attack on oneself. Winning a fight by whatever means usually results in residual fallout that comes around again to haunt us; and neither avoidance or winning at all costs is the high calling we hear from the Bible.

There must be a better way to handle conflict. That is what this book is about: resolving conflict, especially around justice and peace issues in the church. The book focuses on limited parts of this great problem of conflict resolution. The focus is on fights. By fights I mean destructive conflicts with few limits as opposed to contests, challenges, creative nudges or problems to solve that do have accepted boundaries. Conflicts are essential to life, but boundless, destructive fights destroy life. This book tries to turn destructive fights into constructive conflicts that provide the energy for creativity and for life.

Of course there are plenty of books on peacemaking and conflict resolution. They are usually divided between theoretical works and practical, how-to manuals. This book tries to do both so that the reader will know both why and how to resolve conflict.

Also, this book is about resolving destructive fights in a just way so that powerless people do not lose in a mediation session. It is not a book on peace at any price whereby the powerful use "peacemaking" as a way to control the powerless. Nor is it about coercion, that is legal or illegal force as a means of peacekeeping. This book is about resolving conflicts after the powerless are empowered to negotiate a fair resolution and it is before coercive forces are called in to "keep the peace." It is focused on resolving conflicts between disputants after they are relatively balanced in power but before the lawyers or the marines are called in to force a resolution.

In addition, this book begins with a theological foundation and assumes that the church as an institution has enormous potential for conflict resolution ministries. To be sure, the church often avoids conflict. Yet the church has highly developed resources in resolving conflicts between God and human beings and between our various selves that do battle regularly within our individual souls. The church also has resources to resolve conflicts between individuals on an interpersonal level. But the resources virtually run out when it comes to social justice and peace issues, that is resolving conflicts within or between groups of people.

This book intends to build on the church's strengths, the rich resources of private and spiritual peacemaking, which we do rather well in the church. Instead of posing spirituality over against social justice and peace (which is self-defeating, and bad theology as well), we will expand on the church's developed abilities on the personal and spiritual level. We will set out a theory in Part One and a practical design in Part Two that builds on spiritual and personal conflict resolution, but takes it further into intergroup conflict resolution.

Finally, this book presents many real disputes, stories or cases of conflicts to enable the reader to practice conflict resolution even in Part One on theory. The reason for this story approach is that the creative resolution of conflict is relatively easy to learn in theory. It is difficult to practice. Stories help us feel our way into how conflicts can be resolved. The stories here are, like most stories, simplified and selected aspects of the complex confusion of real life. Most of the names and some of the sequences and circumstances have been changed. Some real names are kept when they reflect positively on the people involved. But on the whole they are recreated narratives, especially the trials of the Reverand Buford Beasley.

Acknowledgments

The Office for Church in Society, United Church of Christ (UCC) commissioned this book to help empower churches to work effectively for justice and peace. In its book, A Just Peace Church, the UCC called for a new way of dealing with conflict beyond the three classical Christian positions of crusading, absolute pacifism and just war. This is a beginning response to that call. However, the book is for all churches, not only the UCC.

This book is indebted to many people in other denominations. High on the list are friends at the Mennonite Conciliation Service: Ron Kraybill, John Paul Lederach and Alice Price who were most generous with their time and the use of their library.

Others who made this work possible are Yvonne Delk, whose life models conflict resolution and my wife, Carol McCollough and my brother, George McCollough, who tirelessly mediated my conflicts with a word processor. I owe much to ideas of mediators from whom I borrowed extensively. I tried to give a longer-than-usual reference to these works in the Annotated Bibliography. But none of these people can be held accountable for what I did with their ideas.

Finally, I am indebted to the members of two of my own local churches, Christ Congregation (UCC and American Baptist) and Barrington Congregational Church (UCC) who tired out the contents of this book before and after it was written.

Part One

What Is Conflict and Its Resolution?

CHAPTER 1

Framing the Subject of Conflict Resolution

Kathy, Ted, and the Flying Omelet

Kathy's son, Ted, was a rambunctious thirteen-year-old. Ted's moods swung rapidly from sullenness to exuberance. Feeling excited, Ted would sometimes playfully hit his mother on the back. Kathy also had mixed, changing emotions. She liked the attention and affection her son gave her with these light punches, but they also irritated her and began to hurt as Ted grew stronger.

Kathy's irritation increased until she became angry at Ted's hitting habit. Unsure about her feelings, or how to tell him to stop, she suppressed her anger and said nothing. One evening, after she'd had an especially hard day, Ted approached her from behind and poked her while she was in the middle of turning an omelet. Instantly she swung around, trying to hit him with the spatula. She missed with this weapon, but her screaming words hit home: "Don't you everrr touch me again, ever, ever. Can't you see I'm handling a hot pan, you brainless jerk! And come back here and pick up these eggs off the floor or I'll knock your block off and you'll go to bed for the rest of your life! You . . ."

A sullen quiet hung over the meal, and for the rest of the evening Ted felt demolished by her rage. Kathy felt guilty and ashamed for overreacting. How could this conflict have been handled better? Have you ever . . .

- wished you had controlled an explosion of your anger?
- wished you had just the right words to defend yourself against an attack?
- wished you had given someone a "piece of your mind"?
- feared you would explode if you said anything at all, so you endured?
- felt you gave in too much to a salesperson?
- felt you were too harsh to a friend?
- wished you had not compromised so much in an argument?
- ignored a person you did not like in order to avoid a fight?
- wondered what the Bible says about your conflicts?
- thought you would leave church rather than enter a church fight?

- struggled long and hard on a social issue and lost?
- won a small victory on a social issue, but were not sure why?
- faced a conflict and reached a solution and reconciled a friendship?

All these things happen to most of us. Who does not wish that he or she could deal better with difficult situations, but sometimes feels inadequate or fears making it worse? Such feelings are as natural as conflict itself. The usual ways we deal with conflict are natural too: we avoid it, try with force to win, or try to cut our losses by compromise or accommodation and hope the conflict will go away. Kathy followed her natural instincts, first to avoid conflict, then to use excessive force. Reason got shelved.

Kathy was trapped because she was not clear about her feelings and what she really needed. Nor was she skilled in calmly making those feelings and needs known to Ted, even if she had been clear about them. The conflict could have been resolved like this:

Resolution

Kathy could have asked herself what her feelings really were and what they indicated that she needed. What did she feel? She felt fear of losing affection and she felt hurt from the punches. What did she need? More affection and fewer punches. So she could have said clearly and calmly to Ted exactly what her feelings and needs were, as, for example: "Ted, when you hit me I appreciate your attention, but you are getting stronger and it's beginning to hurt. Let's try hugging more rather than hitting." She hugs him. It works. *A key rule for resolving conflict is knowing yourself, your feelings, and your needs.*

This book is about facing conflict as a positive and natural part of daily life, understanding how conflict works, and training ourselves to respond constructively to it. Such constructive response is not natural, but it's possible. Resolving conflict constructively is a learnable skill. Although it is not natural, constructive resolution can become second nature to us, replacing fear and violence. Indeed, we can learn to welcome conflict as a friendly, constructive challenge to becoming better, stronger persons.

A first step in understanding conflict is to measure the broad scope of conflict resolution and clarify on what aspect of it we will focus. Kathy's and Ted's conflict was between two people. But conflict is pervasive, is constant, and is present on every level of daily life: individual, interpersonal, intragroup (for example, church, community conflict), and intergroup (for example, international conflict).

This book will focus on a particular aspect of conflict, that is, how churches and church people deal with conflict arising from involvement in social issues. But this focus needs to be put into a broader perspective of conflict because these levels are all tied together. Our next example is of a personal or internal conflict over a social issue in the life of the Reverend Buford Beasley, pastor of Old First United Church.

Reverend Beasley's Battle for His Soul

Buford Beasley struggled hard with the decision to commit civil disobedience and consequently go to jail. He had followed the news about the warfare in Central America for a long time. The negative parallels to the Vietnam War were obvious to him. They boiled down to a continuing history of his country bullying a tiny country by sponsoring general mayhem in the name of abstractions like "national interest" and "anticommunism." Moral issues, of which he considered himself a guardian, played no useful part in these policies.

He had done his civic duties of voting, letter-writing, and visiting his congressional representative to protest the involvement. But all his efforts did not stop the government from sending military aid to promote the fighting or even seem to make any difference.

Beasley kept on writing and preaching against our involvement, apparently in vain. Many in his church were getting tired of it. But it seemed insane to him that anyone could believe that a tiny, impoverished country could threaten the most powerful country in the world. The only explanation he could find was that his representatives in congress were afraid of appearing like "wimps" by not "being tough on communism." And "wimps" don't get reelected. To him that was hardly a reasonable basis for their position on foreign policy. Then Beasley realized that he was not innocent either, for he helped pay for the war with his taxes. The thought of his taxes buying guns to kill innocent people kept his conscience busy late at night. He would doze off and dream of standing before the celestial tribunal on Judgment Day to account for his sin of paying for such violence. He would mumble a defense about having done his civic duty. Then the judge would reply sarcastically, "So you preached a sermon and wrote a few letters and then ate a steak for dinner? Send him down. Next!"

Then Beulah Schuman, chair of the social action committee, told him about their denomination's sponsoring a protest at the Capitol rotunda in Washington, D.C. It was to be a demonstration and service of penance for our Government's policy in Central America. There would be an opportunity for protesters to commit civil disobedience. The plan was to kneel in penance and prayer in the rotunda of the Capitol. This was not just a silent prayer, but a kneeling prayer that was against the law in this place.

He thought, Oh, no, God, please don't ask me to do that. I hate jails. I'm too busy to go to jail. I'll get fired from my church. I'll make my friends mad at me for acting self-righteous. I'll get molested and have to eat horrible sandwiches of bologna on stale white bread.

Other pastors he knew, and Beulah Schuman, committed themselves to civil disobedience. Now he had to make a big decision. The battle of his soul was on. Two parts of him were like two different people who sought two different goals. One wanted to stay out of trouble and make only the ordinary witness. The other, his conscience, sought to do what his denomination called "extraordinary witness," meaning civil disobedience. Such personal decision-making is the catalyst for personal conflict. Before one has to make a big decision, these conflicting goals can lie around peacefully in one's soul like lillies in a pond. But forced to a decision, they spring up like alligators slashing about, fighting for their lives. So with Beasley. The battle of his soul raged. How could he get some peace?

Resolution

He lay awake at night as two parts of himself argued over whether or not to do civil disobedience:

"Yes, you must do it. What will you say when the next generation asks you what you did to stop this war?"

"No; good organizers don't go to jail."

"Yes; it's your duty."

"No; it's a waste of time, something you are doing to prove your moral purity."

"Yes; you have tried all other legal citizen efforts."

"No; it will not even slow down a single bullet or make a bit of difference to the government."

"Yes; you must lay your body on the line, as the Bible says."

"No; it's a futile display of pride. You want to be a hero."

"Yes; a deed will make your words count for something."

"Stop!" said a third voice to these fighters in his head as he sat up in bed. "Get up, get a piece of paper, go sit down and process all this, and make a decision once and for all so we can get some sleep." Beasley obeyed the voice, got up, and found paper. Beasley asked the third voice, "Should I sit in the chair or on the couch?"

"Shut up, and get busy. What are your feelings about going to jail?"

"I feel . . . worried."

"Why?"

"I could go to jail for a year, lose my job, and make my church suffer a lot because of my absence, I think."

"What are you afraid of?"

"Of being humiliated and losing control of my life."

"What do you need in all this?"

"I need to do all I can do to stop the war without forsaking my other responsibilities."

Then he wrote down all the "yes" and "no" arguments. He knew he had to commit civil disobedience for his conscience' sake. But what about the other need, to be responsible and keep his job and care for his church? He decided that more research was needed to test this second need by discussing the possible consequences of a long jail term with the church. To his surprise, they all said, "Go for it." They seemed not only willing but ready to welcome his absence. He could not find anyone who would give an excuse to stay out of jail. So it appeared that he could meet both needs.

The conflict of two different goals clashing was over. The decision was made. He finally got some sleep. The resolution made what followed not so hard. The battle of his soul was over. He was at peace.

This story illustrates the *first rule* in conflict resolution: that even in personal, internal conflicts *one needs to take the time to identify one's feelings and then ask what one's feelings are signaling* about one's needs and interests. A *second rule is to express one's needs and interests.*

This was a personal conflict which has similar dynamics to interpersonal conflicts. Two parties (or selves) pursue different goals. When those goals clash, there is conflict. The clash of goals is one definition of conflict. Now let us look at another interpersonal conflict.

Fred's and Marsha's Bathroom Brawl

Fred and Marsha are a husband and wife who both have demanding jobs. Their mornings are hectic. Both shower, grab breakfast, and rush to work. Marsha usually gets up first for her shower in a room next to one with the bathroom sink. She usually does her hair and finishes making up at the sink as Fred showers. Often she reaches into the shower room for her towel or washcloth while Fred is in the shower. Sometimes she leaves the door open, causing a draft on Fred. At first Fred simply reached out of the shower and closed the door, not wanting to have a fight on a hectic morning. The third time this happened, he reached out and slammed the door, hoping that would get his message across to Marsha. It didn't.

Finally, the fourth occurrence came on an especially hectic morning. Fred felt the cold draft, saw the open door, and emerged from the shower like a raging Neptune from the deep, shouting at Marsha for her "chronic thoughtlessness" and "sneaky attempts to give him pneumonia, cause his death, and collect on his life insurance." Marsha screamed back, "You're crazy for exploding at a tiny thing like that. Go see a shrink! You're making me late for work!"

This is a typical conflict: an initial irritation builds tension, and natural ways of dealing with it are used—avoidance, then verbal force. But nothing is settled. The relationship is strained and the problem will continue. What would you do?

There ought to be a better, learnable way to handle these petty conflicts and the big conflicts as well. There is.

Resolution

Fred got a quick glance of himself in the bathroom mirror as he charged out of the shower. It was not flattering. It did not reveal his best self-image.

As he thought about it through the day, he realized how foolish he had looked. It was humbling. Humility has spiritual advantages well known to the saints. It enables repentance. It gives one insights unavailable to the raging fool. One such insight is a precondition to conflict resolution; namely, that conflicts can be seen as solvable problems, not only as battles to be won or lost against demonic forces from the underworld. One rages against depraved, demonic forces and becomes like them. One reasons with another human being and becomes more human.

So Fred's humility allowed him to see Marsha as a real person who had needs and feelings just as he had. If he respected her human needs, perhaps they could work out this petty bathroom routine that had turned into a brawl. He decided to try. After dinner that night he asked Marsha for time to work on it. She agreed.

He proposed that they clear the air, state their concerns, and see if they could solve this problem that was getting out of hand. Marsha said that all she wanted was to not feel like a child being disciplined and to get dressed with a minimum of hassle in the mornings. Fred said that he felt hurt when the cold draft kept occurring when he was in the shower. He felt that his needs were not respected. Then they threw out various ideas on how to solve the problem. Marsha said that it was no big deal—she could just shut the door. Fred said that she should not have to remember it that early in the morning. He could install a towel rack in the sink room for her, and she would not have to worry about the door at all. Marsha agreed to buy the rack and Fred installed it. Problem solved.

In the first story, the rule was: Know your feelings and fears. The second story revealed another rule: Take the time to ask what these feelings are expressing about your needs and interests. This last story illustrates a *third rule: A resolvable conflict must be seen as a problem to be solved, not a battle to be won or lost.*

Buford Beasley's Battle for Peace

Now we come to a more complex conflict. A church conflict involves many more people, a whole organization, and one accustomed to avoiding conflict. After all, we come to church for peace, don't we, not conflict? Or is there another option? Here is an example of resolving a church conflict.

Reverend Beasley went to a conference on peacemaking. He was inspired by the speaker and returned to his church determined to find ways to help his church get more involved in peace issues. This peace conference focused on nuclear war and called on churches to join in a national program to stop nuclear testing.

Beasley always believed the Bible preached peace, so he did just that himself the next Sunday. The congregation had grown used to such sermons, so Beasley received only the usual polite responses to it. He concluded that the general feeling of the congregation was: "Well, the pastor is doing his thing again. As long as he doesn't commit me to something, let him do it." Beasley decided to press his case more. The following Monday at the church council meeting he presented a proposal to vote for support of the test ban. He expected easy passage. He was wrong.

The obvious connection he made between the Bible, the church, and peace was not shared by all council members. Fred Morse said that the vote would "split the church"; Agnes Strickland said, "You're moving too fast"; but Beulah Schuman liked the idea and told Fred and Agnes that they should have listened to Reverend Beasley's sermon on peace and should read the Bible more carefully. That set off a countercharge of "self-righteousness" against Beulah. The debate got more and more tense. No resolution seemed possible. Mildred Morse, council chair, observed that the council was evenly divided on the issue and concluded that a "cooling off" period was needed. She asked that someone move to table the test ban proposal "for further study." The motion passed.

The "further study" could be a time to deal creatively with this conflict or it could turn into a very hostile battle which could, if not handled well, "split the church," as Fred Morse said, and lead to Beasley's dismissal.

How can this conflict be handled creatively? If we can figure that out, perhaps we can gain some insight on how to deal with larger conflicts.

Resolution

Beasley went back to his study after the council had tabled his proposal to support a test ban. He prayed for guidance and reflected on what had gone wrong. Clearly Agnes was right, at least for the council. He was moving too fast. This may have been a delaying tactic by Agnes, but it was a fact now. So the issue was what to do next. Maybe it was not movement, but fast movement, that was the problem. He was determined not to polarize the council or to make the issue into a win/lose battle.

The next day he talked to Beulah, who had supported the proposal. He asked her if she would convene a group to begin the "further study" called for in the tabling motion. She was glad to do it because she was eager to make her point for a test ban. But Beasley was more cautious. He explained the need to get more people on board. So he asked her to be sure to include Agnes, Fred, and others who might not initially support the idea. She also needed to get Mildred, the chair of the council, to officially appoint her to this task. The key was to enlist church leaders in solving the problem without polarizing them into hard positions.

Beulah got Mildred to make the study group official, pending final approval at the next council meeting. She called the group together to meet at her house for two hours. She made it clear that they would not decide for or against the issue itself. They would only decide on how the study would take place. Six people showed up, including Beasley.

The church valued open-mindedness and was proud of its reputation for "willingness to hear all sides" and to be convinced by reason. This led to the plan to hold a four-session course. One session was to be on "The Bible Speaks to Today," led by the minister. The second session would have a proponent and the third an opponent of the test ban. In the final session the group would decide on what recommendation to make to the council. Broad inclusiveness was stressed. So the course was scheduled six weeks away, with time for numerous announcements to the whole church and recruitment of fair presentations on both sides.

The course drew eight people. By the last session the conclusion was no surprise. The vote of the study group was unanimous to recommend that the council vote for the test ban proposal. The council did so with an endorsement to send Beulah to the regional social concerns task force of the church, with a call for it to vote as the council had done.

This story illustrates a number of conflict resolution rules. By slowing down the movement, but pressing steadily and inclusively, Beasley and Beulah were able to help people on all sides to feel respected and heard. *Respect for people* is a *fourth rule*. Also, the story illustrates a *fifth rule: Avoid polarization into hard positions* and keep the values of open-mindedness and a fair hearing for all sides high on the list. The church learned that peace and conflict are not opposites. Instead of avoiding conflict or falling into destructive conflict, they resolved this conflict creatively.

Mediation in Civil and International Warfare

The church and individual believers have many opportunities to be peacemakers beyond the church itself. Even in open warfare, the church can have a role to play. This is well illustrated in the part played by the All Africa Council of Churches (AACC), an affiliate of the World Council of Churches (WCC), in the 1970s in the Sudan civil war. Here a war had raged for seventeen years between the northern Sudan population of Arab Muslims and the southern Sudan population of black non-Muslims (both Animist and Christian).

Countless attempts had been make to end this war when Burgess Carr became the General Secretary of the AACC in Nairobi, Kenya. He had been a leader in the establishment of the WCC Program to Combat Racism, which tries to prevent white oppression of blacks. Now he was challenged to help end a war in Africa between nonwhite Africans who were Muslims and Christians.

The account of how the WCC/AACC went about making peace in Sudan is told in great detail by Hizkias Assefa in his book *Mediation of Civil Wars*.[1] Assefa is a professor and conflict resolution consultant at La Roche College in Pittsburgh. He documents the long history of this conflict and the many complex political, cultural, and military movements involved.

Essentially northern Sudan had dominated the south and was fighting an endless war with rebel groups in the south.

Assefa reports that Carr and the AACC contacted the Sudanese government initially to deal with relief aid to the thousands of refugees from the south caused by the war. Carr pointed out that the aid would do little good, however, if the fighting itself continued. So he asked the Sudanese government how the churches might help resolve the conflict.

Carr was allowed to call various groups together to see what could be done to end the war. In addition to the northern government there were the southern rebel representatives, called the Anya Nya, and various international legal experts, as well as the emperor of Ethiopia, Haile Selassie. After two years of complex negotiations the final negotiating sessions were held in Addis Ababa, hosted by Haile Selassie.

One of the final blocking points between the representatives of the two adversaries was where northern troops would be located in the south after the war. This problem in the negotiations followed a long, complex problem over the number of troops each party would be allowed to maintain. The southern Anya Nya representatives insisted that the northern troops be confined to their barracks. The northern representative insisted on the troops being dispersed to various points in southern Sudan.

Assefa reports that after a caucus of the southern delegates, they concluded that dispersed northern troops would be to the southern advantage because of the difficulty of transportation and mounting an attack. So the southern delegates agreed to the final point of dispersed troops. Assefa summarizes the spirit of the final agreement:

> Thus, around midnight everyone agreed over the military/security issue. At this point, Carr stood up and started to pray aloud, rather than silently as he had done whenever a major issue in the negotiation was settled. He said that he was crying as he prayed, and some members of the delegation were also crying. According to Niilus, Carr, and Bwogo, one of the Generals in the Northern delegation confessed that he was crying out of remorse for the slaughter between brothers all these years. Another Minister from the government's delegation lifted Carr up into the air out of exuberance.[2]

This settlement, called the Addis Ababa Agreement on the Problem of the South Sudan, would now eventually be ratified by each of the heads of the disputing groups on March 27, 1972.

Assefa goes on in his book to spell out a long list of reasons the WCC/AACC was able to mediate this conflict when government and international bodies could not do so. The WCC/AACC could avoid the problem of being seen as another government interfering in the internal affairs of Sudan. It could play a scapegoat role and thus help the warring parties to save face.

The church had valuable knowledge of the country through its relief work. It had the credibility of being politically neutral and could, as a church, raise moral issues—all advantages unique to the church which empowered its peacekeeping role.

Both the church as a body and individual believers can make a difference. Countless attempts to mediate an end to the war in Nicaragua were made during the writing of this book. One aspect of the peacemaking in the final stages of the war was made by former President of the United States Jimmy Carter. By a number of accounts his efforts throughout the night of the presidential election in Nicaragua on February 26, 1990, were critical. One account reported in the *Washington Post*[3] told how Carter, who led the official United States Election Observer Team, was able to help guarantee that the election results would be honored. Carter served as a trusted mediator between Daniel Ortega, who lost the election, and Violeta Chamarro who won it. Throughout the night Carter visited both parties. He first called on Ortega and heard his concerns: that Chamarro not release preliminary results of the voting early or show signs of gloating over the defeat of his party. Carter then went to visit Chamarro and he shared Ortega's concerns, which Chamarro honored. She later gave a conciliatory victory speech calling for reconciliation with the followers of Daniel Ortega.

Carter has been involved in such mediation efforts since he successfully negotiated the Camp David Accords between Israel and Egypt in 1978. He continues to find opportunities to mediate international conflicts as a dedicated Christian peacemaker from his base at the Carter Center in Atlanta, Georgia.

These two conflict mediations illustrate how two Christians, Burgess Carr and Jimmy Carter, have successfully acted as peacemakers in civil and international wars. In addition it is helpful to note that Roger Fisher, of the Harvard Negotiation Project and coauthor of the book *Getting to Yes*, helped both Carter at Camp David and some of the Nicaraguan negotiations.

The Harvard Negotiation Project, through the work of Cynthia Sampson, has documented how other church leaders have successfully negotiated international and civil wars in the recent past:

> The Pope mediated an agreement, signed in 1984, between Chile and Argentina on the Beagle Channel; . . . Quakers played a mediation role in negotiations during the Nigerian Civil War from 1967 to 1970 . . . Anglican Special Envoy Terry Waite negotiated the release of missionary hostages from Libya in 1985.[4]

We can learn a number of things from these efforts: First, the church has a role in conflict resolution on all levels, from the internal conflicts of the soul to international warfare. The question is, are we prepared in the church to do such conflict resolution on any level beyond the individual soul? This book is one attempt to help fill this vacuum.

A second learning is that conflict resolution will fail if some of the parties to the dispute are absent from the negotiating table. The party in the Nicaraguan war that was absent from many previous, failed attempts at peace was the United States. It has invaded Nicaragua a number of times in this century. Most recently the U.S. established, armed, and trained the Contra rebels. So it is only a fantasy to pretend that the U.S. was not a party to the dispute and could thus be excused from the negotiating table. Carter's official involvement during the election in Nicaragua apparently helped with that problem.

A *sixth rule* in resolving conflict is: *Recognize the church's opportunity to do peacemaking.*

A *seventh rule* is: *Get all parties who are in a dispute to the negotiation table.*

Summary

These five stories of conflict suggest many important things. Conflict is a constant factor in our lives, although its intensity and our personal involvement rise and fall. Conflict is many-leveled. It is internal, interpersonal, and cuts across all human groupings such as churches, communities, and nations. Conflict is unavoidable. It comes with life.

So *rule eight* is *accept conflict as normal.* But contrary to popular belief, conflict does not have to be framed as a win/lose, victor/vanquished, violence/pacifism, fight/flight, either/or battle. Rather, conflict can be framed as a life-giving necessity. Conflict can be seen as a normal and positive reality when we apply these general rules:

1. Know your feelings and fears.
2. Know your needs and interests.
3. See conflict as a problem to solve, not a war to win or lose.
4. Respect people.
5. Avoid polarizing or positioning.
6. Claim the church's peacemaking role.
7. Get all disputing parties to the table.
8. Accept conflict as normal.

These generalizations are only a few of the many present in other conflict stories in the next chapters. Each is an attempt to counter our usual win/lose instincts.

Two final points about the approach here: The stories told at the beginning covered a wide range of conflicts. They illustrate the very broad scope of conflict that is difficult to untangle. Deeply personal emotional conflicts are involved in all levels of disputes, from a personal decision, to an interpersonal argument, to international warfare or a church squabble.

This book intends to empower the church with the understanding and skill to resolve conflicts justly. By story and practice it seeks to help us overcome our destructive instincts for fighting or fleeing to gain the constructive power to survive in the real security of God's shalom, a just peace. We will next move to get our bearings and foundation from the Bible.

CHAPTER 2

The Bible
and Conflict Resolution

The Bible is all about conflict. But conflict in the Bible is set in a context of meaning that leads to conflict resolution. There is conflict from the most intimate laments of Job to the cosmic imagery of Ezekiel and the eschatological visions of Revelation. The Bible is about ultimate conflict and ultimate resolution. The Exodus resolves the conflict of slavery for the Hebrews, but is followed by conflicts in the wilderness. The history of God's people in the Promised Land is a history of warring kings whose reigns were judged more by their conflicts with God than by their battlefield victories or defeats.

Creation itself was seen as a great chaotic conflict brought to resolution, after which even God rested. More stories of conflict follow between God and Adam and Eve, which were resolved by their expulsion from Eden. Cain kills Abel, resulting in his life of wandering. The Bible deals with all kinds of conflicts, from constructive ones (Mary's wonderment at the Annunciation) to humorous irritations (Balaam's donkey) to disastrous floods (Noah's story).

Yet, however conflictive the Bible is, there is a clear context and meaning for all these conflicts. This meaning is the key to the resolution of conflicts. The meaning of conflict in the Bible is that God is God and human beings are accountable for what they worship. If they worship no other things or beings but God, then conflict can be constructive. If they worship other gods, disastrous conflicts result. Yet human beings remain free to choose whom or what they will worship as God, and they are, by virtue of that free choice, accountable for their choices and the consequences. These two points (the call to worship only God and human accountability) are stated and assumed in the First Commandment ("You shall have no other gods before me," Exod. 20:3). They are keys to the Hebrew Bible and are repeated by Jesus in the great commandment: "You shall love the Lord your God with all your heart, and with all your soul, and with all your mind" (Matt. 22:37).

Jesus' second commandment is, "'You shall love your neighbor as yourself.' On these two commandments hang all the laws and the prophets" (Matt.

22:39–40). We can add to this summary of the Bible's teachings that these commandments are the keys to resolving conflict also.

Let us build on these basic biblical foundations—(a) no other gods, (b) neighbor love, (c) human accountability—and study what happens when we do the opposite. That is, let us look at the consequences when we do not worship God, and do not love the neighbor or accept human accountability. These concepts give us the basis for how to resolve conflict. Three biblical texts we will study here help us focus these concepts deeply on their rich meaning.

First, when we fail to love God and our neighbor, as Jacob did when he cheated his brother Esau, we must repent and face this failure and the cheated one before we can be restored to a right relation with God. Second, when someone else fails to love us and begins a conflict with us, Jesus tells us how to resolve the conflict, as we read in Matthew 18. We have also in Jesus clear evidence that conflicts can be resolved, with a clear example that a human being: (a) can worship God alone, (b) can love the neighbor, and (c) can be accountable. The author of Ephesians asserts this basis for conflict resolution with unmistakable clarity. Once we were without hope for overcoming violence and chaos, "but now" hope is real. The dividing wall of hostility has come down. Let us look closely at these texts in the Bible.

When We Fail to Love
(Genesis 32—33:4)

The paradox of human nature is that we are accountable for our lives, but we also try to avoid being *held* accountable. The Bible says this in the story of the first man and woman. Adam and Eve hid from God rather than be accountable for their disobedience. Jacob practiced the same conduct when he hid in Haran from his brother Esau, after cheating him out of his birthright. After many years, Jacob could no longer resist God's call back home to resolve the conflict with this brother.

Jacob must face the conflict and get right with Esau and with God. The ancient story of Jacob's struggle to overcome this conflict is still enlightening for us because of its rich complexity. Jacob now wants to make up for his loveless cheating of Esau. But that cannot be done with a simple "I'm sorry." Rather, Jacob is required to go through a conversion, to offer his wealth and his life to Esau, to become handicapped, and to experience a soul-wrenching nightmare, so severe that he believes that he has faced God head on and has become a new person with a new name, Israel. Jacob's failure to love his brother requires him to repent, in the deepest meaning of the word, and completely turn his life around. This is often the case in conflict resolution. When we fail to love, we must repent and make amends. But the word "repentance" has been overused and made into a shallow effort to apologize and forget it all. A deeper understanding is required for true conflict resolution.

Once when the Reverend Buford Beasley was preaching on this passage he decided to consult an expert in the Hebrew scriptures, Professor Walter Brueggemann. The encounter itself was an experience in conflict resolution because Beasley was so easily tempted to simplify the complexity of what the Bible means by true repentance.

He said to Professor Brueggemann:[1] I am looking for the meaning of the Jacob and Esau story.

Professor: Well, first of all, the story has many meanings. I don't have a bumper-sticker answer for you.

Beasley: Good, I'll settle for more. I want a scholarly answer. What is the meaning of Genesis 32:1—33:4?

Professor: "In these chapters, the narrative resumes the story of the Esau conflict, left unresolved in 27:45. In that verse Jacob fled for his life, empty handed. Now by the command of God (31:13) he returns to Esau and the land as a prosperous man (32:5)."

Beasley: Exactly what I thought. What about his struggles with angels?

Professor: "These include a brief theophany (32:1–2), a fearful prayer (32:9–12), and an extended encounter (32:22–32). There is little doubt that the two theophanic episodes (32:2, 22–32) have had an independent life of their own and have been incorporated into the narrative . . . . But finally, our interpretation is not permitted to treat these pieces separately. We must discern the intent of the whole picture. We are offered the remarkable juxtaposition of an account of an anxious, human reconciliation together with one of the Bible's most imposing religious encounters."

Beasley: Precisely my sentiments. I am glad to hear that we should treat it as a whole. But how does Jacob's wrestling with an angel, or whatever it is, relate to his fight with his brother?

Professor: "On the one hand, Jacob is still estranged from his brother. On the other hand, he is blessed by God."

Beasley: So Jacob is both estranged and blessed. He is called home, but his estrangement stands in the way.

Professor: I think you are catching on. "Jacob approaches the meeting with extreme deference, the kind of deference appropriate to a wrong-doer in the face of the offended. . . . But something is at work here beyond Jacob. The power of primogeniture against which he had struggled . . . seems to endure. He cannot have his way by force. The formula of deference here is, 'If I find favor in your eyes' (v. 5), used subsequently three times (33:8, 10, 15)."

Beasley: Jacob is forced between God's call and his brother's possible violence. This moves him to humility and penance.

Professor: "Because of his shrewdness, Jacob can *plan*. Because of his vulnerability, Jacob must *pray*. In verses 9-12 [of chapter 32] we are offered the only extended prayer in the book of Genesis."

Beasley: So this passage is a double feature, with a fight on two fronts, with his brother and with God.

Professor: How many times do I have to tell you?

Beasley: Well, isn't this really a story of the whole people of Israel and their efforts to claim a homeland—not just two brothers fighting?

Professor: You are jumping ahead, but "the fugitive character of Jacob is understood as the exile of the whole people of Israel."

Beasley: I say it is the story of all fighting brothers and sisters, especially those who have taken the birthright of others: the rich from the poor, the oppressors from the oppressed, all the shrewd Jacobs from the guileless Esaus.

Professor: Please sit down and be quiet.

Beasley: Yes, sir.

Professor: "Jacob has to struggle with the stranger at Jabbok before he is blessed and renamed 'Israel.'"

Beasley: The stranger is really God, isn't he? But how can a human prevail against God?

Professor: Can you back off for a minute? "The stranger did not win (v. 25). But he did not lose either. And so he will not grant as much as Jacob asks . . . . Jacob has gained a great deal, but the name of God has not yet been given. (That must wait for Moses—Exod. 3:14)."

Beasley: Now he is Israel?

Professor: "When daylight comes, the stranger is gone and so is Jacob. There remains only Israel, who has not had a good sleep that night."

Beasley: That's for sure! And he is wounded too.

Professor: "There will be no cheap reconciliation. On the way to the affronted brother, Jacob must deal with the crippling (and blessing) God."

Beasley: Jacob is so scared of Esau, he dreams that he is wrestling with him and God. They are the same, right?

Professor: Wrong. "Not for a minute does the narrator confuse God and brother, heaven and earth. But it is seen that the most secular and the most holy overlap. Permission to be Israel and not Jacob depends on wrestling and prevailing. But it also requires meeting the brother. Perhaps it takes meeting the brother to regard the limp as a blessing."

Beasley: Well, what precisely is the relation between Israel, God, and Esau in a nutshell or on a bumper sticker? . . . Just kidding.

Professor: Do you have a Bible?

Beasley: Well, I . . . May I borrow yours?

Professor: Here, look up 1 John 4:21. What does it say?

Beasley: Let's see. It says, "Those who love God must love their brothers and sisters also."

Professor: "Love of God and love of brother belong together."

Beasley came away from his meeting with Professor Brueggemann with a much deeper understanding of repentance and how necessary it is for healing the conflict between Jacob and Esau and between all people. He got so much out of it that he did a whole Lenten series of sermons on it.

The use of the word "repentance" in this book intends to refer to the same rich meaning given it by the Brueggemann interpretation. Failure to love leads us to acts that require us to repent, as Jacob did. That is, we must do more than say, "I'm sorry." Rather, repentance involves profound struggles with oneself, with God, and with others, wounding, renaming, and making amends, as God required of Jacob.

When Others Fail to Love Us
(Matthew 18:15–20)

When we fail to love, we must repent in order to resolve a conflict. When others fail to love us, what do we do? Again the answer from the Bible can be summarized in one word, "Forgive." But that word "forgive" is just as complex as the word "repent." Let us examine its rich meaning in Matthew 18:15–20, a passage that also can be a basis for a practical guide to conflict resolution.

This passage in chapter 18 falls in the middle of the three main sections of the Gospel. The first, after the genealogy and birth narrative, is Jesus' Galilean ministry; the second, where this passage is found, is Jesus' journeys and teaching of the disciples; the third is his passion, death, and resurrection in Jerusalem. Chapter 18 itself is long and complex. It begins with the disciples' arguing over "Who is the greatest in the kingdom of heaven?"

Jesus instructs the disciples by holding up a child and the child's humility as the model of greatness and heavenly example. Then in all three Synoptic Gospels Jesus warns them against causing these "little ones" to sin. If you do cause them to sin, it will be worse than cutting off one of your limbs or going down to the sea bottom wearing a millstone. Only Luke shares the lost sheep parable with Matthew, but both make it clear how important it is to Jesus that the "little ones" be protected from temptation and also brought back and welcomed if they, like sheep, go astray.

By verse 12 the "little ones" seem no longer to refer to children but to anyone who is tempted and lost. Then by verse 15 it is your "brother" (*adelphos*) or as the New Revised Standard Version of the Bible translates it, "member," who sins against you who must be dealt with. Some ancient manuscripts do not have "against you" and only say "your brother who sins." Later, in verse 21, Peter asks Jesus what to do about one who sins against him as an individual. The instructions are clearly both for individuals and for the whole church.

Jesus presents concrete steps for dealing with conflicts with those persons. We should be clear that the perspective is not that of one who fails to love others like Jacob in the Genesis story. Rather, it is presented from Esau's point of view, from that of one who is hurt by another's lovelessness. It is not a matter of repenting and making amends to someone else, but rather of confronting the person who has hurt us and of forgiving that person. And it is not a matter of simply keeping a law. For Jesus pushes us beyond strict observance to deeper, more complex human sensitivities which affirm the offending persons while correcting their behavior. If we are to resolve conflict by loving not only our neighbors but also our enemies (5:44), then we certainly need some specific help on how to do it. That is exactly what Jesus does in this passage. He teaches us how to forgive.

One would think that such practical help would by now, after two thousand years, have been put into practice somewhere. But we are still trying alternately in our softheadedness to grasp Jesus' teaching about loving enemies and in our bullheadedness to ignore it completely. We must keep trying to grasp it.

Jesus' first instruction is to go directly to the offending person and point out what you think the person has done wrong. If the person listens, you have gained a friend. This step one can be compared to Luke's much briefer version. Instead of Matthew's "listen" (*akouo*, to hear, harken, heed, understand), Luke (17:3–4) requires repentance (*metanoeo*) before forgiveness is granted. Matthew is softer and much more elaborate. He reports that Jesus gives us three more steps to take. If step one fails, then take one or two witnesses with you (v. 16). If the offending person still does not listen, then take step three; that is, take it to the church. Only after three tries does one give up on the offender. In Luke's report the person must be forgiven seven times. In Matthew it is seventy-seven times. These verses in Matthew 18:15–17 deserve extended exposition because they are fundamental to conflict resolution and because now, as well as then, nothing is more destructive to church life and to friendship than a smoldering conflict that won't go away. So let us look at the passage in more detail.

Step One: Go Directly

Step one, in verse 15, tells us to go directly to our offending brother/sister to speak in private. The text is quite explicit about privacy, saying "the two of you" and adds "are alone" for emphasis. Note that Jesus does not say to go to a third party and start complaining about the abuse you have gotten. He does not tell you to start undermining your enemy in any way you can. Nor does he tell you to bottle up your anger and keep quiet about it or wait until sweet revenge can be gotten safely through passive aggression.

Rather, he says to go directly to that offender and tell him or her face to face, in private, with no one else around, "alone," what you think about the behavior. Then if the person listens, a wonderful reconciliation happens. Then, like Jacob, you have been united with a brother or sister, and you may also see the face of God in such a reunion. You will have resolved the conflict and will have "regained that one."

Very often the conflict is only a misunderstanding calling for no more than a brief effort to clear up communications and certainly less than an ecclesiastical council or a court case. For example, when Frank Simmons, a member in Old First United Church, noticed that the pastor, Buford Beasley, abruptly got up and left an important church meeting that Frank had arranged, it got to him. But Frank did not go directly to the pastor after the meeting and tell Beasley how little he appreciated his absence. On the contrary, Frank went other places with his anger. He let Beasley's offense be known to just about everybody else but Beasley. He told most of the members on the church rolls, some transferred members, and a few of them who were, by then, resting in their heavenly reward. He told most of the saints living and dead except the one against whom he had the complaint.

After many days and considerable speculation about the pastor's terrible habits and incorrigible behavior, Beasley heard from the grapevine what his high crimes were supposed to be: "wanton, willful, malicious disregard of church responsibilities." Finally, the accused got a chance to attempt to justify his behavior at a council meeting. But all he had to say for himself was that the expected array of food offerings had not arrived for the meeting and that he therefore had left the meeting and had gone out to the store to buy food so the guests would not go hungry. Then, as they met, he alone prepared the meal for them as if it had been laid out well in advance. No one knew where he was or what he did because no one (not even Frank

Simmons) had bothered to do what Jesus very clearly told us to do: "go and point out the fault when the two of you are alone."

Step one is: Go directly to the person who gives you trouble. Do not stop, do not pass the buck, and do not raise an army. Go to him or her directly, alone. This very often settles the matter, because very little face-saving, ego, or risk is at stake. You simply speak your piece, which can very well turn out to resemble the peace of God.

Step Two: Take Others Along

Step two is taken only when direct, private encounters have failed to resolve the conflict. Then the stakes are higher, because step two moves from two-party negotiation to third-party mediation. Mediation is necessary when and only when negotiation between two parties fails. Yet you still do the same thing, going directly to the offending person and speaking directly to the person. Only this time you "take one or two others along with you" (v. 16). The procedure echoes Deuteronomic law (Deut. 17:6 and 19:15), which requires at least two or three witnesses to verify a charge against someone before you start piling up stones for the wrongdoer's execution. (See also Hebrews 10:28.)

The instructions in Matthew are less like a people's tribunal or court case and more like a mediation panel. Even one witness may be enough. The witnesses' presence is "so that every word may be confirmed." Logically, that would include the words of both parties to the conflict. All words, even the offended person's, must stand up to the impartial third party. Also we can assume, because people take the time to be witnesses or mediators, that they are committed to a peaceful resolution of the conflict. Their commitment and impartiality are often all the additional ingredients that are needed to mediate and settle the dispute. Note what the passage does not tell us to do. It does not tell us to absorb the abuse even if the offender is bigger and meaner. Nor does it tell us to write the offender off as a lost cause or wish he or she did not exist anymore or gang up on the person or manipulate someone else into doing the attacking for us. There is not a word of instruction about storming out of the room and slamming the door behind you, or slamming the door in front of you for that matter. Jesus gives us absolutely nothing to console our hurt feelings, nor does he give us one single pet for our peeves.

Step Three: To the Church

Then and only then, after we have tried steps one and two and have failed, do we make the matter public in the whole church. That is step three. If the witnesses/mediators have not settled the dispute, maybe the pressure of the larger church can bring about a settlement. In each step the stakes get higher, more face has to be saved, and more risks assumed. But even in the Bible there is not a hint of doing what we often think of doing first, namely "take 'em to court." No, with all these steps in the attempt to resolve the conflict, not one single lawyer is ever called in. But taking it to the church suggests going through the authorized channels and following established grievance procedures. There is no hint of indirect attacks.

Step Four: Forget It

The final step is taken only if steps one, two, and three have been tried and have failed. This step is, "Let such a one be to you as a Gentile and a tax collector" (v. 17). Some scholars believe that this verse may have been added later, because it appears inconsistent with the rest of Jesus' words in this passage. Does it mean that the offender is condemned or excommunicated? This certainly would not fit with Jesus' words calling for infinite forgiveness, nor would it be consistent with Jesus' blessing of the house of the tax collector, Zacchaeus (Luke 19:9). Matthew himself is thought to have been a publican, or tax collector. Nor would this fit with the hope given to the Gentiles. (See Matthew 12:21, from Isaiah 42:1–4.) If the words are authentic, it would appear to tell us, as Jesus does in Matthew 10:14, "Shake off the dust from your feet," and move on when offending people will not listen to you. The conflict is not worth any more effort. Some conflicts have to be left to God. The conclusion that this phrase is a warrant for excommunication does not hold up. Rather, Jesus' final word is "forgive." Forgive seven times. Then seventy-seven times.

Conflict resolution requires us to turn around and frame the problem differently. That may mean the deepest kind of struggle with God and deference to those we have hurt; that is repentance. But when others fail to love us, and hurt us, we do not seek revenge or damages. Yet we do not meekly absorb their abuse either. Rather we go to them to face them and tell them how we are hurt by their actions. If they listen (Matthew) or repent (Luke), we forgive. There is one more key biblical word that is basic to conflict resolution: hope.

But Now, It Is Possible
(Ephesians 2)

Destructive conflicts begin in our failure to love and others' failure to love us. The last two Bible passages have focused on each separately. That is, we repent of our failures that have caused conflicts *or* we forgive others their failures. But most conflicts involve both our failures and others' failures, the need both to repent and to forgive by both parties. They are mixed together in everyday life.

Furthermore, most conflicts get even more tangled up when other, third parties get involved, quickly deepening conflict into lifelong feuds and warfare. Indeed, such warfare has been the way historians have organized human history—one war after another. The Bible itself reads that way in the books of Kings and Chronicles. It is not hard to become fatalistic when we see how persistently warlike human beings are. Most national foreign policies are based on the assumption that war is likely, if not inevitable. But the Bible has a different foreign policy. First of all, it does not rely on nations or on the nations' defense for security. Rather, the Bible seeks global security, a vision of peace and justice for all people. There is one word in the Bible that summarizes this vision. That word is *shalom*. To be sure, the word is much overused and misused today, but *shalom*, usually translated as "peace," is still a key biblical word for this vision.

Such a vision is considered so unrealistic, however, in discussions of foreign policy and conflict regulation among nations and within nations that it is routinely dismissed before it is ever even brought up. It is assumed in all such "realistic" peace efforts that human beings are a basically depraved lot who can survive only under a shield of fifty thousand nuclear warheads or more . . . maybe.

Of course, there is more than enough human depravity around to make this perspective convincing, with one important exception. That exception is the core of the biblical message. The word *shalom* actually became flesh, embodied in a human being who proved that it is possible to live in love, justice, and peace. This is the message throughout the New Testament. But the letter to the Ephesians is the most systematic summary of that all-important message that takes exception to fatal despair over human depravity. Human history may look as if it is all sound and fury signifying nothing, "but now" we have proof that love of God and neighbor can actually be lived out by a human being who is totally accountable to God. That's what Jesus did. If so, then we have hope. It can be done. We are not so totally depraved that destructive conflict is inevitable.

The Ephesians Summary

Ephesians summarizes a vast breadth of ideas, mostly Paul's, into this: We no longer need to live the terrible hostility that has been our painful lot. Now something new is given. It is now possible for humanity to overcome destructive conflict and to live in peace. In this passage it is a peace that transcends the battles between the Jewish Christians and Gentiles. The Gentiles are the sojourners who are far off, "aliens," "called the uncircumcision," and "strangers to the covenants of promise" of Israel, without hope and "without God." They are the *outs*. The *ins* are the Jewish Christians who are inside the promises of Israel, "near," "unalienated," "the circumcision," and "with God."

But now it is all different because Christ Jesus has preached peace (*shalom*) both to the outs and to the ins. The laws and the temple wall that divided the ins and the outs have now fallen down. We are reconciled in one body, ending hostility and bringing peace. It is not a matter of one side winning and the other losing. Instead of a victory and defeat we have peace without victory, because both sides win. Both are made into one new people.

Both are part of the household of God, like equal stones supported by the cornerstone, Christ. The household then becomes a holy place where we all live in unity. In spite of our differences, "there is one body and one Spirit, just as you were called to the one hope . . . , one Lord, one faith, one baptism, one God and Father of all" (Eph. 4:4–6).

The writer of Ephesians tells how to bring such peace and unity by framing our conflicts not as divisive problems but as "gifts" (4:11) and by "speaking the truth in love" (4:15) in the ethical exhortations in the rest of the book of Ephesians. Yet we still need help knowing where to begin, because the theological abstractions in Ephesians call for some daily experiences for people who don't make a profession out of theology. Let us look at two of the ideas that help us overcome conflict. One idea is the inclusion of the outs. The other idea is that Jesus and his blood have somehow made this all possible. A good way for us to get concrete is to look at our church life itself and the people in it.

Including the "Outs"

Ed and Marsha Turner have a relatively happy marriage.[2] But that was not always the case. That is, they were not always married to each other or happy. It is their second time around. Also Ed's daughter, Jane, by his first wife, did not adjust well to Marsha, his second. Not that Jane and Marsha did not try to get along. They did, but there were formidable obstacles. Jane and her dad had gone through a lot together after her mother died, and she had moved back home to look after him, giving up a good job to do it.

Then in came Marsha to change the old order. Jane moved out again but still lived nearby, visited often, and fought regularly with Marsha and her new ways that kept changing Jane's old home. Not that the fights were screaming matches. They were not—not on the outside at least. Rather, all the screaming matches were held indoors, inside each person's soul. On the outside they tried to outdo each other with politeness and favors. It was a cold, icy war. Meanwhile, Ed kept trying to accommodate and compromise: "We'll do Thanksgiving Jane's way and we'll do Christmas Marsha's way." Both were getting mad at Ed for causing the whole mess to begin with and for not ever taking the right side in the war.

Finally, Jane broke the iceberg when she exploded at her dad for his caving in to the "tacky Christmas decorations that made the house look like Sid Martin's used car lot." Unknown to Jane, Marsha overheard the blast and let her displeasure at it be known to her with a one-and-one-half quart flow of tears. Jane was speechless with embarrassment. She left not knowing what to do next, but she could not get over the bad feelings and the worry about how Marsha and her dad felt. So she called up for a session with Rev. Beasley, who by now had heard all about it. But he listened anyway as Jane explained how she really did like Marsha as a person and knew that the new order was here to stay, but the feelings would not go away.

Fortunately, just expressing them helped. All Reverend Beasley said to her was, "Tell this to Marsha." She did, the next Saturday morning in the old house in the old kitchen. Jane told Marsha how sorry she was and how she really did want to be friends. Marsha accepted her apology, and Jane and Marsha became new people committed to work at their relationship. "So he came and proclaimed peace to you who were far off and peace to those who were near . . . . So then you are no longer strangers, . . . but you are . . . members of the household of God" (v. 17).

This little domestic squabble is hardly comparable to the big battles of the early church over who was in and who was out in the current theological debate. All the theological ingredients are present, nevertheless: the battle between the ins and outs, between the old order (commandments and ordinances) and the new order, the hostility, the dividing wall, the end of the old order, the preaching of peace to both sides—Jane, who was in but is now out, and Marsha who was out but is now in. Also, conflict resolution in the household cannot be reached by one defeating the other. Both must win; and the only way both can win is for both to become new people. They did, even though they did not talk much theology to do it.

The people who are hopeless outsiders and strangers and sojourners can be included because we now have a new thing on earth. There is a way to end destructive conflict and achieve unity, and it is what God has always been drawing us toward. Now it is fully realized. That is one idea of Ephesians.

Proof Positive

The second idea we will focus on is that this unity and peace is possible because of Jesus. "But now in Christ Jesus you who once were far off have been brought near by the blood of Christ" (v. 13). What does this mean?

It means that war is over for those who really believe it can be. Those in power and those out of power now have a new way, a common ground on which to find peace. It is not now a matter of the powerful, who write the rules and the laws for their own benefit, finally enforcing them over the will of the powerless. It is not a peace lightly healed, a peace brought by oppression. Nor is it a matter of the powerless finally succeeding in a violent revolution by throwing the tyrants out. Before now it seemed that we had only these two options: tyranny or revolution. "But now" (the most important words in the passage), but now, the rules have changed. It is a new game. But now there is a third option. The wall of hostility dividing the ins and the outs, the powerful and the powerless, the haves and the have nots, has been abolished. The exclusive clubs are opened up. The promising deals have gone sour. The inside traders have been stopped. The old game of win/lose, winner take all, is ended. How so?

It happened like this. Nobody believed that it was possible for human beings to break the cycle of violent victory or the cycle of hopeless defeat. If they were attacked, they usually counterattacked violently if they could, and the cycle of violence and counterviolence spiraled out of control, even unto this day. The cycle of hopeless defeat went the same way, but in reverse. Victims who could not counterattack became habitual targets of violence and never could break out of the habit of losing. So hopeless defeat became a habit for the powerless, while loveless, violent victory became a habit for the powerful. What was needed was someone who could break both habits, someone who had enough hope to break out of the victim-as-target habit and someone who had enough love to break out of the loveless-violence habit.

That is what Jesus did, and that is the reason he is called "our peace" (v. 14). Jesus proved that it is possible to take all the hostility and violence, all the abuse, betrayal, misunderstanding, slander, and all the ugliness that human depravity can devise to hurt someone. He took it all and still refused to fall into the habit of loveless counterviolence or the habit of the hopeless, defeated victim-as-target. Rather than retaliate in kind, he lovingly forgave his murderers while hanging on their nails. Rather than fall into hopeless defeat, he hung in there with hope to the end. That is what it means to say, "in his blood," and "through the cross." So the hope that we can live in peace and justice is born. Peace is possible. We are not condemned to constant habits of violence and defeat, of endless, destructive conflict. The cycles have been broken. All we need now is the faith to follow the example. It can be done because Jesus did it. Now we have no more excuses. It is a matter of breaking the habits of loveless violence and hopeless defeat, for "he is our peace" (v. 14).

Here is a chart that summarizes this chapter:

Constructive Conflict
(a)No other gods   (b)Neighbor love   (c)Human accountability

Keys to Conflict Resolution
(a)Repentance   (b)Forgiveness   (c)Hope

Destructive Conflict
(a)False gods   (b)Hate of neighbor   (c)Denial of accountability

In summary, the Bible commands us to worship God only and to love our neighbor. Those commands assume that human beings are able, response-able, and accountable for doing this. It also records how often people fail at it. If we could successfully love God and neighbor, then conflict would be a constructive and creative experience. Since we do fail at love, conflict turns destructive and spirals out of control. So the Bible also tells us what it means to repent of this failure, this defeated hopelessness and loveless violence. It tells us that it is possible to love God and neighbor and that it is possible to forgive others who fail to love us. In addition, the Bible shows us that love of God and neighbor can actually be (has actually been) accomplished. That is, Jesus has shown that *shalom* love is not simply a future vision but is valid and possible "on earth as it is in heaven." These biblical foundations give us hope that peace is possible and conflict is not inevitably destructive or violent, that by building on them, we can make conflict constructive and creative.

CHAPTER 3

What Is Conflict?

Paul and Nancy, the Odd Couple

We will begin to define conflict by observing a conflict between two colleagues in a church. Paul and Nancy were ministerial colleagues in a multistaff church. Both reported to Harold Vetman, the senior minister. They worked together and sorted out who did what tasks under the general supervision of Dr. Vetman, who left the details to them. Vetman did most of the preaching, and left town frequently for high-level meetings.

Paul and Nancy did most of the calling, education, fellowship, and committee work. They had different work styles which complemented each other, at least at first. Nancy's style required frequent meetings to clear signals and make sure that she and Paul did not trip over each other. Nancy often asked Paul to meet to sort out details. She liked to get things pinned down. She pressed Paul for detailed plans and commitments.

Paul had less need to meet. He was confident that he could work most things out as they arose, and he preferred to work independently. After all, they had worked out separate assignments. He was responsible for confirmation class and adult Bible class, calling on shut-ins, and the men's group. She worked with the education committee, the women's guild, the youth groups, and the social action committee. Both did general and hospital calling, weddings and funerals, and assisted in worship.

Initially they found each other's differences challenging and stimulating, an opportunity to grow and a chance to learn from each other. But after a few months on the job Paul began to get irritated that Nancy pressed him to plan things farther in advance than he wished to commit himself. Both had hectic schedules and felt overloaded with pastoral duties. Paul felt Nancy's attempts to meet so often were her way of asserting too much authority over him, but he did not say this to Nancy. Rather, he began to be late or occasionally to miss their meetings. Sometimes he would forget; other times he explained that there were car troubles, illness, or weather problems causing his delays or absences.

Nancy got more and more frustrated. Since they did not meet to plan often enough for her, and because Dr. Vetman was usually gone or inaccessible, she did not know what to do. Then more serious slipups began to happen. Each thought the other was covering a luncheon at church. Nancy got a call from an upset parishioner asking why she was not there for the opening prayer. She rushed over, missing her afternoon preparation time for a trip of the social action committee that she was leading to a legislative briefing. She covered the luncheon but was furious at Paul.

Back at the office, she tried to reach him without success. Just before she was to pack up the van for the briefing, she got a call asking her to find Paul so he could meet with a couple who expected him to discuss their wedding plans. Nancy made two more calls and found him. She gave him the information about the couple, but he said it was his day off and the couple had misunderstood the meeting date. He would try to get back to them, however. Nancy complained about the luncheon mix-up. Paul said that he was sure Nancy had assumed that responsibility. Nancy then said to Paul, "Your irresponsibility has gotten totally out of control. You really do have a problem. I want to meet with you on Tuesday to iron this out." Paul tried to calm her down by asking what the matter was. She was so angry that her mind went blank. She could not remember details, so she just said, "If Tuesday is not good, Paul, you name a time. It's very important that we clear up our assignments. If we can't, I'm going to do it with Dr. V." Paul agreed on Tuesday at ten A.M.

How would you handle this conflict if you were Nancy or Paul? How can they develop a better working relationship? This is what conflict is: two or more interdependent goals, intentions, or work styles clashing. There was no quick fix for the conflict between Nancy and Paul. Seen from the outside, it might appear to be a petty squabble over different work styles that could easily be worked out so they could move on to important matters like the church's work for justice and peace. It was a clash of styles, but it was far from petty, and it was difficult to resolve. In addition it had begun to consume their energy and seriously interfere with their work. When Nancy finally got to the legislative briefing, she could not listen to what was going on because she kept thinking about what she would like to do to Paul. Paul felt constantly judged and condemned by Nancy. He thought he could never do anything right in her eyes, so why try? Just avoid her, he thought. Maybe she will get frustrated enough to leave. Both wished the other would either disappear or suddenly change, perhaps after a severe scolding. Neither was a real option, of course. Both felt hopeless about their relationship.

Resolution

Both Nancy and Paul sought help by talking to friends, but in the fishbowl atmosphere of a parish they had to be careful how much and what they confided to others. Furthermore, talking to others did not change the problem.

They felt hopeless because each was sure the other one had to change but was convinced that would not happen. They became fearful of each other and of their own antagonism. They communicated less and less and tried to avoid each other more and more. They were afraid that their anger would get out of control and explode in an embarrassing overreaction. But suppressing that anger and avoiding each other was exhausting and difficult to do in this church. They were stuck with each other and were finally forced to try to negotiate a better working relationship. It took three tries before it began to work.

First, Nancy got Paul to sit down on Tuesday and talk about the dispute. Nancy was ready with a long list of Paul's missed meetings and delinquent behavior. During the two-hour meeting he was on the defensive, trying to answer how each of Nancy's charges against him could be explained or justified. Nancy pressed Paul to agree to meet twice a week for scheduling and clarifying assignments, but neither felt satisfied with the session.

A second attempt at what can be called "administrative arbitration" solved an immediate issue, but not the overall problem. Paul failed to finish his part of the annual report on time. Nancy was editing it. In desperation, she decided to take the matter to Dr. Vetman. She arranged a quick meeting of the three. Dr. Vetman listened for a while and simply asked Paul for a new schedule for doing the report, then left for another important meeting. Both still were angry at each other and embarrassed at their own violent thoughts about each other.

The third try came after a mix-up during worship, when both stood up to give the pastoral prayer. Finally, a friend told Paul that their conflict was becoming obvious to all the church and that they had better resolve it, or else. This moved Paul to do something himself. He knew that if Nancy initiated a negotiation session, he would feel it was somehow rigged against him. He feared he would just get more of her condemnation. He resolved that matter by asking a mutual friend to mediate the dispute, tested the idea with Nancy, who agreed, and set a time for them to meet. A third party who they thought could be impartial gave him the needed courage to face Nancy.

They met in a neutral office and, guided by the mediator, laid out both sides of the simmering dispute. Nancy brought in a long list again, but did not present it because Paul went first and cast the dispute in terms of attitudes and styles of work. He admitted that his attitude could improve, but on his own terms and if Nancy would "back off." Nancy was ready for any sign of hope and consented to let Paul initiate their meetings. They agreed to communicate at least three times a week and to meet with the mediator in a month to evaluate their progress. Both felt they had finally begun to get somewhere.

This type of conflict is very common between work colleagues, roommates, and classmates. It is the interdependent, odd couple who are thrown together to do something and must go through adjustments of their work styles or end the relationship. Though sometimes humorous to others, such a relationship is extremely painful to the persons involved. Furthermore, when staff are involved it is quite destructive to the church and to its mission of justice and peace. If the ministers can't work together peacefully, it is hard to preach about peace in the church or reach out to others to work for justice. This dispute illustrates what a conflict is. Understanding conflict is a start toward resolving it. Here are some definitions of conflict:

- con = together, *fligere* = to strike; *con fligere* = to strike together
- "Two pieces of matter trying to occupy the same space at the same time"[1]
- "That condition which always exists when two or more interdependent parties interact"[2]
- The active striving for one's preferred outcome which, if attained, preludes the attainment by others of their preferred outcome, thereby producing hostility"[3]
- "An expressed struggle, perception of incompatible goals, perception of scarce rewards, and interdependence coupled with interference are the common element underlying all conflicts."[4]

All these definitions could be applied to Paul and Nancy's dispute. I prefer to use the simple definition of conflict as *goals clashing* because it is easy to remember, and it includes both constructive and destructive conflict.

Constructive and Destructive Conflict

Constructive conflict refers to the clashing of goals that challenges one's energy, creativity, or competitive spirit. It usually leads to constructive ends. Destructive conflict is also a clashing of goals, but it depletes one's energy, creativity, and the will to reach constructive ends. This happens when people are demeaned and attacked in a conflict. To be sure, there are points of overlap when a conflict appears to be destructive but turns out constructive, and vice versa. Some conflicts go on so long that no one can know their final results. But the distinction applies to most conflicts and will be spelled out below in detail under "Levels of Conflict." First, let us look at conflict dynamics.

The Dynamics of Conflict

The dynamics of conflict are the typical processes of interaction that happen in a conflict. I will present three views of the dynamics of conflict and then list the different levels of conflict. These views are helpful in order to grasp the meaning of conflict by understanding how it works from different perspectives. The first can be named conflict characteristics.[5]

Conflict Characteristics

When A clashes with B it is very common for both A and B to avoid talking to each other. Rather, they both go to C and D to talk about the problem and win support. Thus Nancy and Paul went to friends to try to solve the problem at one point rather than going directly to each other. In a typical conflict, indirect communication is evident. Note these other characteristics:

1. Indirect communication begins.
2. Personal animosity develops.
3. Parties focus on the last insult.
4. Polarizing happens.
5. Extreme positions are assumed.
6. The issues multiply and fuse.

After they stopped communicating with each other and went to friends instead (1), Nancy and Paul developed personal dislike for each other and stopped viewing their different styles as complementary (2). Rather than focusing on the problems, each thought about the insults they received from the other; for example, Paul's unreliability and Nancy's demanding attitude (3). Each person expected a solution to come from the other party rather than by changing their own behavior, thus polarizing into two alternatives: change or else (4). The more the dispute spiraled out of control, the more extreme the positions became (5), and the more the issues were expanded and became confused (6). Such dynamics have to be changed to be resolved. To name the dynamics is a good start toward their resolution. This list implies a parallel list of resolutions: (1) direct communication, (2) problem solving, (3) focus on root causes, (4) multiple possible solutions, (5) moderation, (6) specific issues. These will be spelled out in chapter 6, "Conflict Resolution.

Hard and Soft Approaches

Another perspective for understanding the dynamics of conflict is found in the popular book by Fisher and Ury, *Getting to Yes*.[6] The authors call for principled negotiating that is "soft on people, hard on problems." But in the dynamics of conflict other destructive things happen. Nancy was hard (tough and assertive) about the problem of the work relationship, and she was hard on Paul. Paul, by contrast, was soft (or laid back, even casual) about their work problem and he was soft toward Nancy, preferring passive aggressive behavior (forgetting, making excuses), which infuriated her. She was hard on problems and hard on Paul as a person. He was soft on the problem and apparently soft on Nancy as a person, at least on the surface. But underneath the surface, Paul was soft on the problem and hard on Nancy. This way of looking at conflict lays out three options. In a destructive conflict we are:

1. Hard on people and hard on problem, or
2. Soft on people and soft on problem, or
3. Hard on people and soft on problem

The clue to conflict resolution is obviously the fourth remaining option: be soft, caring, and respectful of the other person, but be hard, assertive, tough on the problem. For Nancy and Paul this would mean treating each other with high regard, listening carefully to each other, taking the problem very seriously, and dedicating whatever time was required to work toward a mutually agreeable solution.

The Conflict Cycle[7]

Now let me draw a third picture of conflict which I've found helpful in explaining its dynamics: the conflict cycle.

1. Goals clash
2. Fear and hopelessness grow
3. People are attacked
4. Adjustments are made
5. Conflict repeats in a spiral

When two people or two groups or two nations have certain interrelated goals, intentions, or directions that they are pursuing, they often come into contact with each other. Because they are different, they rarely fit together smoothly. When these differences become apparent and the parties perceive a delay or block in attaining their goals, a warning signal goes up. Because human beings have evolved by responding to these warnings with either avoidance or aggression (flight or fight), that is the natural pattern to follow. Nancy felt like fighting Paul. Paul took flight from her. Both feared the other and lost hope in the relationship (2).

Finally Nancy attacked Paul verbally, and Paul "attacked" himself in defensiveness but subtly attacked her with passive aggression (3). Temporary adjustments were made (4), but the conflict spiraled on (5). By understanding this dynamic process of destructive conflict we get clues for its resolution. There is no way to avoid conflict (goals clashing, 1); but we can replace fear and hopelessness (2) with courage and hope, and attacks on people (3) with attacks on the problem. More on this in chapter 6. We still need to define more terms. This is because there are different levels of conflict.

There are two general levels of conflict, constructive and destructive. In the early days of Paul and Nancy's relationship they experienced a creative, challenging level of conflict. Their differences challenged each other to grow and to solve their scheduling problems together. They experienced each other as helpful, and their differences as positive. They did sort out their duties and areas of responsibility. Even good-natured competition gave

Levels of Conflict[8]

CONSTRUCTIVE

LEVEL	OPPOSI-TION IS SEEN AS	DOMINANT ATTITUDE	COMMUNI-CATION	MEANS OF RESOLU-TION	LIKELY RESULT
Creative Nudge	Chance to grow	Excitement	Free flow	New creations	Win/win/win
Challenge	Problem/ mystery to solve	Stimulation	Cooperative	Support/ collaboration	Win/win
Contest	Competition	Determin-ation	Selective	What rules permit	Win/lose

DESTRUCTIVE

LEVEL	OPPOSI-TION IS SEEN AS	DOMINANT ATTITUDE	COMMUNI-CATION	MEANS OF RESOLU-TION	LIKELY RESULT
Dismissal	Invalid	Disinterest	Only that required	Avoidance	Temporary suppression
Fight	Enemy to defeat	Anger	None direct	Limited cold war	Win/lose/lose
War	Enemy to destroy	Righteous fury	Only to deceive	All out, few limits	Lose/lose
Annihil-ation	Evil to obliterate	Possession	Condem-nation	Suicidal ter-ror, no limits	Lose/lose/ lose

energy to their exchanges. Their dominant attitudes were excitement, stimulation, and determination to do their jobs. The communication with each other was free and cooperative before it gradually became selective. Their goal was to serve the church together so that both accomplished their tasks, with the result that they and the church benefited. I call that a "win/win/win" situation. Both of them, as well as others, win when conflict (diversity) remains constructive.

The means they used to reach these goals and results were to develop creative solutions through support and collaboration. Soon, however, their relationship became a contest, in which they followed the given rules or norms of behavior but stopped cooperating and sought rather to win over each other.

This competition could have been constructive, but as the conflict sank into a destructive relationship, they became more and more angry at each other. Dismissal is the first level of destructive conflict. It denies or tries to deny the other's existence. Then they sank into a fight level, which still had limits, as in a cold war. Paul and Nancy never reached the next level—war—in their behavior, only in their feelings. Here there are few limits at all; the only goal is to win for oneself. The last level is the most destructive, as it seeks to annihilate and obliterate the "enemy." Of course, none of their behavior reached this level, but neither could deny occasionally feeling this way.

When one's opponents are dismissed, they are seen as invalid. On a fight level, they are viewed as the enemy to defeat. On a war level, one seeks not only defeat but destruction of the enemy. In the last destructive level of conflict, annihilation, one is possessed with the passion to obliterate the enemy, which is seen as an inhuman, evil force. On this last level of conflict the only communication is curse or cosmic condemnation. It is so out of control that not only do both sides lose, they take others with them. This is a lose/lose/lose situation.

In a less frenzied but destructive conflict, as one on the dismissal level, the adversaries grow to disdain each other. Occasionally, Nancy and Paul felt righteous anger and even fury as the conflict reached the fight level. Their communication decreased from the minimum required, to indirect, and then to suspicions of deception. Both sought to avoid the other by means of temporary suppression. On the fight level, one seeks to win by making the other lose. The means are a cold, limited war. On the war level both sides lose.

Summary

To sum up, we have seen that conflict is a normal, natural, and good aspect of life. It is necessary for constructive, creative life. It becomes destructive when we reject diversity and try either to force our goals and intentions onto diverse others or flee from the diverse others and refuse to relate to them. Lacking hope, we fight, or lacking courage, we take flight. To put this dynamic theologically, by fighting we play god and try to control the diverse other. Or by fleeing we deny that we are accountable for ourselves, let alone for the other. When we play god we thereby deny that the real God is the only god, and we deny love to others and reject it for ourselves. We try to live without God and without love. We end up in a hopeless fatalism. We are in need of repentance, forgiveness, and hope, which are the bases of conflict resolution and constructive conflict. In this chapter we defined conflict as goals clashing and gave three ways to look at the dynamics of a conflict—the six characteristics, the four hard/soft approaches, and the conflict cycle—then we laid out seven levels of conflict.

There is yet another critical aspect of conflict. That is, power. We will examine power and empowerment in conflict resolution in the next two chapters. For power is a key issue, especially in the church's work on peace and justice issues. All these aspects of conflict need to be understood and analyzed in order to get at conflict resolution.

CHAPTER 4

Power in Conflict Resolution

Conflict resolution is a useful process for people who are more or less equal in power. But what about trying to resolve a conflict between people and groups who are not balanced in power: a parent and a child, an abusing husband and an abused wife, management and unorganized labor, a big company and a little consumer, or a superpower and its client state? It is a truism that the powerful do not give away power to the powerless. So is the reverse a truism: "No one can negotiate without power to compel negotiation."[1]

If that is the case, then does conflict resolution run aground on this problem of unbalanced power? For it appears that there can be no conflict resolution between people and groups where there is a power imbalance, and virtually every conflict has some power imbalance. Many experts in the field spend considerable time on this knotty problem. Some say that mediators of conflict resolution cannot be neutral because they must take sides and empower the low-powered party. They call for "power balancing" of this asymmetrical power relationship. Others insist that neutral impartiality is an absolute for mediators, regardless of the asymmetrical power of the disputants. For them empowerment of either party would corrupt their neutrality and usefulness as a mediator and derail the whole process of conflict resolution.

The problem exists on all levels of conflict resolution. The Interfaith Conciliation Center held a conference in 1986 to focus on the issue of resolving conflict in family disputes where there is a power imbalance. A report on the conference says, "Advocates for women and children in crisis . . . assert that the power inequities among family members in conflict present too great a risk for fair resolution." The conference agreed that ending violence has overwhelming priority because violence is nonnegotiable and that power imbalances between parties "can make mediation non-viable."

Mediation supporters stressed its value as compared to our dysfunctional court systems. Opponents stressed that mediation assumes "some level of equality between parties." And men very frequently have the "upper hand" in family power and "mediation offers little in terms of enforceability or follow-up."[2]

Power imbalance frustrates mediation in social conflicts between groups as well as in families. Dan Dodson of New York University put the problem bluntly to clergy, calling on them to *start* conflicts, not just neutralize them.

> If the *minister* is concerned with changing the social arrangements within this community so that more people enjoy more freedom, he must be prepared to induce conflict to secure the change. He must have enough perspective to understand that his preaching and his educational program will not change social arrangements in which people have unshared privilege.
>
> The church leader must also understand that the tide of social circumstance washes up on his doorstep a lot of confrontations in which he does not create the conflict, but must deal with it. Too often the church wants to play a mediating role in such controversies. It talks much of dialogue, reconciliation and arbitration. It wants to be the peacemaker. It strives for a neutral position on matters where neutrality represents moral compromise. It too often finds itself as the broker for the power arrangement of the community as it negotiates with the powerless.
>
> Religious leadership must understand that it is a disservice to try to stop conflict before it has restructured relationships. The only way the powerless can force the powerful to share power is to organize conflict-producing confrontations in which they can force their interests into the communal decision-making process. [Otherwise] . . . any group coming to negotiations without power is coming as a beggar.[3]

How do we deal with this tough issue? How can we resolve conflict if it appears that we must "induce" conflict when the two parties in conflict have unbalanced power? In a word, isn't *inducing* conflict and *resolving* conflict a *contradiction?*

In order to answer the question, we will begin with the story of Cathy. Then we will define power and analyze the dynamics of power in an unbalanced conflict so we are clear what we mean by unbalanced power. We will untangle the different levels of power and the social arrangements or deals set between the power abuser and the powerless. Our theses are:

Power is the ability to influence outcomes.
Power is exercised on many levels.
Power abuse requires powerlessness and vice versa.
Power is not zero sum.

After we have defined and analyzed the dynamics of conflict in an unbalanced power arrangement in this chapter, we will examine some steps for balancing power in chapter 5. Now, the story of Cathy.

Cathy Got Fired

Cathy was a schoolteacher until she quit teaching to have children. When the children went to school she sought to return to teaching but found only part-time work with no benefits and little pay. She substituted in public school and taught courses part-time in a college while she continued to seek full-time employment. But she could not find such a job in schoolteaching.

She had always been active in church and finally decided to take a part-time position as director of religious education at a church, in the hope of getting a full-time job in this area. In order to do well, Cathy took courses in religious education and worked hard. After two successful years at this job, a full-time position opened up in a church nearby.

The church had eleven hundred members. It was about one hundred years old. The minister had been there seven years. He was forty-four years old and popular with his congregation. He had a high regard for order in the church, for formality in the service of worship, and for his preaching. The organist had been there a year and was competent at the organ and at directing the choir. The position of religious education director had been empty for a year when it came to Cathy's attention. The position was recommended to Cathy by a seminary professor with whom she had studied. By now Cathy was almost desperate for a full-time job, and this job looked good to her.

It was not far from her home. The equipment was adequate and the building was well kept. The membership appeared to be friendly. The church seemed to care about education. When it was offered, Cathy eagerly said she would take the job.

The church job had a general, one-year contract, which said that she was obligated to give two weeks' notice if she decided to leave before the contract was renewed each year. It listed the pay and the vacation days and named the pastor as her supervisor. She signed it without much thought. She was thankful to have a full-time job.

She started work with her usual enthusiasm, but quickly learned that the pastor wanted more than a religious educator. He really wanted an associate minister to relieve him of some of the many tasks that were burdening him—assistance in worship, calling on the members, the confirmation class, and committee work.

He also wanted a confidant, because he was going through some hard personal struggles and needed someone he could talk to without fear of exposure. At first Cathy felt flattered at the extra work and his personal sharing. She assumed that both were expressions of the pastor's confidence in her abilities and her professional competence. It never occurred to her to refuse the extra work or ask for extra pay for these additional chores, or that knowing his secrets would become a burden to her and eventually make her vulnerable. After a while she began to see that all these extra tasks and listening sessions took time from her assigned job. She began to feel stress in getting all her work done.

Cathy, however, felt good about the hard, time-consuming job. She felt it was her mission to serve, and serving the church normally meant "going the extra mile." Besides, the pastor was complimentary about her work, even though he seemed to be preoccupied and hardly knew what she did. She felt it had made her day when he would tell her that she was the best educator he had known. She could put up with a lot when she felt valued this way.

When Cathy brought up issues to him that she was concerned about in the church, he would laugh and say, "That's the way things have always been around this crazy place." Then he would change the subject. If Cathy pressed an issue like the large amount of calling that came her way, or asked him which members should get priority in her calling, he would tell her not to worry, he would take care of it and let her know his decisions. But he did little about it.

Cathy asked the sexton one day if he would put her name on the door of her office. He said he would, but never got around to doing it. After two reminders, Cathy stopped pressing for this token of her identity. She considered that it was not worth a fight and concluded that perhaps she was only trying to glorify herself by advertising her name. So she settled for the title Director of Religious Education on the door without her name underneath it, even though the pastor, the organist, and the sexton had their names and titles prominently displayed.

The pastor's personal difficulties did not seem to diminish after she listened to him for hours. They seemed to get worse. By now Cathy felt drawn into his problems, but also stuck, because she was sworn to keep them confidential. She told no one, even though they interfered with her work. When the pastor's difficulties led him to be late or to miss an appointment, Cathy would make excuses for him or do the work herself if she could. After all, she said to herself, he has been good to me; he has taken me into his confidence, and I owe him this much. In addition, the pastor had suggested that they (he, Cathy, and the organist) were colleagues and should protect one another when problems arose. She felt a strong bond of personal loyalty to him and had no problem doing what he suggested.

But conditions continued to get more stressful. Cathy hardly had time to do her education work, and she felt it was getting cut short. Her preparation time got less and less and she felt that her performance suffered. Finally, she decided to confront the pastor. She asked to talk to him, but her nerve failed her when he told her that he was going to list her name on the Sunday bulletin next to his and the organist's names. He also was thinking about hiring a retired minister part-time to help in the calling and counseling.

The gestures only bought time, however, because nothing essential changed. In addition, the organist began to complain to Cathy about his poor salary and about the music committee's decision to ask him to start a junior choir and to be in charge of choir camp next summer.

Cathy asked the committee chairperson about the extra work given to the organist and was told that the organist was responsible for getting these extra assignments. The reason was that he had done such a good job with the senior high choir that the junior high youth wanted their own choir. Also, the camp committee was desperate for a leader and, being single, he was considered to be more available. When the committee politely told her to stick to her own work and leave the music up to the organist, Cathy felt embarrassed and ashamed of herself. She also began to feel anger at the organist who she thought had put her up to protecting him. Then the committee challenged the organist on the matter, suggesting that he might be causing trouble. He in turn got angry at Cathy and would not speak to her for weeks.

The pastor sought to relieve the tension between them by calling them together and clarifying the issue. By now Cathy, thinking she had gotten herself into a terrible quagmire, began to blame herself for all the trouble, even her attempts to help the organist or the pastor in their difficulties. So when the pastor told the organist and her to stick to their own jobs in music and education, Cathy took this to mean that she was being reprimanded again and told to mind her own business. When he also told her that she need not take the time to attend the general church board meetings because he would handle it himself from now on, Cathy really began to doubt herself. Now she would not have access to a great deal of the important information and decisions made by the board until the rest of the church knew them.

Cathy began to see that she was being treated like a marginal appendage, and she began to feel like one. She asked herself, Is this because I'm a woman, or because I try to help and nurture people? Am I really that marginal a person around here? Cathy went over and over these self-doubting questions. Usually she concluded that she was to blame for the troubles, that she needed to change, to work harder and to show them she was not the incompetent person they seemed to think she was.

But the more she tried, the worse it got. The pastor took over the confirmation class from her, one week before the end of the course. By now she was even grateful for this, although she got no recognition at the service of confirmation. She had taught the class for seven months.

Finally, after eleven months on the job, the time came for the renewal of Cathy's contract. She knew that there were problems, but she expected to be rehired without question. She got the shock of her life when she read the pastor's evaluation and recommendations. He told the personnel committee in his review of Cathy that she had a hard time adjusting to the job, that she never seemed to have time for all her work and was poorly organized, that he had heard many complaints about her performance, and that he therefore did not recommend that her contract be renewed. He suggested that she quietly resign so that no one would be embarrassed. He also offered to write her a good recommendation for another job.

Cathy was stunned and lost. Why? What had gone wrong? How could she have failed so badly? Was she really that bad a person? Was there no recourse, no appeal to a higher authority in the denomination, no personnel review? She got out her contract and really read it for the first time. There was no legal or administrative recourse. Or was there?

Resolution

It was clear that Cathy had no legal grounds for fighting the decision, but Cathy was not powerless. She still had choices. The first choice she had to make was whether to leave quietly or not. Cathy struggled mightily with that choice. To accept the pastor's proposal would seem to affirm the unjust decision. Deny it, and she would probably lose his recommendation. She decided she did not even want his recommendation and that justice required her to make him come clean on the evaluation. This was a key decision because it gave her a beginning of self-esteem that she needed to keep going. She would not become invisible and quietly disappear.

She told the pastor the next week that he would have to fire her and come clean with his vague evaluation. Both he and the church would have to be responsible for their decision. She would not cooperate in her own dismissal.

Cathy made them face up to their decisions. She felt good about that. The church board struggled long and hard, because Cathy insisted that she be given a hearing. She still did not expose the minister's secrets. Yet the church did not renew her contract.

This job was over now. But she still was not powerless. She had more choices to make. The basic one now was self-rejection or self-esteem. Would she use the pain as evidence that fate willed her to be a victim, or would she use it for her future? The decision not to cooperate in her dismissal by resigning gave her just enough self-esteem to begin the process of accepting the pain and slowly, gradually learning from it, even using it as a source of power. With counseling and supportive friends who listened, she was able to move on. She decided to begin again in a new field. She went to work at a college and started at the bottom. She carefully read the college's policies on hiring, firing, and advancement.

Cathy learned from the church experience and advanced rapidly at the college. She now holds a high administrative position there. The pastor moved on soon after this. Cathy does not know where to and has not tried to find out.

Power Is . . .

Clearly there was an unbalanced power arrangement in this relationship between Cathy and the pastor. If a conflict mediator had entered this conflict, it would have been difficult for him or her to mediate the conflict because Cathy had so little power relative to the pastor. What would you do as Cathy or as a mediator? Two essential points need to be made about this and all unbalanced power relationships.

First, the definitions of power come in a great variety: from mechanics ("power tools, power brakes"), to law ("power of attorney"), to hype ("power breakfasts"). One dictionary defines power as "the capacity to act" or "the ability to do." But power also means the ability to prevent action. Saul Alinsky reminds us that power is "not only what you have but what the enemy thinks you have."[4] Other widely used definitions include awareness of one's own intentions and interests, so that power is defined as: "the capacity to produce intended results" or "the ability to make one's interests felt in communal decision making."

Another book could be written to sort out more complex definitions of power. However, it is adequate here simply to assume these aspects of power in this standard definition: the ability to influence outcomes. In this definition one may or may not actually determine the outcome, but one has some effect on it, to enable or to prevent it, intended or not. In other words, power is a quality one has that enables one to make a difference, to influence outcomes one way or another.

Levels of Power

Cathy was virtually powerless on the level of job outcome because she could not change the outcome of the dismissal. She was not completely powerless on other levels, however. She could influence the outcome of the interpersonal relations, her own future, her own attitude, her own self-esteem, and her ability to learn from this painful experience. She was powerless on some levels and powerful on other levels. Therefore, it is essential to distinguish different levels of power. Five general levels of power have been named by Ron Kraybill of the Mennonite Conciliation Service: existential/religious, self-esteem, social esteem, process, and outcome.[5]

The existential level of power means having basic meaning for one's life in the face of ultimate reality. It is the foundation of all power. To be powerless at this level is to lose meaning in life and feel that one's existence is finally inconsequential. It is the religious sense that one has a purpose and one's existence makes a difference eternally. In a word, no other god is in charge of one's life. We do make a difference. We are loved by God.

Cathy doubted this occasionally, but hung on to it, finally affirming that she did matter and she was not to be dismissed quietly. The existential/

religious power was the ground for her awareness of the injustice and the assertion of her courage or personal power of self-esteem.

The next level of power is the level of self-esteem. Cathy rallied her power to reject the marginal, throwaway treatment of the pastor in which he asked her to resign quietly. That quiet resignation would be convenient for him, but it would be demeaning to Cathy and unjust as well. Because she had enough power on the existential level, she was able to sense the injustice of it, and because she had enough courage and power on the self-esteem level, she refused to cooperate by disappearing for his convenience and for the demeaning offer of his future reference. Cathy had existential/religious power, and she had the power of self-esteem.

For a while she had had the power of social esteem. That is, she felt affirmed in the church and in the small circle of pastor and organist. She felt that she made a difference in the church and with the pastor. In fact, Cathy felt greatest power here in the interpersonal relations that were the high focus of her energy on the job. One might observe that this focus on interpersonal relations obscured for her the institutional power of process and outcomes. This is not uncommon for both men and women. Theologian Letty Russell observes that women who enter the professional ministry have special difficulty dealing with institutional power and authority. Her point is that power is "standpoint dependent."

> They are called to their first parish and decide to exercise authority as partnership. You know what happens, it doesn't work. Why? Because the new pastor does not realize that power is standpoint dependent. She cannot decide to share power and work in a process of empowerment until her authority has been recognized as legitimate by the congregation. She has the legitimacy of employment and ordination, but the congregation may not perceive her as legitimate because she does not fit the accustomed Father role.[6]

Russell uses the phrase "standpoint dependent" to mean that one's position in a social structure helps determine one's power, but it also suggests different levels of power. The partnership or relational level (what Kraybill calls "social esteem" level) of power is what women were traditionally taught to specialize in, i.e., as helpmates, helpers, caretakers, and nurturers of children and men. This is absolutely essential to human life. But it is not the only level of power, and Cathy was abused because she had too little power on the next two levels, of process and institutional outcome.

The process level of power refers to *having a say* in the decision making, whether or not one achieves one's desired outcome. It is voice and/or vote. It means participation in the process of choosing what happens in a situation. Cathy slowly discovered how little say she had in the church (i.e., power in the process of decision making). The pastor limited her access to the church board meetings, where members did participate in the decisions. She was cut out of most power on this level and was dependent on him even for information about church decisions. She did get access to the church board after she demanded to get a hearing on her dismissal, but it was, of course, too late to influence the outcome.

Finally, she had virtually no influence on the outcome of this decision about her job. The outcome level is usually what people mean by power, that is, the capacity to produce an intended result or to gain one's interests in a communal or institutional context. On this level Cathy was powerless, nor did she concern herself about it as she casually glanced at the contract which locked her out of legal or administrative recourse. One could argue that this was no fault of Cathy's, but rather a setup exclusively to protect the institution. She was desperate for a job and was hardly powerful enough to argue for a better contract. True enough. The point is still the same, however. Regardless of the one-sided, unfair contract, the story illustrates the different levels of power and how her focus on relational power contrasted sharply with her virtual powerlessness on the level of participation in the process and in the institutional outcome. In addition, one could argue correctly that Cathy had the power on the social esteem or interpersonal level to expose the pastor's secrets, which might have influenced his future in the church. That could have been institutionally powerful on the outcome level. She did not use this power. It might have resulted in some revenge, but probably not in Cathy's continued employment there.

It is critically important to recognize that there are different levels of power in a conflict. For even if Cathy was nearly powerless on the last two levels, she was powerful on the first three, and that power saved her future and apparently resulted in a much better job in the long run as well as greater self- and social esteem. Often defeats like this job dismissal can be beneficial to a person *if* one has the power on the existential/religious level and self-esteem level to keep learning and growing beyond the defeat and powerlessness on the process or outcome level of power. Of course, this compensation is frequently used as an excuse for power abuse on the institutional level, but that alone does not preclude the value of the distinction. Courage and hope are existential/religious sources of power that overcome fear and hopelessness in destructive conflicts.

Cathy's faith in herself and her sense of her eternal significance and meaning gave her the power to turn the painful experience into a learning experience, a defeat into a valuable step toward a better future. Yes, the injustice was not rectified, at least not to human understanding. But justice and righteousness, suffering and pain finally come to rest with God. God's Spirit in turn gives us the courage and hope to move on after we have done all we can to resolve a conflict justly. (See Matt. 18:15–17.)

The levels of power are built on each other in a pyramidal structure, as in this summary chart:

LEVELS OF POWER

Power: the ability
to influence
outcomes

5. Outcome
4. Process
3. Social esteem
2. Self-esteem
1. Existential/religious

Power Arrangements

The second theme in this chapter on the dynamics of power in conflict resolution is that power abuse requires powerlessness, and vice versa, powerlessness requires power abuse. Neither exists without the other. It always takes a slave for there to be a master and a master for there to be a slave. A dependent person or group must have a dominant person or group. They need each other. And both the abuse of power and powerlessness are corrupting. In order to balance power and resolve conflict, these social arrangements need to be understood.

This is true in all social groups but easier to see in the interpersonal relationship of Cathy and the pastor. She clearly was dependent and he dominant. But they needed each other on all levels of power. It is in this symbiotic relationship that there is hope for balancing the power. Cathy and all dependent people have the *power to stop cooperating* in the abuse of power. So they are not, strictly speaking, powerless. ("Powerlessness" is used here for convenience, but it is not a precise usage because finally we all have the power of God's love if we ask for it.)

The pastor, by contrast, obviously abused his power in relation to Cathy. But it was necessary to have Cathy or some other person in a powerless position under his supervision for him to do so. Likewise, in order for Cathy to be dependent, the pastor had to play a dominant role. It became a social arrangement like this:

DOMINANCE←——→DEPENDENCE
Power Abuse←——→Powerlessness

This is an unbalanced power arrangement, which needs to be changed in order for there to be a just resolution of the conflict. The power balancing would involve empowering Cathy or any dependent person in any unbalanced relationship. If Cathy were empowered adequately, the relationship would move from dominance/dependence to interdependence and from power abuse/powerlessness to power sharing. Power sharing does not mean equal power between Cathy and the pastor. It does mean responsible use of power—power used only up to the level of authority granted by the authorizing body, in this case, the church.

DOMINANCE←——→DEPENDENCE——————→INTERDEPENDENCE
Power Abuse←——→Powerlessness————→Power Sharing

The dynamics of power in an unbalanced power arrangement are quite elaborate. But understanding power and unbalanced power in conflict resolution requires knowing some of the ways it works. This writer has listed a large number of power arrangements, or "social control mechanisms," played out between dominant and dependent groups in the book *Morality of Power.*[7] Here are a few:

Power Arrangements
On an Existential/Religious Level of Power

Power arrangements are the games of institutional power politics. I will list these arrangements, three sets for each level of power, as they were used in our story. There are many more, and they function in different ways in other power struggles.

There are basic conditions of power arrangements that parallel the existential/religious level of power. At this level, the dominant person or group insists that the present power arrangement is the God-given norm. The dependent person or group accepts it as given, beyond question. It is divine fate. The initial work contract that Cathy signed gave her no protection. It only protected the church and the pastor. It was accepted by all as the given, nonnegotiable, basic condition.

The second assumption is that the dominant one makes *all* the institutional rules, and the dependent one believes and cooperates in these rules of the present power conditions. Theologically, the power abuser plays god and the powerless one cooperates by assuming he or she is condemned to this fate. The pastor said "not to worry," he would take care of it. Cathy cooperated.

Existential/	DOMINANCE◄————►DEPENDENCE————►INTERDEPENDENCE
Religious	Power abuse◄————►Powerlessness————►Power sharing
Level of Power	
	Play god◄————►Assume condemnation————►No other gods
	Make all rules◄————►Cooperate————►Higher law, God rules
	Status quo is norm◄————►Fatalism————►Shalom vision

If there were power balancing, fatalism and the tyranny of the status quo as norm would be overcome with a vision of justice and peace, that is, shalom. If powerless persons stop cooperating in their own oppression (as Cathy finally did stop, by not leaving quietly) and the dominant power abuser comes to acknowledge a higher rule or law than himself or herself (such as God, for example), then the basic conditions of the unbalanced power relations are transformed. It makes very practical sense to say that God rules when all parties acknowledge the higher vision and rule or reign of God. This is the reign of God that Jesus talked about over and over. When we truly affirm that power is finally grounded in God, then we have no other gods. When we forget this, we dominate, play god, and abuse power over the dependent ones. Then they also do not acknowledge God's power and assume they are condemned to accept the abuse. The power abusers play god, and the powerless play along. This power arrangement assumes a false god in the given conditions. Change is not possible. Fear and hopelessness rule. Then conflict is always destructive.

Power Arrangements
On a Self-esteem Level of Power

On the power level of self-esteem, a number of power arrangements are at work: arrogance/self-hate; blame the victim/blame yourself; and co-optation/privateering. The pastor arrogantly blamed the victim, Cathy, and wrote it down in his evaluation of her work. Cathy went along with it until the final effort of the pastor to get her to leave her job quietly. Up to that time, Cathy hated and blamed herself, and she kept trying to fix herself by working harder. It did not work. Power balancing or empowerment happens when blame of others and self-hatred and self-blame are overcome. The Bible calls this forgiveness.

The pastor co-opted Cathy into his personal problems, not only by all the hours of listening he asked of her, but by getting her to cover for him. Cathy thought that covering for him would help her privately. That is, she expected to win his favor (privateering) at the church by overdoing the assistance one colleague normally does for another. But she went beyond assistance. Covering up for his problems corrupted Cathy and trapped her in a tangle of his corruption. As in all cases of powerlessness and power abuse, both are corruptive. Balanced power and empowerment would transform the social control mechanisms of co-optation/privateering into a higher loyalty to the church and the good of the whole, rather than private and manipulative power misuse. Repentance from and forgiveness for arrogance and self-hate are essential for self-esteem.

Self-esteem	DOMINANCE←——→DEPENDENCE——→INTERDPENDENCE
Level of Power	Arrogance←————→Self-hate————→Self-esteem
	Blame victim←————→Blame self————→Forgiveness
	Cooptation←————→Privateering————→Higher loyalties

Power Arrangements
On a Social Esteem Level of Power

On the next level, of social esteem or interpersonal power, three power arrangements can be observed: superiority/group anarchy, pit the victims/fight each other on the one hand, and protect/obey on the other. Cathy and the organist were pitted against each other, and they cooperated by fighting each other. The pastor's superior position gave him the power to assume superiority. Anarchy reigns between the less powerful. In larger group conflicts this arrangement is also called "divide and conquer." The pharaoh used it against the Hebrew foremen and taskmasters in the fifth chapter of the book of Exodus. The colonial powers used it to subdue the colonies.

A transformed balancing of power would result in an interdependent relationship between dependent and dominant people, in which both fight common problems, not each other.

Protect and obey is a power arrangement even blessed by the church for centuries in marriage and in the wedding ceremony. Though it is being replaced now, it is alive and well throughout many unbalanced power arrangements. The pastor said to Cathy and the organist that they all should protect each other. Cathy, in response, had no problem obeying him. But his protection failed at the end. When it did, she stopped obeying him.

A solution would have been for the problem to be dealt with openly by all the people involved, and for Cathy to have the power to protect her schedule and workload herself rather then depend on the pastor's control. The power of social esteem is essential for group life, but the extreme of power abuse leads a dominant group to assume superiority and a powerless, dependent group to live in anarchy.

Social Esteem	DOMINANCE←——→DEPENDENCE——→INTERDEPENDENCE
Level of Power	Superiority←——→Group anarchy————→Group esteem
	Pit the victims←——→Fight each other————→Fight problems
	Protect←————————→Obey————————→Self-protection

Power Arrangements
On a Process Level of Power

On the level of power in which people have a say in the process of decision making, we will mention three power arrangements: all decision making/no decision making; limit access/play dumb; and steal identity/deny identity.

The pastor controlled the decision making on the process level and limited Cathy's access to the church boards. But, rather than question this power play, she accepted it and turned on herself with self-doubt and feelings of being marginalized. She did not take the next step that dependent people sometimes take, that is, fouling up the procedures with passive aggressive tactics of forgetting, or playing innocent, dumb, and childish. But this happens in unbalanced power arrangements. Balancing of power here would result in full access to information, boards, and whatever is needed to do the job.

Another mechanism that cuts a person out of the appropriate exercise of power in the process of decision making is stealing identity/denying identity. Cathy never got her name on her office door, and the pastor played with her name being in the worship bulletin. Names give identity and demand respect. The church limited her name use as compared to the other staff's. But Cathy cooperated by not demanding that her name, and thus her identity, be treated equally. The oppressed, like slaves, are robbed of their names, history, and culture, to keep them totally dependent so they cannot participate in the process of power as interdependent persons. Lack of access and identity limits or precludes participation in decisions. Power-abusing dominant people control access and identity in order to control all decision making. Stealing a person's or a people's identity destroys self-esteem, hope, and a sense of meaning. So fatalism rules.

Balancing power on this level would mean celebrating person's identity and honoring it appropriately.

Process	DOMINANCE←——→DEPENDENCE——→INTERDEPENDENCE
level of power	Make Decisions←——→No Decisions————→Full Participation
	Limit Access←————→Play Dumb————————→Full access
	Steal Identity←———→Deny Identity————→Celebrate identity

Power Arrangements
On an Outcome Level of Power

The last pairs of power arrangements are related to the level of institutional power outcomes: win/lose; segregate/know place; and zap/vanish. Cathy's "place" changed from what she initially agreed to. That is, she was hired as an educator, but her place, or role, became confidant and powerless assistant to the pastor. Although the place or role is not a physical location in Cathy's case (except for her office without her name on the door), powerlessness often leads to segregation and apartheid. This arrangement benefits only the dominant power abuser. The dependent powerless person or group gets only increased misery from segregation. But as long as the powerless accept "their place" as their given fate, nothing changes. They lose and the power abuser wins.

Balanced power in this case would lead to an arrangement of just integration. Cathy would be empowered to return to the tasks she had agreed to do at the beginning or to negotiate new tasks, receiving appropriate increased benefits for any additional work she may accept.

The other pair of power arrangements we will mention relating to power on the level of outcome is zap/vanish. The pastor tried to zap Cathy so she would quickly vanish without a fuss when he asked her to resign. "Vanish" here means avoiding any public visibility. Dependent and oppressed people sometimes cooperate in this zapping by accepting the invisible role. Illegal immigrants, lesbians and gay men, and other oppressed people often vanish for the very good reason that they are violently attacked when they become visible. But this continues the win/lose arrangement. The goal is for all to win power on the level of outcomes.

Cathy was powerful enough on the existential/religious and the self- and social esteem levels of power finally to stop cooperating with the abuses of power. Simply by not cooperating she became visible. She could have quietly left the church and vanished, but she finally said "no" to the zap/ vanish game. She stopped cooperating in the power abuse, made the pastor's actions visible, and held him accountable for his abuse. She did not change the final outcome of the dismissal, but she used the power she had to assert her human dignity and deny being made a disposable, invisible person. Balancing power between dependent, powerless people and dominant power abusers leads to the assertion of visibility and the ideal, interdependent relationship. The win-all, lose-all deal is transformed to a win/win power relation.

Outcome	DOMINANCE←——→DEPENDENCE——→INTERDEPENDENCE
Level of	Win all←————————→Lose all————————→Win/win
Power	

Segregate←————→Know my place————————→Integrate
Zap←————————→Vanish————————→Assert visibility

Both Inducing and Resolving Conflict

In sum, unbalanced or asymmetrical power is a grave problem in conflict resolution. It is an apparent contradiction to call for both inducing conflict and resolving conflict, even though destructive conflict is inevitable when there is an imbalance of power. The solution to the apparent contradiction is in two theses of this chapter: First, there are different levels of power which result in a complex situation of both inducing and resolving conflict. It is not an either/or contradiction, but a both/and paradox. For example, Cathy induced conflict on the outcome/institutional level of power when she refused to resign. But she resolved her internal existential/religious and self-esteem conflicts. She was at relative peace with herself. Also, she increased her existential/religious, self-esteem levels of power as her outcome level of power declined. So there is no necessary contradiction when one says that conflict resolution both induces and resolves conflict. Both can happen at once but on different levels of power and conflict. Or one may induce conflict at one time in order to gain enough power to attain a satisfactory resolution later.

The final thesis that helps solve this apparent contradiction of inducing and resolving conflict in imbalanced power arrangements is the symbiotic arrangement of the powerless/dependent person or group and the power abusing/dominant person or group. Because they are interconnected, they need each other, and they have a strange (even demonic) cooperative relationship. But in this symbiotic tangle is hope for both dominant and dependent people. The powerless and dependent person or group can stop cooperating, and that changes the demonic game. Then the power begins to shift. Other options appear. Power is unhooked from a zero sum, win/lose battle to an infinite sum relationship. Let us look at that.

Power Is Not Zero Sum

It is well known in textbooks, but rarely elsewhere, that power in conflict is not necessarily an either/or war in which every loss of one side is a gain for the other side and every gain for one side is a loss for the other. This all-or-nothing warfare is called "zero sum" because nothing (zero) is left over. For example, if you win 51 percent of the votes, I must have only 49 percent. If I get 60 percent, you must get only 40 percent. This kind of thinking is ubiquitous in sports, in politics, in the Alinsky approach, and in warfare. But this does not have to be the way one thinks.

Power, especially if viewed as multilevel, can be an infinite sum game. For example, Cathy lost the power of her job on an outcome level, but gained power on a self-esteem and existential level. In the long run (and possibly infinitely) she gained a new and better outcome by getting a better job. So power in conflict does not have to be won and resolved in a zero sum battle. To do so denies that power comes from God, infinitely. But power can be viewed not as a 100 percent pie but as an infinitely expanding circle finally resting in God.

100% Pie—Power as Zero Sum   **Power as Infinite Sum**

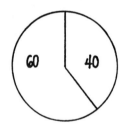   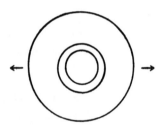

It is essential in a discussion of power balancing to recognize that the different levels of power mean that power is infinite sum. That is, there is no finite limit to power. Rather than zero sum, the approach to power balancing of Jesus, King, and Gandhi, for example, results in both the powerless and the power abuser gaining more power. How can this be? In the next chapter we will explain how empowerment can empower all people and illustrate that the types of empowering action and the different processes for power balancing depend on the levels of power one seeks. A summary chart (opposite) illustrates these levels of power and some of the power deals that are played out between the dependent and dominant people. These power arrangements are zero sum deals. As empowerment occurs, power expands. In the next chapter we will build on these understandings as we lay out how to balance power in conflict resolution. (The chart should be read from the bottom up.)

Levels of Power and Power Arrangements

Levels of Power (read from bottom up)	Power Arrangements		Goals of Empowerment (power balancing)
	DOMINANCE←——————→DEPENDENCE————→INTERDEPENDENCE		
	Power abuse←————————→Powerlessness————————→Power sharing		
Outcome	Win all←————————————→Lose all————————————→Win/win		
	Segregate←————————————→Know place————————————→Integration		
	Zap←————————————————→Vanish————————————→Assert visibility		
Process	All decisions←——————→No decisions————————→Full participation		
	Limit access←——————→Play dumb————————→Full access		
	Steal identity←——————→Deny identity————→Celebrate identity		
Social Esteem	Group superiority←——————→Group anarchy————————→Group esteem		
	Protect←————————————→Obey————→Common security		
	Pit the victims←——————→Fight each other————→Fight problems		
Self Esteem	Arrogance←——————————→Self hate————————→Self-esteem		
	Cooptation←——————→Privateering————→Higher loyalties		
	Blame victim←——————→Blame self————→Forgiveness		
Existential/ Religious	Play god←————————→Assume God condemns————→No other gods		
	Make all rules←——————→Cooperate————————→Higher law/God reigns		
	Status quo is norm←——————→Fatalism————————→Shalom is norm		

CHAPTER 5

Power Balancing in Conflict Resolution

Levels of Empowerment

In the preceding chapter we examined the dynamics of power and the paradox of inducing conflict as we try to resolve conflict. We concluded that the different levels of power help explain the paradox of doing both. Also, the power arrangements explain how the powerless and the power abuser must cooperate to maintain the relationship. However, in this cooperative dependency lies the hope for change. When the powerless can stop cooperating and the power abusers can be blocked, the change begins to happen.

Now we will move from the dynamics of power in an unbalanced relationship to a study of how we go about empowerment, or balancing power (I use the terms balancing power and empowerment interchangeably); that is, the stages and steps in different levels of empowerment. Empowerment was represented by the arrow "———→" in the last chart that showed the dominant (power abuser) and the dependent (powerless) moving to a relation of interdependence (shared power).

First, we will name a number of empowering actions and illustrate them with real experiences of three activists. Then we will spell out stages and steps in the different empowerment procedures that move powerless, dependent people and power-abusing, dominant people to interdependent power sharing.

Please note here the difference from the common use of "power," "empowerment," and "action," in which these words usually refer to action like community organizing or direct action. In this common usage, power and action are radically separated from spirituality and individual discipline. By contrast, here spiritual action and power are connected directly with all other kinds of action. They are interdependently related on different levels of power and empowerment. Here is how some common types of action relate to the levels of power:

LEVELS OF POWER	TYPES OF ACTION
Outcome	Direct action
	Resistance
	Community organization
Process	Advocacy
	Community building
Social esteem	Service
	Education/Issue
	Education
Self-esteem	Self-discipline
Existential/Religious	Worship

Like the levels of power, the types of action are pyramidal in that they support and rest upon each other. If one does not have the spiritual power of existential/religious affirmation, one can't go far in self-esteem, nor act to make a difference in society. Likewise, some types of action, such as spiritual renewal, worship, and meditation, are critical for other types of action, such as self-discipline, community building, and advocacy. Now let us look at how these types of action have functioned in Clara Rader's life. The focus is on the action of public advocacy, but the foundations of worship, self-discipline, education, service, community building, and issue education are evident.

Clara Rader

Clara Rader (her real name) is quiet at meetings except for a few pointed, but gentle, words that go right to the heart of an issue. She appears to be shy and accommodating. On first meeting one expects her to say little and make sure others are comfortable, just as some people think a pastor's wife is supposed to do.

Clara Rader is a pastor's wife, but she does not fit the popular image. She works with, not for, her husband, Bill Rader, the pastor of St. John's United Church of Christ in Boalsburg, Pennsylvania. She got involved in peace and justice actions well before her children, a son and daughter in their late teens, left home. In 1983 she was commissioned by her church conference to work part-time on outreach. Her pay, she says, was "very part-time."

Outreach for her includes persistently and relentlessly pressing her elected officials to vote for peace and justice legislation. They know and respect her well-documented arguments and undiluted faith, even though they often disagree with her views on issues. For example, a while back her congressional representative had consistently voted for "Contra aid"— money voted by the U.S. Congress to overthrow the Nicaraguan government. She organized a letter-writing campaign. When he would not respond, she arranged for a group to visit his office. When he would not see them, she got an article about that refusal into the local paper. When that news hit his desk, it finally got his attention. He came to a town meeting of 350 people that Clara had organized. After that he voted against Contra aid at least once.

Now she is working patiently and effectively through a Peace Academy she helped establish, the United Church of Christ Justice and Peace Network, and IMPACT, which does public policy organizing and mobilization, mainly on national legislation. Why did she get involved? Clara explains it this way: "When I was thirteen years old at Dunkirk Family Church Camp, our youth adviser, Lavon Baylor, challenged us to think how much good could be done if we used the massive military budget for social programs." Then in college she went on a church caravan to work in the inner-city area of Cincinnati. She saw in the "reality of poverty the possibility of resurrection." She could not understand how people in the white part of town could not see what was happening in the black inner city.

After she married Bill, they took a church and began to preach and work on this kind of resurrection. That church did not understand their actions and suspected their motives. "When we were fired we were working on a local church human relations group, but the church said it was for other reasons." The injustice of this process devastated Clara, who had learned a gospel of peace and justice from the church. Now it seemed that the church rejected her and Bill for preaching the same gospel in word and deed that it had taught them.

They moved to New Haven, Connecticut, where Clara earned a master's degree at Yale. Then they went to Basel, Switzerland, where Bill earned a doctorate in theology. Looking back on the firing, she still sees resurrection as she saw it in the poverty of Cincinnati. She says, "The personal experience of injustice is a good ingredient for getting involved in social action."

Analysis

Clara's personal experience of injustice in the firing by the church eventually strengthened her personal faith in a God of peace and justice and gave her the existential/religious power to act for justice and peace on many levels. The first was the worship of this God of justice and peace. Worship is the ultimate and basic act of valuing or giving worth to the core of one's faith. It is the foundation of one's power to act on other levels. The other levels of action are built on this core act.

• WORSHIP

Self-discipline is another level of action. To be at peace with oneself and to be fair (self-accepting) to oneself is an essential gift of God. We normally seek to nurture this by spiritual disciplines such as reflection, meditation, music, self-improvement, and creative self-expression. Clara said she responded to the devastation of being fired first with anger and then by returning to the discipline of school. Much later, she said, she recognized the gift of resurrection that had been there in the midst of disillusionment and pain.

- SELF-DISCIPLINE
- WORSHIP

Community building is another level of action that is critical to one's faith expression. Although solitude in the religious life is important, we all need the love of friends, relatives, or the church to hold us together. To be at peace with friends who are fair (just) is to be in community. It is to belong and to be at home. Clara and Bill worked closely together, supporting each other at each step. "Finding larger communities of support within the church was an essential part of my healing," Clara said. Building community was essential to their action. Then it was possible to think of loving enemies. Jesus says that loving your friends is easy. What about your enemies?

- COMMUNITY BUILDING
- SELF-DISCIPLINE
- WORSHIP

Religious education is another level of action, in which we teach and learn about the community of faith, both living and dead. Our identity with the community requires us to understand the Bible, theology, and our history. To be at one with scripture and the saints is to be at peace with one's faith community. Justice means a fair respect for and careful attention to all that the church stands for. For Clara and Bill that meant getting a strong religious education that honors the past and is relevant to the present.

- RELIGIOUS EDUCATION
- COMMUNITY BUILDING
- SELF-DISCIPLINE
- WORSHIP

Nearly all believers participate in some form of service. Most see service to one's family and church as a requirement of faith. Most want to reach out farther to lend a helping hand to the unfortunate, the poor, and the sick. Disaster relief and development are widely accepted as part of our mission in life. Bringing justice and peace on this level of involvement means a voluntary distribution of goods and services to those in need. Clara did this in her service in Cincinnati. But she also learned that there is still more to acting for justice and peace.

- SERVICE
- RELIGIOUS EDUCATION
- COMMUNITY BUILDING
- SELF-DISCIPLINE
- WORSHIP

Service is essential, but it is not enough. Service does not ask why injustice happens. It does not ask what caused evil to occur or who made the decisions that resulted in human pain, hunger, war, and poverty. This is the next level of action.

Issue education focuses on the social structures or root causes of injustice and poverty and strife. These causes are distinct from the results or symptoms that they cause. Such a focus of issue education was in the question that Clara was asked at church camp. That was: "Why don't we spend less on military and more on social programs?" To act on issue education is to look for the causes, to look for who decides what happens and where power is used to effect good or evil in the institutions in what the Bible calls "the rulers . . . the authorities" (Eph. 6:12) of the world.

When we ignore issue education, we ignore some of the facts and some of the means that can end suffering. God's justice and peace, which we seek, cannot be excluded from our concern. When we learn the root causes of human pain, like the injustice that Clara experienced, we do what we can to expose it and change it. When her representative refused to be accountable to his district, she exposed his negligence to the local newspaper.

- ISSUE EDUCATION
- SERVICE
- RELIGIOUS EDUCATION
- COMMUNITY BUILDING
- SELF-DISCIPLINE
- WORSHIP

Public advocacy action is a means of being an active and responsible citizen. But it means much more than merely voting. It means constant analysis of the causes of injustice and of the centers of decision making that bring about injustice and strife; that is, issue education. It means organizing letter-writing campaigns, demonstrations, visits to elected officials, media work, public speaking, skill training, fund-raising, and many more activities. Clara's persistent effort to make her representative respond to the people is a good model of public advocacy to follow. To avoid this level of action is to accept authoritarian rule by default. The exercise of public advocacy is a citizen's right. But it is that and more to a believer for whom advocacy is a means to justice and peace; that is, to God's will.

There are other levels of involvement, such as community organizing, resistance, and direct action. They are used when public advocacy is thwarted. For example, if Clara's representative had persisted in ignoring the people, more organizing, resistance, and direct action might have been called for. After all the ordinary means of action have persistently failed, faith may call us to extraordinary action, such as resisting conscription into the military or resisting paying taxes that buy weapons.

Faith may call us, as it called the faithful in the first century, to not cooperate with the state and to block a persistent evil such as racism with direct action in sit-ins or strikes or boycotts. Arrest and jail can result from resistance and direct action. So they can never be entered into casually. Yet they remain important acts of Christian conscience, as we have learned from the examples of the apostles, who were in and out of jail because of their faithful witness.

- DIRECT ACTION
- RESISTANCE
- COMMUNITY ORGANIZING
- PUBLIC ADVOCACY
- ISSUE EDUCATION
- SERVICE
- RELIGIOUS EDUCATION
- COMMUNITY BUILDING
- SELF-DISCIPLINE
- WORSHIP[1]

Why do believers become activists? To be realistic, we have no choice. We are always acting on some level. The only issue is at what level. They are all connected. All are needed and all are appropriate actions for religious reasons. They are means to seek God's rule of shalom, justice and peace. Tragically, many believers refuse to move their actions for God beyond service, if they get that far with it. It is so easy to limit our moral life to loving those who love us. Jesus called us to move beyond this level, to love even our enemies. Like Clara, most of us who have so much are called far beyond this private world.

Bertha Gilkey

This story is about a person who is a community builder and organizer. The life of Bertha Gilkey (her real name) illustrates how she built on her basic power of existential/religious meaning, using all of these actions, to fight the world of powerlessness and power abuse in housing projects. Bertha Gilkey was born in a St. Louis housing project. She was the third of fifteen children. Her mother had the first child at age eleven. Growing up, she was abused by a grandfather and raped by her mother's boyfriend and sent out to earn her way at age fourteen.

She did. She said, "I was supposed to end up pregnant, in jail, on welfare, another statistic. But I did something with my life." She made her living, got a college degree, and now has two children in college.

Now she uses the pain and powerlessness of her experience to help other poor people in housing projects. She is in great demand as a person who can clean up housing projects that have been taken over by drug dealers and addicts. She helps residents to restore projects to be safe, drug-free, pleasant environments.

In a *New York Times* article[2] on Ms. Gilkey, the reporter says that she has spent the last twenty years rehabilitating the worst public housing projects in the country. She has managed to do what federal, state, and local governments, with the help of hundreds of millions of dollars, have failed to do—make public housing safe, clean, decent places for people to live. State officials agree. What's her secret? It is people over buildings, and her own power to model how she did it herself. In her words, "The government always fails because it works on buildings, not on the people. First you have to give people back their pride, their dignity, make them feel good about themselves. Once you do that, the whole environment changes. Then it's easy to fix buildings."

Ms. Gilkey comes to a project such as the hopeless crime- and drug-ridden project called Miller Homes in Trenton, New Jersey. She comes for three straight days a month over a half year or so. She builds a community by group gospel singing and lectures on legislation, how to read a lease, run a committee, and protect the property. She listens to the residents' stories. She organizes floor captains to clean graffiti, check garbage, and police elevators. She gets retired carpenters to teach their skills, starts a day-care center, a Cub Scout troop, a tutoring program, a tenant screening committee. Skills in cleaning, gardening, even trash disposal are taught. She gives tests to make sure residents have learned her lessons. Pride returns to the project because Ms. Gilkey has turned her own pain and powerlessness into strength and empowerment for others.

Analysis

Bertha Gilkey used many of the types of action we cited, from worship (gospel singing), to self-discipline (she even gave tests to the residents of the housing project), to education (how to fix up a building), to service (helping each other clean up the building), to community building (meetings that build hope and courage), to issue education (lessons on reading a lease), to advocacy (housing legislation). All the actions empowered the people of the housing project to fight off violence and injustice and to assert their power on all levels.

The powerful outcome is a safe, clean, and secure housing project. Bertha Gilkey did community organizing to fight off criminals as well as fighting off the powerlessness in the residents.

Bill Goldsmith

This story illustrates all the same actions, but focuses more on conflict management between government officials and a group of inner-city churches after they were empowered through community organizing.

Bill Goldsmith (his real name) earned a master's degree, became an electronics engineer in the Navy, and then a nuclear engineer at Oak Ridge, Tennessee. When he and his wife lost their daughter, he began to ask hard questions in a disciplined religious search for meaning in life. The search for answers led him to the study of philosophy at the University of Tennessee and then theology at Princeton Seminary in Princeton, New Jersey. But before graduating from the tree-lined campus in this wealthy town, Bill felt a call to move on to its nearby opposite—the run-down, crime-ridden city of Trenton, New Jersey. Bill explained why he got involved in community organizing:

> God has given me eyes to see the pain and causes of divisiveness in the past. God has given me ears to hear the voices of hope for a new community—based on a vision that esteems the dignity of all human life. God has given me a mouth to speak a prayer of thanksgiving to our Lord and Saviour who never abandons us and stands ever-ready to perform miracles in our midst.

In Trenton, he interned as a community organizer, slowly bringing together eighteen churches in the city under the guidance of the Interfaith Organizing Committee. He thoroughly researched the history of the economic and political reasons for the city's decay. Together the churches began successfully to fight for streetlights, to make city officials clean up abandoned houses that were used as "drug stores," to push out crack dealers, and to begin to reclaim the city house by house, block by block. Black, white, and Hispanic residents began to change the city through organization, hope, and hard work. The powerful outcome of this level of empowerment is documented in Trenton newspapers. One of the actions was to get the city to clean up and board up vacant houses to prevent their use by drug pushers. The *Trentonian*,[3] a local newspaper, reported that on May 19, 1986, before meeting with the owners of the houses, the church and residents of the Cadwalader-Stuyvesant community had targeted about a hundred abandoned houses. But at this meeting they specifically aimed to get two of the worst houses boarded up by confronting their owners. These two houses were owned by a local bank and the New Jersey Department of Corrections. Representatives of each were invited to the meeting in one of the churches. In preparation for this meeting, the residents were organized and ready to present the facts about problems in the houses and to demonstrate their power to make a difference.

The representatives of the owners came and faced eighty determined and angry residents who demanded action from them, according to the *Trenton Times*.[4] They wanted specific commitments about when the cleanup and boarding up would happen. They got what they came for. The person from the state department agreed to have the trash cleaned up in one week and the windows and doors boarded in two weeks.

Typically a community organizer works to empower others like the angry residents and to avoid publicity for himself or herself. In Bill Goldsmith's story we see all the actions and levels of power at work: community organizing (he spent two years empowering the poor before the eighty determined residents faced the officials); advocacy (he advocated the cause of the poor for a safe environment); issue education (he researched the power structure of the city); service (his organizing included helping people in their daily survival); education (he went from electrical engineering to philosophy to theology to community organizing); self-discipline (he disciplined himself to search for meaning after his daughter's death); worship (Bill is a lay minister who gives God the credit for his eyes, ears, and mouth, and for a savior who performs miracles).

Stages and Steps of Empowerment

The types of actions listed above were only named briefly. But each type of action for empowerment has a number of elaborate steps on each level that helps move the powerless and the power abuser to a point of interdependent power sharing. Letty Russell has drawn up a general list of stages that dominant and dependent groups usually go through as they move toward the ideal of interdependence.[5]

The powerless begin in a stage of the "happy slave" who is unaware of the forces of power abuse confining him or her to dependence. Paulo Freire calls this condition "submerged consciousness." The second stage for Russell is that of "emulation," in which the powerless imitate the behavior of the power abuser because the latter is still the norm and standard of value. Then the rage stage happens, when the powerless become aware of the abuse and act to throw out the values of the abuser as they move into their own cultural identity, which is stage four. Finally, upon discovering their own identity, they move to a stage of pursuing a new awareness and ability to act and take charge of their own lives. These stages can be detected in liberation movements, as powerless people get organized and take pride in their culture and manage their lives. This is what Clara Rader, Bertha Gilkey, and Bill Goldsmith helped people to do.

Letty Russell observes that people in a dominant power position can also go through stages of awareness and liberation.[6] She lists the first stage, in which the power abuser sees the powerless as a "joke." When this is overcome, the powerful become "liberal experts" who want to help without empowering the powerless. When this is rejected, they go through an "armor stage," then turn toward their own "identity" formation in the soul stage, and finally, in the last stage, become self-accepting and ready to challenge the status quo.

Stages of Empowerment

The Dependent:
　Happy slave, emulation, rage, identity, new humanity
The Dominant:
　Joke, liberal expert, armor, soul, self-acceptance

These stages give a helpful, general picture of degrees of empowerment. But each level of power and the action for empowerment also has progressive steps that are often taken to empower people for that particular action. I will lay out some very broad processes followed in each action. There are many varieties of procedures, which differ widely, each with its own advocates. We will avoid these technical debates, however, because our purpose is to get only a general view of how power balancing or empowerment is done on the different levels of power and actions for empowerment so that just conflict resolution can happen.

Basic to all levels of power and actions for empowerment is existential/ religious power and the many forms of action it takes under the broad term of "worship." One generally accepted set of steps in public worship in Christian churches is the following: (1) call and invocation; (2) confession and pardon; (3) Word and Sacrament; (4) dedication to new life.

The steps are the usual, formal structure which intends to empower us existentially and religiously with the deep awareness that we are significant in the universe. God knows and cares about us. We have meaning and purpose in our existence. We are called to take the journey toward the vision of justice and peace. But we confess our failures, receive forgiveness, open our hearts to God's word and Christ's sacramental presence, and rededicate ourselves to a new life, empowered by courage and hope in the knowledge that we are valued by God. Clara Rader saw God at work in the slums of Cincinnati and in her painful rejection by a church. Because she had the power of existential meaning and continued to act in worship, she had the vision of resurrection in the midst of fear and hopelessness. She refused to play the games of the power arrangements which at this level are fatalism and cooperation with injustice. We fight temptations of false gods, bitterness at people, and denying accountability with repentance, forgiveness, and hope.

The second level of action for empowerment is self-discipline. It takes endless forms, but one common process is: (1) awareness, (2) acceptance, (3) celebration, (4) use.

One becomes aware of oneself, one's unique calling, and one's weaknesses and strengths. This often happens in a painful experience like Clara's rejection at the church or Bill Goldsmith's loss of a child, which sent him to search for answers to the meaning of life and self-discovery. Eventually, one must turn, or repent, and accept who one is (forgiveness) and discipline oneself to growth and responsibility, rather than to blame oneself or others for one's condition. Celebration here means moving beyond self-blame and beyond holding back one's gifts of expression and offering one's true self as a gift to others. Using our gifts for others is the goal of self-discipline that is based on a religious foundation.

Education is another level of action for empowerment. Clara, Bertha, and Bill all took unusual responsibility for their own learning. A common process for empowerment on the level of education is: (1) Assumptions are questioned; (2) concerns are raised up; (3) issues are posed; (4) knowledge is tested.

Much of our learning requires us to discipline our minds to question assumptions in an area of study which we previously took for granted: Clara was challenged at youth camp to question the assumed national military priorities. Bertha questioned the assumption that she was supposed to end up pregnant, in jail, on welfare, a statistic. Bill questioned the assumption that Trenton was a hopeless city. Much education simply stops here, at a test of knowledge. But there remain three more steps in issue education: facing problems, learning the structures of power, test of will.

Empowerment on this level seeks to move us toward solvable problems. Paulo Freire calls this "problemization." Saul Alinsky says simply, "If it's not solvable, it's not a problem." Another step is learning about the structures of power as Bill did in his research on who benefited from the powerlessness of Trenton's poor. The third step moves beyond a test of knowledge to a test of will; that is, doing something for society with one's knowledge, not simply passing a test for a grade. These three additional ingredients (problem solving, examining power structures, and test of will) distinguish schooling education from issue education. The latter examines the power structures and asks why some are powerless while others abuse their power. Issue education challenges one's will to act and seeks to solve real-life problems rather than only theoretical ones. Students, for example, can be empowered by higher loyalties rather than being co-opted into lucrative but unjust corporate enterprises (that is, "privateering"). Rather than fighting peers "up" the ladder of success for materialistic rewards, one fights against social evils that destroy the common good.

On the level of action called community building, empowerment for social esteem is sought. Empowerment on this level rests on a list of ingredients that are present when a group is able to effect behavioral change in its members and also develop powerful bonds within the group. The members of a group may be average people, addicts, alcoholics, obese people, or chronic offenders. The ingredients for successful behavior change are: (1) structure; (2) strong group support; (3) letting go to a higher power; (3) catharsis; (4) transfer; (5) success.

Most of these ingredients were present in Bertha Gilkey's work in housing projects. She established a firm structure and supported but held residents accountable for their learning with her tests. She created a warm, gospel-singing, hand-holding environment, encouraging residents to let go of their burdens to God's care. She allowed residents to air their problems and needs. She insisted they transfer the self-esteem and dignity they felt in the meetings to their whole lives. She, like Bill Goldsmith, knew how small successes empower and encourage community groups to move beyond these small successes, such as trash cleanup and boarding up vacant houses, to successful reclaiming of housing projects and whole communities.

The processes involved in public advocacy focus on getting people empowered to participate in governmental functions, particularly legislation. A common series of advocacy steps are: (1) issue awareness; (2) organization of constituency; (3) skill-training; (4) mobilization; (5) lobbying; (6) media support.

Clara Rader's work illustrates this well. In the Peace Academy she helped found in her area, issue awareness is a prime function. The citizens of her congressional district were organized enough to get 350 people out to talk to their representative. The IMPACT and UCC Justice and Peace networks offer skill-training events which she helps organize. Mobilization and lobbying of the constituency happen around key legislation. And media work helps get and keep lawmakers' attention.

On this advocacy level of empowerment action, we seek to provide full access to citizen rights and full participation of citizens in the processes of government. Whereas the power arrangements seek to limit and deny access as well as to steal and deny the citizen rights that identify us as members of our society, advocacy empowers us to celebrate and demand our full identity and access to government of, by, and for the people.

Finally, we come to community organizing as another empowering action that builds on the former actions and levels of power but focuses on successful outcomes. However small the outcome of boarding up two houses may seem, it is a large step toward a big vision of reclaiming a whole city. Essentials in the process of community organizing as named by Saul Alinsky[7] are: (1) The first step to community organization is community disorganization; (2) push a negative long and hard enough until it breaks through to it's counter-side; (3) bring together a community of people committed to a multi-issue agenda; (4) do what you can with what you've got.

There are a number of other "rules for radicals" in his book by that name. But these will be sufficient to suggest some procedural steps that seek to empower a community to take charge of itself.

Alinsky, more than most activists, insisted that you cannot resolve conflict between people whose power is unbalanced. The powerless must gain the strength to "compel negotiation" with the powerful. The first step in gaining such power is to disorganize—disrupt—the social power arrangements between the powerless dependent and the power-abusing dominant groups. The powerless have to break out of their powerlessness and their segregated ghettos and social positions and become visible by challenging the power arrangements. The poor have very little but numbers. But *organized* numbers are powerful, particularly if they push their "negatives until they break through to their counter-side." That is, they become an advantage. Bill and Bertha did not lead the poor into distant, ideal goals. They focused on the local negatives: trash, addicts, abandoned houses. The news accounts now represent the negatives as positive accomplishments.

Bill and Bertha also used large meetings to get people to work together and "do what they could do with what they've got." Bertha enlisted retired carpenters and gardeners. They did not seek other outsiders to do their work for them. However, they did break out of their segregated social positions to demand their rights and to demand responsible actions of officials. It takes a lot of slow, hard work over years to empower the powerless to break out of patterns of marginal existence (zapping), but it's all a part of balancing power, or empowerment on all levels of power.

Resistance and direct action are also available actions that seek to end cooperation with injustice. Direct action goes farther, seeking to block the processes of injustice, as by engaging in civil disobedience to stop Contra aid.

Summary

This broad analysis of the process of empowerment on five levels of power and through ten types of action is necessary to understand how conflict can be resolved when the conflicting parties have unbalanced power. It is too easy to assume that we are powerless if we do not have a say in the process or do not belong to a group, or to blame ourselves because of low self-esteem. But the bottom line of empowerment is that we are blessed by God with the power of love, hope, repentance, and forgiveness as our bridge to worship of God alone, neighbor love, and accountable lives. On that basic ground of power we work through these and other levels of empowerment to claim our responsible place as empowered citizens of our communities, nation, world, and even the commonwealth of faith.

So empowered, we are not controlled by the arrangements of power abuse and powerlessness. When empowered, we are not dependent or dominant. We are interdependent, power-sharing people who resist all fatalism and resist all cooperation in anything less than the vision of shalom, of justice and peace. A chart summarizing the steps of power balancing or empowerment follows.

Levels of Power, Action, and Empowerment

(read from the bottom up)

LEVELS OF POWER	ACTIONS THAT EMPOWER	STEPS OF EMPOWERMENT
Outcome	Direct action Resistance Community organization	Disorganizing, pushing negative, mass organization, doing with what you've got
Process	Public Advocacy	Awareness, organization, skill-training, mobilizeing constituency
Social esteem	Issue education	Assumptions, concerns, issues, problems, testing will
	Service	Awareness, education, collection, distribution
	Religious Education	Assumptions, concerns, issues, testing knowledge
	Community building	Structure, group support, letting go, catharsis, transfer, success
Self-esteem	Self-discipline	Awareness, acceptance, celebration, use
Existential/Religion	Worship	Call and invocation, religious confession and pardon, Word and Sacrament, dedication to new life

CHAPTER 6

Conflict Resolution

Summing Up What Conflict Is

Now that we have laid out these different aspects of what conflict is, we have the basic ingredients for understanding conflict resolution. We began chapter 1 by noting how conflict is constructive and essential to life, but how conflict also becomes destructive. This is true in our most personal relations to ourselves and to God as well as our relations in families, churches, communities, and nations. In chapter 2 we looked at how destructive conflict is handled in the Bible. Assuming some of the given perspectives of the Bible (no other gods, neighbor love, and human accountability), we explored in depth three passages where conflict resolution happens: through repentance (when we fail to love), through forgiveness (when others fail to love us), and through hope in God's presence and in human accountability (conflict can be resolved even between the worst enemies; Christ showed us how). These theological concepts attempt to explain a mysterious transformation that happens when destructive conflict turns to constructive conflict. We turn (repent) from hopelessness and fear to hope and courage. Instead of attacking people out of fear, we attack problems out of courage.

We defined conflict as goals clashing in chapter 3 and explored in detail three views of the dynamics of how constructive conflict becomes destructive, and the different levels of conflict. Then we examined the issue of power in conflict, dealing with the problem of unbalanced power, which complicates and often precludes resolution. Chapter 4 untangled the different levels of power and showed how power abuse and powerlessness work together. Then chapter 5 showed how power can be balanced so that a just resolution of conflict can be brought about. We called this power balancing "empowerment." We laid out ten types of empowerment based on the levels of power and the stages and steps frequently used in each level of action and conflict, in different groupings from personal to intergroup.

This two-chapter study of power was necessary before we could examine conflict resolution, because it is clear to most conflict mediators that true conflict resolution does not happen until those who are in conflict have dealt with power imbalance. Until then, repentance, forgiveness, and hope cannot do their work. As a psychologist said of destructive conflict, a "constrictive construct" must become a constructive conflict.

After Empowerment

Once empowerment has taken place, then resolution can happen. However, another problem frequently occurs here. Activists often stop at empowerment, assuming that a balance of power is sufficient to win a war. It is not. Evenly matched warriors often kill each other off. Or a violent revolution often simply replaces one tyrant with another one. The game has to be changed and elevated to a process in which balanced forces solve problems rather than try to win wars. That calls for the skills of conflict resolution.

It should also be clear by now that much confusion in conflict resolution can be sorted out by distinguishing what levels of conflict we are trying to resolve. It is necessary too to determine the number and degree of involvement of people who are party to a conflict. That is, a personal conflict is different from an interpersonal, intragroup, or intergroup conflict. We will proceed, therefore, with stories of conflicts in each of those four groupings.

Meanings of Resolution

Another clarification of language is useful at this point in defining resolution because there is much elasticity of word usage in this field. Words such as "reconciliation," "negotiation," "mediation," "arbitration," "management," or "regulation" of conflict are frequently used interchangeably to refer to resolution, but not always. One way to deal with the confusion is to discern slight trends in usage, then decide which words to use and use the words in a consistent pattern.

I have noted a tendency (but by no means a consistent one) to equate conflict resolution in these groupings in the following way:

- Personal conflict resolution as conciliation or reconciliation
- Interpersonal conflict resolution as negotiation or bargaining
- Intragroup conflict resolution as mediation or arbitration
- Intergroup conflict resolution as management or regulation

To be sure, mediation and arbitration are needed in interpersonal conflict to settle disputes (and even on a personal level at times). Mediation usually involves a third party who helps two parties resolve a dispute themselves. In arbitration the third party decides on the resolution. When an interpersonal dispute, such as a divorce, reaches the warfare level, arbitration often is required. Also, an individual may be so conflicted, to the point of mental illness, that a psychiatrist or judge will have to arbitrate a resolution.

The need for outside coercion relative to internal self-regulation varies with the level of the conflict. The lower the level, the greater the need for third-party power to assure that the agreements are reached and carried out. The higher the level of the conflict, the more a conflict resolution will be self-regulating. Graphically it looks like this:

Creative nudge
Challenge
Contest
Dismissal Fight
War
Annihilation

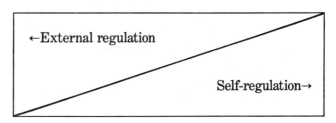

The resolution of a high-level conflict requires little to no external regulation, but has a high degree of self-regulation, whereas a fight or a war has low self-regulation and requires a high degree of external regulation, and, in the case of war, third-party coercion. Also, one can expect much greater self-regulation in personal and interpersonal dispute resolution than with groups. But in the case of a lower-level, personal conflict (for example, mental illness), external management may be necessary here too. The reverse is also true. External regulation is more often required in intergroup dispute resolutions. Yet higher-level conflict is self-regulatory and even groups can become reconciled allies. But both regulation and reconciliation vary with the level of the conflict. Graphically, the relationships look like this:

Coercion   Intergroup Intragroup Interpersonal Personal
                  management   mediation   negotiation reconciliation

Creative nudge
Challenge
Contest
Dismissal
Fight
War
Annihilation

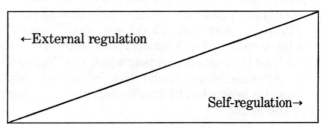

For purposes of this book, which deals with resolving conflict short of outside coercion, we will use the following words to describe the different levels of conflict resolution:

Groupings	Conflict Resolution
personal	reconciliation
interpersonal	negotiation
intragroup	mediation
intergroup	management

Now we will tell and analyze stories of resolution in each grouping and draw principles of resolution from them.

Beasley's Rest
A Story of Personal Reconciliation

The Reverend Buford Beasley had saved Monday to rest. He was exhausted and desperate for "down time." He felt a head cold lurking around, ready to get him. "I have done plenty already this month," he said to himself, "I now deserve a rest. I preached five times. I revved up our financial campaign, visited everybody in the hospital, and spoke twice to the women's guild. My throat is sore, my back aches, and my brain is numb. Now I can relax on Monday."

He could have, that is, if Bob Moore hadn't gotten to him after the service of worship during coffee hour. Bob directed the local peace coalition. "The coalition is holding a press conference tomorrow downtown. Can you come and speak?" Moore asked him. Beasley thought, Oh, no. There goes my Monday! I'd have to think up quick sound bites for a media speech, get in the car again, drive downtown, get lost trying to find the meeting, be nice to strangers, stand before cameras and newspaper reporters' asking questions as if they are average citizens. This is exactly what I do not need!

He asked Bob if Beulah, current chair of the social action committee, could do it.

"No, she is visiting her sick dad."

"How about Warren, cochair?" Buford inquired.

"No, he's out of town," Bob replied. And I have done it too much. All the reporters know me. We need new faces on camera."

Beasley struggled for a while, seeking to avoid the conflict. The best he could come up with was, "I'll call you later. I've got to think about it."

A battle began to break out in his soul between his conscience which said, "Do it" and his health department which said "No, don't do it; you need the rest." After church and lunch he decided courageously to face the conflict head on. He went to bed for an afternoon nap. But it was no use. The conflict kept him awake.

Conscience:	It's your duty.
Health department:	Don't be a purist. You'll get sick.
Conscience:	You lazy slob. Do your duty.
Health department:	You already did it. You deserve rest.

Resolution

Finally, the discomfort of the conflict exceeded his fear of either option. He got up and tried to sort out the real issues. He asked himself, What are the real feelings, fears, and needs here? Answer: Worry, hassle, guilt. What do I fear? Answer: Getting sick, wearing out, and getting worse and the hassle of finding a new, strange place downtown, facing reporters. What do I need? I need to minimize hassle and avoid guilt."

Once he had named these needs, another solution, other than the polarized options, to do it or not do it, dawned on him. The third option was to do it with Bob. Bob could worry about all the driving and finding the place, introduce him to the strangers, and brief him on procedures. In other words, let Bob help with the hassle. That felt better. He thought, I could do it for my conscience's sake, but I could limit the hassle for my health department's sake. He called Bob to test the idea. Bob said, "Sure. I'm going anyway. I'll pick you up. I just wanted a new face to speak on the issue." Beasley's need was to limit hassle. Bob's need was to get a new face before the camera. Beasley's face would do. So they made a deal. Problem solved. He had reconciled two conflicting parts of himself. It worked.

Analysis
The Theological Connection

Theological concepts help explain conflicts like this one. Of course, few people refer to theological language to explain how they move from destructive to constructive conflict. Yet it is reasonable to affirm that such language as hope, courage, accountability, even love, are critical ingredients at a key point in conflict resolution. That point is where we take a step back from the downward spiral of destructive forces and turn away from the pit of hopelessness and fear. Repentance means turning away from hopelessness and fear and turning toward hope and courage. Seeing a problem in a new way, with less personal antagonism, is the beginning of forgiveness. These basic psychic/spiritual shifts, along with hope for resolution, are as necessary as they are mystical in origin. We really don't know where they come from or how to obtain them. Only metaphorical language can evoke images of these real experiences at the turning point from destructive to constructive conflict. But they are real experiences.

No one doubts the need to move beyond personal antagonism, or the need to turn one's perspective (or have it turned) around so that a conflict is perceived differently, or the need to possess a positive anticipation of resolution in spite of discouragement. We may not call these needs "forgiveness," "repentance," and "hope," but that is what they are. Even if so-called nonreligious persons do not use this theological language, can they maintain that it is farfetched for others to do so? It does not appear to be so to this writer.

We can further claim that forgiveness, repentance, and hope are themselves based on the assumption that human beings can change and turn away from destructive conflict toward creative conflict. That is, we are accountable. Also, they are grounded in an eschatological vision of a unity known in the Bible as love—a love that, in turn, is grounded in God, who holds it all together. That is, the grounding is a faith in God whose own faithfulness discourages our having faith in any other source—no other gods.

Conflict Resolution Dynamics/
Conflict Resolution Characteristics

Beasley's struggle to make the decision whether or not to attend the news conference came to focus during an attempted afternoon nap. Most of the characteristics of a destructive conflict listed in chapter 3 were present then. Different parts of his soul had antagonism against each other. A lot of indirect communication was going on until he faced the real issue. The pro and con forces were becoming polarized and extreme. Multiple issues confused the decision making.

Finally, his battling selves made him so uncomfortable he had to push beyond the antagonism to solve the problem, and get beyond insults to the root causes (his feelings and needs). The destructive-conflict spiral was turned away from a battle between two sides to win and toward a problem for both to solve. Both sides laid out the root causes (needs and feelings of both sides). They were called back from extremism and a polarized zero sum solution. He could then see that there were more than two options—more than going or not going. He finally saw a third option: that he could go under certain more favorable conditions. The confusion of multiple issues was also clarified into specific issues of how to get to the news conference and other arrangements distinct from the actual speaking before cameras. When the characteristics changed, he was able to find a less stressful solution and to salve his conscience.

Hard/Soft Approaches

Using the Fisher and Ury categories of hard and soft, Beasley finally got to a point of being soft on the combatant aspects of himself and hard on the problem to be solved. But this did not happen until he went through the other destructive approaches. He was hard on himself and the problem, soft on both, and hard on himself and soft on the problem before he finally became more gentle on himself and focused on the real issues at stake. When that happened, a third option was allowed to come into view.

The Conflict Resolution Curve

Another way to understand conflict resolution is the spiral/cycle scheme. The spiral/cycle scheme as laid out in chapter 3 (see illustration, page 00) is an image of destructive conflict in which one goes on the defense when conflict happens and (1) goals clash. One then (2) feels fear and hopelessness, and (3) attacks oneself or others in order to (4) reach an adjustment. The conflict only subsides briefly, but then spirals on out of control. This is what happened in the personal conflict around Beasley's decision to go to the news conference. Finally, in the afternoon, something happened so that the spiral was broken. Instead of feeling dominated by the fear and hopelessness, he allowed their expression in the illustration that follows (2). Rather than attacking the various sides on the issue, he attacked the problem, reduced the size of it to reality, and explored other options (3). Then a tentative resolution was agreed on, pending its acceptance by Bob. The spiral/cycle was broken and became a curve. The conflict was resolved (4).

1. Goals clash

2. Expression in courage-hope

3. Attack problem

4. Resolution

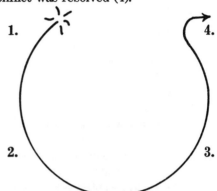

Levels of Conflict

Beasley's struggle with himself also moved down the levels of conflict and back up again. The request to speak at the news conference produced a conflict, as his goal to rest clashed with Bob's goal to get him there. He did not welcome it as a creative nudge or as a challenge, but saw it as a contest, then as something to dismiss. "Couldn't someone else do it?" The conflict almost reached the fight level, with Bob and his fighting selves becoming "enemies."

But the level of conflict moved back up the scale when he realized that there was a third option, in which Bob could help him handle some of the hassle. He reached an acceptable compromise in which his fighting selves, as well as Bob, got something of what they needed. This personal conflict became a constructive challenge in which all won something.

Ann and John
A Story of Interpersonal Negotiation

Ann and John had been married five years and lived in a small apartment with their young son. They attended a church-sponsored marriage enrichment weekend and tried afterward to practice some of the conflict resolution skills they had learned.

Ann was committed to help solve ecological issues and tried to recycle their kitchen wastes. John agreed with her commitment up to a point. But that point was passed when he kept finding the kitchen counter occupied by drying cans and bottles to be recycled. He said to Ann, "I can't use the kitchen when you leave that stuff all over the counter. I support recycling it, but I can't even get to the counter to fix breakfast. It's really getting to me."

Ann: OK, I'll try to say this right. We are supposed to paraphrase each other. Do you want me to do that?

John: I guess.

Ann: You are frustrated because you want the kitchen to be neater. Did I get it?

John: Well, mostly. Can't you move that stuff out faster?

Ann: Well, let me say that I thought the kitchen was clean. The recycling center says the cans and bottles should be clean, so I rinse them off, but then I dry them because I don't want to trap water in the containers, which are too heavy for me to carry as it is. I'm pretty hassled with child care, office work, and housework.

John: Why do you wait so long to get rid of them?

Ann: John, your shouting scares me. Look, I paraphrased your concerns. Now it's your turn. Besides, it's really out of my way to go by the recycling center very often.

John: You clutter up the kitchen because you want to dry the bottles and cans so they won't be so heavy. How's that?

Ann: Well, you ignored my feelings.

John: Ignored? I did not hear anything about feelings.

Ann: Try.

Resolution

John: You feel hassled, and the bagful of cans and bottles is too heavy for you.

Ann: Much better. So, what can we do?

John: I need a neat kitchen and you need help with the trash.

Ann: Don't you ever drive by the recycling center?

John: OK, I get it. How often do you take them?

Ann: About once a month.

John: I'll take them once a month too, so they get out of here every two weeks. But, I want you to please get them off the counter.

Ann: If you'll help load them when I take them and take them yourself once a month, I'll keep them off the counter.

John: You've got a deal.

Analysis

The reader may wonder what such a small conflict over bottles and cans has to do with big issues of justice and world peace. The answer is, everything. Of course, we should not get so upset about trivia when the world is falling apart. But, whether or not we should, we do. Learning how to handle the small conflicts helps us handle the big ones. After all, our fore-bears, Adam and Eve, got in trouble over a seemingly simple piece of fruit. And Henry IV fell because a single nail, horseshoe, horse, and so his king-dom were lost.

Levels of Conflict

John began it with a challenge, then moved it to a contest and fight level by insisting that Ann justify the "clutter" and "stuff" and by asking her "why" questions. An automatic response by Ann would naturally be to defend herself. But their conflict resolution experience suggested an alter-native to defense, namely, paraphrasing. By paraphrasing John, Ann was able to turn the conflict spiral around. She moved the fight level back up to a challenge level when she insisted on both paraphrasing John's concerns and then asking "What do we do?" If she had stayed on the defense, she would only have asked, "What did I do wrong?" John was a bit slow to move back up to a challenge level, but he eventually got there.

Conflict Resolution Characteristics

The destructive conflict characteristics were there at first; for example, per-sonal antagonism rather than problem solving. (Note the accusing language: "You leave. . . ." "Why can't you . . . ?" "Why do you wait so long?")

The indirect communication as such is not present in this dialogue, but clearly John had stored up some anger and internal indirect communication. Fortunately, the direct communication began before the conflict dropped to a cold-war level. Personal insults were near the surface in John's words—words that attacked Ann for cluttering the house. She was a bit patronizing in her words "much better" and a bit manipulative when she asked "Don't you ever drive by the recycling center?" But John was not insulted because her training helped her avoid counterattacking with more insults.

Rather, she went to the root cause of John's frustration and her hectic schedule. John came on sounding as if the solution was polarized. Ann should keep the kitchen neat or else. He was not yet extreme but it took Ann's open-ness to avoid polarization and keep the tone moderate. They eventually focused on specifics—a neat kitchen, help with the recycling—rather than on multiple issues.

Hard/Soft Approaches

Note the hard-on-people, soft-on-problem beginning. John was out to work on Ann, not on the messy kitchen. But she deflected the attack and even-tually got it onto the problem of "What can we do?" She did this by para-phrasing, which is an excellent way to be soft on people. In it, one shows respect for the other's concerns and feelings and helps move the attack on people to an attack on the problem.

The Conflict Resolution Curve

The destructive spiral was present at the beginning. The different goals clashed: John's neat kitchen versus Ann's clean, recycled waste (1). He had feelings of hopelessness regarding his inability to get breakfast made conveniently (2). So he attacked Ann (3). She was fearful of his attacks (2). But Ann turned around a typical defensiveness and forgave (or at least overlooked) John's attack on her "clutter." She had hope for a constructive resolution to the conflict. She called for a paraphrase before the destructive conflict spiral got out of hand. A real fight would likely have happened if Ann had counterattacked.

The paraphrasing allowed each to be heard and allowed both to name the real problems. They solved it rather easily once they got beyond the feelings of hopelessness and fear. They negotiated a deal quickly whereby Ann would keep the bottles and cans off the counter and John would help ease Ann's hassled feelings of being overburdened. John got his goal of a neat kitchen, and Ann got her goal of help with the recycling. It was a win/win resolution.

Carl Versus Frank
A Story of Intragroup Mediation

Intragroup conflict refers to conflict involving more than two people and taking place within a group, rather than conflict between two or more groups. An intragroup conflict may and often is between two people, but it is not always, whereas interpersonal conflict (as Ann and John's) is exclusively between two people. In intragroup conflict, two or more people in the group may fight it out, but others are involved, either in the results or as mediators or both. This was the case when Carl and Frank got into a shouting match over who would get invited to a conference on poverty.

Carl and Frank were colleagues in an ecumenical community organization. They met frequently to evaluate past efforts and plan future ones. The head of the agency was Doris, who had given them freedom to work at their own pace but who required frequent reporting and signal clearing at monthly meetings.

At one such meeting Carl was reporting on plans for the poverty conference for which he was responsible. Frank asked Carl to name who was coming to the conference. Carl read off the names of those invited.

Frank: Hey, wait a minute. Isn't Maxine invited? Maxine should come—she is a key player.
Carl: Last year she came the last day and left early.
Frank: She had two kids at home. What do you expect?
Carl: I expect people to stay the whole time. We have to pay their way.
Frank: We've got to have Maxine. She is the way you get to the whole coalition.

Carl: Can't do it.

Frank: The hell you can't! Just get on the phone, that's all you've got to do. I talked to her last month. She's OK. She's got help from her mother for the kids, and she'll be there.

Carl: Are you trying to take over this project? If you want it, you can have it and all the headaches, the no-shows and the budget crunch. But if I'm responsible, I decide on who's coming.

Frank: That's the typical uptight crap you always do. You can't hear anything. Count me out.

Carl: Your absence is the best news I've heard all day. I hope I can also count out your usual behind-the-scenes backstabbing, too.

Doris: OK, that's enough. Both of you cool it. This meeting is over. But I want you both in my office at nine on Thursday to settle this.

Resolution

Meanwhile, Doris talked to Carl and Frank separately. She listened to their views and heard some of the past history of their conflicts. She was also aware of how each had his supporters and how this fight was only a recent outbreak of an agency-wide problem. Their hostility toward each other was boiling over and beginning to entangle others in the agency. On Thursday she sat down with Carl and Frank.

She focused on the issue of who was to be invited to the conference, and said, "I want to hear from both of you." There is only one rule: No interruptions. Who is first?"

Carl: I said it the other day. If I am in charge of the conference, I think I should decide who comes.

Doris: You mentioned no-shows the other day.

Carl: Sure. I can't stay in budget when I have to pay for empty hotel rooms. The person Frank wants showed up late and left early last year. Why risk a repeat? That's just being stupid.

Doris: Maxine?

Carl: Right.

Doris: You seem to have some strong feelings about Frank. Let's get them out.

Carl: OK. To put it bluntly, I'd like him off my case— butt out. He's got a thousand ideas he wants other people to carry out for him. Now he wants to control this conference. I've had it.

Doris: Now, Frank, I appreciate your holding back. I'm sure you're eager to have your say.

Frank: Damn right! This individual here . . .

Doris: Why not speak directly to Carl?

Frank: Well, Carl, you think I'm trying to take over. I'm not. All I did was to suggest Maxine, and you exploded. Can't you even take a suggestion? Come on, give her a chance.

Doris: Hold it, Frank. Let's try this. Tell Carl what you heard him say first. Then we'll get to your side.

Frank: He . . .

Doris: To Carl.

Frank: You don't want to invite Maxine because she did not stay the whole time before. You don't want to risk it.

Doris: Carl, did Frank express your concern?

Carl: In part. But I want him off my case, too.

Frank: You think I'm interfering, and you are frustrated at that.

Carl: Exactly, and if you . . .

Doris: OK, let's hear more from Frank and, Carl, you can report what you heard him say.

Frank: Well, I think Carl ought to be a little more flexible. The woman has kids, she's poor, and she's not always on time. But she can make things happen. We need her.

Doris: How do you feel about this, Frank?

Frank: Feel?

Doris: Feel.

Frank: I feel Carl ought to loosen up, to put it politely.

Doris: Forget Carl for a minute, and your ideas. What are you feeling?

Frank: I feel . . . I don't feel anything about it. I'm just worried we'll miss out on Maxine's contribution because we're so uptight.

Carl: You are concerned to make the conference work?

Frank: That's all. I can't understand all the "feeling" fuss. You want a successful conference. Maxine is key. So why not invite her? It's that simple.

Doris: OK. Now you both want a successful conference. Carl, do you agree that Maxine has something to offer?

Carl: Sure, if she will show.

Frank: She'll show.

Carl: Who says?

Frank: I say, and I guarantee it!

Carl: How?

Frank: I'll sit with the damn kids if I have to! When you want something, you go get it.

Carl: OK. If you guarantee she'll show and stay, I'll invite her.

Frank: That's what I just said!

Doris: We seem to be getting an agreement. You both agree we need a successful conference and that Maxine should be there. Carl, you agree to invite her if Frank will assure she'll be there. You mean for the whole meeting, I guess?

Carl: The whole meeting.

Frank: I keep saying she'll be there.

Analysis

Let's look at the power issue in this story before we follow our previous pattern of analyzing the characteristics, the hard/soft aspects approaches, the conflict cycle, and the levels of conflict. In the first fight dialogue, Carl and Frank got into a power struggle over control of the conference. It became a zero sum power struggle at one point, at least for Carl. He wanted total control of the invitations or total release from the project. He assumed Frank wanted to take it over. Whatever Frank gained, Carl expected to lose. Frank also withdrew from contributing his ideas at one point. Doris opened up the power assumptions in her mediation of the conflict. By finding some common ground (desire for a successful conference, Maxine's value for that end) she helped them back off the either/or, all or nothing, zero sum game.

Frank returned to contribute, and Carl agreed to invite Maxine. Although Carl and Frank had equal power in the agency's structure, Carl had more power on this project because he controlled the invitations and budget. No one ever doubted that. But in the fight scene, Frank used the tactic of uproar to counterbalance the power on the process level. Doris equalized their group esteem and process power by granting them equal voice in the mediation session.

Conflict Characteristics

The dynamics of the first conflict illustrated the characteristics of a destructive conflict. Both Carl and Frank expressed personal antagonism and insults rather than seeking the causes or solving the problem. Their accusations of "typical uptight crap" and "backstabbing" are examples. They ended with polarized options around control of the invitations and extreme, rather than moderate, positions. The issue became generalized into competing styles of work, budgets, and no-show policies.

The characteristic of indirect communication can be seen in the mediation when Frank and Carl talked to Doris rather than to each other. Then Doris asked Frank to talk directly to Carl. The destructive traits changed to constructive traits during the third-party mediation of Doris after a cooling-off period. She guided them to a specific issue, moderate position, root causes, multiple solutions, and common ground.

Hard/Soft Approaches

In the first fight the men were clearly hard on each other, virtually ignoring the real problem. In the second session Doris helped them find and express their real interests rather than their polarized positions. Neither of the disputants became very personable (soft) with the other. That would be expecting too much of them. But when Carl latched onto Frank's guarantee of getting Maxine to be present at the conference. satisfying his interest problem was solved.

The Conflict Resolution Curve

These two encounters between Carl and Frank vividly illustrate the conflict cycles. The clash of goals (1) came when Frank challenged Carl's invitation list. The hopelessness and fear (2) of losing control to Frank flowed out unchecked with Carl's charges of takeover, and were enhanced by Frank's sarcasm, such as "just get on the phone." These attacks (3) on each other got them nowhere, of course. Fortunately, they had a mediator, who could also be an arbitrator if she had to use her power to coerce a settlement. She called a mediation session, telling them to be present on Thursday. So an adjustment (4) that could spiral on was aborted. Rather, a just and peaceful settlement was reached.

In the mediation session Carl and Frank had a clear structure, a firm mediator, and a safe environment in which to get to the real problem and solve it. This context gave them hope. Both expressed their fears and needs and backed down from a diehard fight for their own solution or for one position. By focusing on the specific issue of Maxine's invitation, they could attack the problem (3) rather than attack each other. By doing this, a simple solution was found. Frank's guarantee of Maxine's presence won him his goal and won Carl's goal of avoiding the risk of a no-show. Both got what they wanted. Their goals no longer clashed. The conflict was resolved.

Levels of Conflict

The conflict began as a fight. Carl and Frank each wanted to defeat his enemy. The dominant attitude of each was anger. Communication was partially indirect, requiring a third-party mediation. They were in a limited cold war. One of them could have won a battle, but the other would have had to lose. The rest of the agency would lose too. The mediator moved the conflict back into the constructive-challenge level by making it a problem to solve with cooperative communication and some collaboration. The result was a win/win. Both got what they needed.

The Story of Intergroup Conflict Management

Intergroup conflict is much more complex than intragroup and interpersonal conflict simply because more people, organizations, and impersonal forces are involved. These complexities can be focused, however, in a conflict management session. Such a session may involve only a small group of people, but they represent larger groups and have to keep them in mind at all times. It is possible for intergroup conflicts to be mediated, negotiated, even reconciled, depending on the level of conflict and on the conflict resolution skills and goals of the people involved. But more often simply managing or regulating such conflicts is as much as we can expect, and that may be enough. This is the case in the fight among church groups over economics in the following story.

A Fight Over Economics

A number of Protestant denominations and the U.S. Roman Catholic bishops produced statements on economics in the late 1980s. Realizing that the economics of poverty had both structural and moral origins and implications, these churches sought to claim the economy as a legitimate focus of moral responsibility.

One such effort was made by the United Church of Christ (UCC). It was a long and very conflictive process of nine years. The goal in the process was placing economics on the church's agenda. One way to do this was to get a pronouncement passed by its General Synod.

The official pronouncement-writing committee (after this, called "the committee") of laity, clergy, economists, and theologians from the UCC spent nine months writing five succeeding drafts of a proposed pronouncement. This followed seven years of committee debate, study by churches, hearings, and feedback on a study paper that had been sent to all churches. Considerable conflict developed between theologians and between economists in the years of developing the study paper. One meeting involved theologians in a lengthy debate on Aristotle as others sat by in mystified exclusion. But by the last year, a new set of disputes arose. They were raised by racial and ethnic groups represented by the Commission for Racial Justice (CRJ), who wanted a stronger challenge to the U.S. economic system, and business people represented by the church's Pension Board (PB), who said the present economic system was the one to "most likely" serve the poor and the gospel.

The pronouncement committee attempted to include both voices in the committee and in its various drafts. But both still felt their positions were not adequately represented in the committee's final draft. By the time the final draft was due, both dissenting groups had written their own competing statements. One way to illustrate the differences can be summarized in two phrases, although such a summary misses many other points. The committee proposal said to "reform the market system." The CRJ statement said to "transform capitalism," and the PB position was that no basic changes were called for—the current market and existing structures would correct social faults. The PB offered no new pronouncement, but mailed out an opposing statement to the churches and sought to block others from passage. While the committee expected the PB to protect the status quo, it was surprised by the CRJ move. Mistrust developed on both sides. Charges of "racism" and bad faith floated about. Hostility among committee members developed, angry letters were sent, and it appeared that nine years of effort would be lost. The committee feared that the Synod would be so confused with two competing pronouncements that neither would pass; thus the PB would succeed with no vote or a delay in voting. The church would remain silent on the critical moral issues of economics.

So the committee sought to find common ground with CRJ and proposed a meeting to test the possibility of combining the "reform" document of the committee with the "transform" document of the CRJ. The meeting was called for ten o'clock to four o'clock in a meeting room of the Interchurch Center at 475 Riverside Drive in New York. Considerable preparation went into this meeting. A three-hour preparatory session was held by staff to discuss and attempt to combine the two documents by the committee and the CRJ staff. The preparatory meeting decided on an agenda and recommended that the heads of the two competing groups cochair the meeting. The CRJ staff redrafted the committee draft and sent it out before the general meeting. They made a crucial decision on the agenda. The most agreed-upon sections of the two documents (each had seven sections) would be discussed first, leaving the most conflictive sections to the last.

The chairpersons were Yvonne Delk, representing the committee, and Ben Chavis, representing the CRJ. Delk opened with a prayer, followed by agenda-setting and logistics. She pointed out the need to speak together, if possible, and give a clear word to the church on the economic issues of our country and world. After a decade of debate, the time had come for the church to take a stand. Chavis made similar remarks, expressing the hope to work together.

The conflict resolution between the two documents began as planned with the least controversial section. That was the section called "A Proposal for Action." Numerous wordings were discussed, along with typos and omissions in the documents. Usually conflicting words from each document were dealt with by finding third options. Finally the group got to the key difference between the two positions: the words "reform the market system" from the committee and "transform capitalism" from the CRJ document. Disagreement over these two phrases threatened to wreck the whole effort. Both sides made speeches in defense of their wording. The committee argued that they were trying to find words that a broad spectrum of the churches could accept and to avoid labels like "capitalism" and "Marxism." Chavis argued that "transform" was a more religious word than "reform" and that we needed to name the problem of capitalism up front. This debate went on for some time, appearing to be headed to a deadlock on the first section, dooming the rest of the sections and the whole effort to combine the documents. If this happened, the chances of success at General Synod were slim.

Resolution

Finally, Delk suggested that they separate the words "reform" and "transform" from "market" and "capitalism" and discuss them separately. After more speeches, Chavis somewhat humorously offered: "I am willing to give on one of the words, if I can have the other. You choose which one." People laughed good-naturedly at the offer, even though everyone knew it was a serious offer and that a stalemate was finally broken. He would eliminate "capitalism" if he could keep "transform." Then the resolution came easily. The wording that all agreed to was "transform the market economy." This allowed CRJ and Chavis to keep the stronger word "transform," but allowed the committee to keep the "market" wording which it had used throughout its document to avoid inflammatory labels like "capitalism." Conflict resolved.

Then the remaining issues were worked through in a similar manner, but more rapidly. Delk encouraged both sides to present the basic interest that their particular wording sought to express. Sometimes one side gave in to the other in exchange for another wording. Often third options were found. The momentum of the early success and the warm spirit encouraged by Delk kept the trading going on all day through six of the seven sections of the competing documents. On a few occasions one side even found itself promoting the position of the other side, apparently unknowingly. Consensus was reached on six sections of the two documents. Even the title, which combined words from both documents, was agreed on. If enough time had been allowed, the momentum likely would have carried the resolution through the final section. But the allotted time expired. The group agreed to tentative directions and asked a subcommittee that it appointed to come up with agreeable language for the final section. Trust was strong enough by now for both sides to sign one document.

Delk ended the meeting by assigning a concluding prayer to a relatively quiet participant. The group stood, held hands, and prayed a thanksgiving prayer for a successful day of hard work in conflict management, and with strong hope for the church to get to work on critical economic issues.

Analysis
The Issue of Power

The power issue was central to this conflict. Neither the racial and ethnic group nor the Pension Board believed the official committee spoke for it in its document. So both went outside the official route to balance power. Both CRJ and PB threatened the committee's success in different ways and for opposite reasons, using a similar method, that is alternate documents, another pronouncement by CRJ and a statement by PB. The committee judged that it would lose the vote of the Synod on the basis of confusion, if not substance, if it did not try to manage the conflict with CRJ. The statement by PB would not be voted on at Synod. Two long and different proposed pronouncements on such a complex and volatile subject as economics would surely confuse Synod voters, who have to make decisions in a relatively short period after considering a huge pile of papers on many other issues.

A number of valuable conflict management moves were made prior to the session described here. These moves helped assure success of the conflict management session. For example, two preliminary rewrites were attempted, a preparatory meeting was held in which each side tested the other's bargaining points, an agenda was agreed upon and wisely designed to move from easy to difficult issues, both executives were present, giving more authority and assurance of follow-through of any agreement, and all parties were given all relevant documents and clear instructions on location and time of the meeting.

Theological Concerns

Theological concerns were present as well. Delk began and ended the meeting in prayer. Although prayer could easily be considered a formality, it was not. Rather, the basics of no other God, neighbor love, and human accountability were affirmed in prayer. That also assumed repentance (a willingness to bargain) and forgiveness (of personal antagonism) and hope (for a united effort). The prayer led in to opening statements that precluded dwelling on past insults, charges, and animosities. Each person was respected. A problem-solving goal was set.

Wherever possible, the groups intended to reach a consensus. If they could not do so on some sections, each party was free to promote its own separate section. Thus all pressure and threats between the parties were excluded. However, Delk and Chavis named another threat from beyond the negotiating group that sought to discredit both documents and to block passage of either pronouncement. This threat from outside brought a motivating and bonding influence to the people at the meetings.

Conflict Characteristics

Direct communication was promoted by having all relevant parties at the table with the full authority to negotiate. Polarization and extreme positions were replaced with multiple solutions, compromise, third options, and moderation. Delk insisted on specifying that separate sections be handled one at a time. At one point four words were even divided into two to break a sticking point.

Hard/Soft Approaches

The conflict was managed in a way that was soft on people. But the well-planned structure of the session resulted in the group's working hard on the problems.

The Conflict Resolution Curve

Prior to this conflict management session, the destructive conflict cycle/spiral had threatened to destroy the whole effort to put economics high on the church's agenda by means of a General Synod pronouncement. The cycle began when goals of different economic perspectives clashed (1) in the first committee and escalated into separate statements. When two groups felt powerless to get their views into the final committee document, the hostility and frustration gathered (2) and were released in the angry charges and counterattacks at individual persons (3). Attempts were unsuccessful to reach a resolution before the due date of the document.

The stakes got higher and defeat was made more imminent before the two groups sat down to manage the conflict with balanced power at the table. Then the constructive conflict cycle was set in motion (1). The hopeful context was carefully set so that each party could express its views and perspectives (2) without fear and be assured they would be heard. Even if they were not agreed to, they would not be ignored. Then the disputing parties could attack specific disagreements and problems (3) rather than attack each other. Finally an agreement could be reached (4) toward a common position to take to the General Synod.

In the final meeting they concluded with a common document. They also developed a plan to work together as a team to seek the approval of their common statement. Again the barriers fell and openness prevailed. Again it was difficult at times to know which side people were on, because various representatives argued points for the other side. By the end there was only one side, seeking economic justice together.

Levels of Conflict

The level of the conflict had dropped down to the dismissal level and then to the fight level. The racial and ethnic groups and the Pension Board members felt dismissed and invalidated, so they stopped direct communication and communicated indirectly by writing separate documents.

However, the conflict management session pulled the conflict up from the destructive fight and dismissal levels to a challenge level, at least between two of the parties. There the conflict could be resolved constructively.

Summary

To sum up, we have studied four cases of conflict resolution in personal, interpersonal, intragroup, and intergroup situations. Each was analyzed according to conflict resolution characteristics, approaches, cycles, and level of conflict. Faith assumptions and power issues were also analyzed. Some parties neatly resolved their conflicts. Others resolved parts, but not all of their conflicts. Nevertheless, the basic ingredients were evident in each. That is, faith assumptions, even when unexpressed; empowerment of low-powered persons and groups; the necessity of moving to the challenge level of conflict; the necessity of respecting (being soft on) people and hard on problems; and the need to break the cycle of attacking people and replace it with attacks on specific problems.

Repentance, from fear and hopelessness to courage and hope, happened.

Forgiveness of personal antagonisms allowed people to attack the problems rather than each other.

In some ways the resolution of conflict is simple. But there are three things about conflict resolution that make it so difficult that millions of people suffer and die for lack of it. One is that there is great confusion and little understanding that there even exists any way out of destructive conflict spirals. A second block to conflict resolution is that even when we know and understand conflict resolution, we do not have the skills, the learned (second-nature) ability, to actually see and do what has to be done to resolve conflict. In Part Two we will practice some of these skills. A third difficulty is the vast differences among cultures and the different ways they handle conflict. We will move to this important issue in the next chapter.

CHAPTER 7

Conflict Resolution in Different Cultures

Resolving conflict is hard work even among people with similar customs, values, and cultures. When it comes to resolving conflict between different cultures, the challenge is greater, but it is still possible, in fact, essential. A key block to cross-cultural conflict resolution is the human tendency, born of our attempt to play god, to assume that our own culture and particular way of resolving conflict is the only way or is a superior way.

This book attempts to account for this tendency or cultural bias by acknowledging that it is written with the dominant, Western, mainline church perspective in mind. That is, it assumes that church members live lives of relatively busy, practical, problem-solving activism.

This, of course, is not always the case in our society. Also there are many other cultures among our churches and elsewhere that honor ceremony, silence, patience, and public reserve much more than the dominant culture does. By being aware of these cultures, we in the dominant culture can be more attentive to the strengths and weaknesses of our own culture. For example, in his extensive study of warfare throughout history, *The Science of Conflict*,[1] James Schellenberg discovered that poor, deprived nations are less prone to start wars. Rather, they are more peaceful than rich nations, which, history shows, go to war more often. Western nations tend to be more aggressive and seek to solve problems in more belligerent ways than other cultures. While there are many exceptions to this broad generalization, it does at least suggest that Western cultures can learn something from other cultures.

There is another tendency that we must guard against. That is the assumption that since we are so prone to cultural biases, it is hopeless to try cross-cultural conflict resolution. This author believes that we must reject this assumption as readily as we reject the assumption that we have the only correct way to deal with conflict. On the contrary, we have no choice but to find ways to resolve conflict across cultural, religious, racial, and national lines if we are to survive. We can begin by learning from other cultures how they handle conflict. In doing that, our own traits become more evident to us and conflict between cultures can become constructive conflict rather than destructive conflict. In this chapter we will examine some general cross-cultural studies but focus on the indigenous culture of Hawaii, where a complex conflict resolution process was developed in complete isolation from Western influences before Western missionaries and others came in the early nineteenth century. I will begin with a personal account of a conflict I had when I first went to the Hawaiian Islands.

The Gift of Story: A Conflict

In Hawaii white, Western North Americans experience being a minority, for they are outnumbered by people of other cultures. Hawaii is a great mix of Pacific Island and Asian people. Yet, even as a minority, white, Western culture has had a dominant influence there. The Christian churches (particularly my own, a descendant of the first Congregational missionaries to Hawaii) are deeply involved in the impact made on the indigenous culture of Hawaii. That impact is well known and is now subject to many complex challenges to "Haoles." Haole is the name originally given to foreigners by Hawaiians. Now it usually means a white person in Hawaii.

As I planned my first trip to Hawaii, I ran into a conflict. I was supposed to give a series of speeches on theology and education to groups of church leaders on a number of the islands. My hosts from Hawaii, one, Randy Furushima, of Japanese and one, Kekapa Lee, of Hawaiian descent, tried to prepare me by saying, "Don't come off like a Haole!" I responded, "What do you mean? I can't jump out of my skin." Then my tutorial began.

They explained, "Don"t come off like a know-it-all expert. Some Haoles come from the mainland exuding arrogance, superiority, and condescension. They seem to assume that their way is the only way and that we will be OK as soon as we learn to do it their way, if we can. It is hard for them to see that the people of Hawaii have a lot to give too." I said, "I think that I'm beginning to catch on."

Then they gave me a stack of books on Hawaii to read before I went. I read a number of them but still felt conflicted. How could I be a speaker without coming across as an expert teacher offering to teach them something? It seemed like an impossible assignment. I suggested we drop my speech and I would just listen.

"No, you must speak. Our host churches will expect it." Furthermore," they warned me, "your listeners will be very gracious to you whether or not they like what you say. It is our way."

That made my conflict worse. I had hoped for corrective feedback so I could improve as I went to different meetings. How could I give speeches without appearing to know more than they do about the subject and without having any direct feedback on how I was coming across by which to improve my talks? My conflict intensity increased as the time for the trip and my first speech drew closer.

I rewrote my talk a number of times but felt that it got nowhere near to accomplishing the impossible standard that my hosts had given me. Then they added a final requirement that made me wish I had not accepted the invitation. They said, "In Hawaiian and Asian cultures gifts are very important." I said, " Yes, I read that they are." Then they added, "You must give your host church leaders a gift."

With that add-on, I was ready to turn around and forget the whole thing. The only problem with that thought was that when they told me we were on a plane that was landing in Hilo, Hawaii, in about ten minutes. My teachers had saved the last bit of my cross-cultural education until this moment, when I had no way to deliver on it, I thought. Even if I could jump out of my white skin and speak with maximum humility and try to keep it short and then listen intently to their views, I could not buy gifts that would have any significance between the airport and the meeting place. I was convinced that they were maliciously teasing me. Was I to hand out macadamia nuts to Hawaiians, or Bibles like the missionaries? How could I bring gifts to these gracious people?

Resolution

If my hosts were teasing me with their strung-out lessons on how not to come off like a Haole, it turned out to be pedagogical, not malicious, teasing. Their answer to how I could give the people of Hawaii a gift pulled together their previous lessons in non-Western communication. They said, "Give them the gift of yourself."

As we got off the plane and headed for the meeting, I agonized once again about what they meant by giving myself. When I asked again, they said, "Give your story."

"What story?" I asked.

"The story of your life and your faith, your religious experience."

This reply did not help my anxiety, only increased it. For I had long ago stopped using personal stories in my talks. That practice had been drilled out of me in graduate education. Such personal references were considered "subjectivity," a derisive judgment I had learned to avoid. I could hear in my head my graduate professors asking me why I might imagine anyone would want to hear such trite drivel as my own life story?

My hosts provided an answer. "In this culture 'talk story' is the gift you give of yourself first, if you want to be heard. It is an act of respect and humility that counters the arrogance of some Haoles."

Fortunately, there was a potluck supper before my speech and it gave me some time to scrap my prepared lecture and to dig out from memory a few experiences about my life that connected somewhat to my original topic.

I managed to get through the speech. I would give it a C grade. But after I worked on it more and gave it a few more times at the following meetings, it seemed to improve and to be received well beyond the polite graciousness. The conflict of cultures forced me to learn a new way of communication in spite of myself.

Cross-cultural Studies

If it takes such extensive tutoring to move one Western mind a few small steps across cultures, imagine how important such learning of cross-cultural sensitivities must be for resolving cross-cultural conflicts on international issues. Fortunately, there are some courses that are taught on this subject. One example is at the Foreign Service Institute of the U.S. Department of State.

Here a manual written by an anthropologist, Glen Fisher, has been used.[2] Fisher points out how we Americans have certain tendencies in negotiating. We down play protocol and special hospitality and seek problem solving, advocacy, and bargaining in public. This approach is an embarrassment to other cultures such as the Japanese who avoid public disagreement. The French expect more elaborate hospitality. For Mexican people, public meetings are ceremonies for rhetoric and performance, not a time for frank dealings and pragmatic compromise as many in North America assume.

Fisher's book focuses on these three countries, but such sensitivities are, of course, required for peacemaking and mediation in other countries as well. North Americans can easily fall into behavior that is distractive to foreigners by doing things such as forgetting titles, speaking too loudly, joking, or joking inappropriately. (President Carter's reference to "Montezuma's revenge" was not appreciated by Mexicans.) By contrast, understanding the value of silence among Japanese is important in negotiations with them.

Although there are many differences among cultures, there are as well similarities that make some conflict resolution processes transferable and make hope for cross-cultural resolution real. Another anthropologist, P. H. Gulliver, a North American who worked in Africa, makes the case for the essential similarity of negotiation processes across cultural boundaries.[3] In order to make his case in his book, Gulliver reports in detail a complex negotiation procedure between two neighbors of the Arusha people in northern Tanzania and one in an American labor dispute.

The Arusha neighbors' dispute was over who owned land and water rights to a property that joined each person's land. It became available when the previous tenant left. Gulliver does a detailed analysis of how a settlement was reached in a sophisticated negotiation session with other villagers present. He compares this process to an industrial labor dispute between the Process Workers of America and the Industrial Processing Company. He concludes:

> Despite differences in the social, cultural and economic context as
> well as inevitable differences in many details, essentially the same

processual patterns are evident. In each case, the dispute occurred between parties who were significantly involved in ongoing mutually advantageous relationships such that negotiations were concerned with both the reorganization and the continuation of the relationship. In both cases, negotiations continued through to a final, agreed outcome and thus extended over the full series of developmental phases.[4]

Even in such radically different societies totally isolated from one another, this study found similarities in their conflict resolution processes.

The case for overcoming cultural differences is borne out by another study, of the seventeen-year-old civil war in the Sudan, referred to in chapter 1. This study shows how the church helped to settle a dispute even between black non-Muslims in the south and Arab Muslims in the north of Sudan. An additional and important difference between these warring groups was a difference in their power. The northern government forces were vastly superior to the southern rebel forces. So it would seem unlikely that, given the religious, racial, and cultural differences, in addition to this difference in power, that a settlement could ever be reached.

The author of this study, Hizkias Assefa, spells out in his book[5] how, in spite of all of these differences, the African Council of Churches was able to mediate an agreement. How should the mediator deal with this power difference: with strict impartiality or with assistance to the weaker party? Assefa responds to this question thoughtfully:

> The mediator's concern for producing a fair result should outweigh his or her strict concern for impartiality. In circumstances of an obvious inequity between the parties, the mediator, by remaining impartial, would be playing into the hands of the stronger party or, by being passive, would only be insuring the imposition of injustice. In fact, in such cases of gross imbalance, the mediator's strict impartiality may not even serve the best interests of the stronger party, since in the long run, an unfair or unjust settlement would collapse from its own weight.[6]

Even after seventeen years of civil war between racially and religiously diverse enemies who were also vastly imbalanced in power, a settlement was reached. This bears up the argument that processes of conflict resolution are similar enough to overcome vast cultural and power differences.

The point was reconfirmed in a number of violent disputes among different groups in the United States in a book entitled *At the Heart of the Whirlwind* by John P. Adams.[7] Adams mediated many violent and near-violent battles in the 1960s and 1970s as a mediator for the National Council of Churches and the United Methodist Church. He embraces the church's role as "scapegoat" which allows the disputant to save face and still back

away from violence. One dispute that involved considerable gunfire and battlefield conditions was between American Indians, federal agents, and vig-
ilantes at Wounded Knee on the Pine Ridge Reservation in 1973. Led by
the American Indian Movement, Indians had taken over a trading post and
were soon surrounded by U.S. agents. A small war began.

Adams, by traveling time and time again across the battlefield lines,
helped mediate a settlement that saved lives. Though he was a white person,
he was able to gain enough understanding of both the Indians' and of the
federal agents' perspective to get both sides to back off from gunfire and
finally to end the standoff peacefully.

The church, he argues, does not always need to take the activist role,
though it should certainly not take an escapist role. Rather, as an impartial
mediator, truth giver, and reality tester, the church can help defuse the
"object-dehumanization" that psychologically allows one to kill. Adams
affirms how hard it is to "fight for non-violence" across cultural lines. It
is a position often misunderstood by the press and by both warring sides.
But that is a good place for the church to be, and it can be done. Though
cross-cultural differences require extra effort in conflict resolution, the similarities of respect for our common humanity and the way a mediator can
play a "scapegoat" and face-saving role help bridge these differences in conflict resolution.

However, the jury is not yet in on exactly how we go about training and
preparing for cross-cultural mediation. John Paul Lederach, director of the
Mennonite Conciliation Service, has done extensive research and training
on the issues of cross-cultural bias in mediation, especially in Central
America. He warns that assuming to be an expert or even using "logical"
processes and role plays from North America in Central America can result
in imposing our cultural assumptions on them. North Americans need to
adapt to the cultural setting by becoming a catalyst rather than an expert,
by using informal rather than formal structures in mediation, by learning
to understand indirect rather than direct dialogue, by attending to personal
relationships more than to getting the tasks done, and by working with complex family and community bounds rather than assuming North American
models of individual autonomy. In short, cross-cultural differences call us
to use an "elicitive" rather than a "prescriptive" model of mediation and
mediation training.[8] The least that such study and experience can give us
is a humbling mirror reflection of how our own ways of dealing with conflict
are relative to our own culture. I will focus on my study of the Hawaiian
process of conflict resolution.

Ho'oponopono

The Hawaiian people developed their own conflict resolution process over
centuries, independent of Western and Christian influences. It is called
ho'oponopono, which translates into making things right and restoring good

relations in families and with supernatural powers. Before Christianity came, these powers included ancestral gods. Westerners should not read "family" here as nuclear family. For Hawaiians, family, *'ohana*, includes many other people, nature, and spirits. E. Victoria Shook has written extensively on *Ho'oponopono* and says that it includes all elements of the world.

> Precontact (pre-Captain Cook) Hawaiians recognized the need to develop ways to maintain harmony among all the elements of their world. This meant maintaining harmony not only between family and social relationships, but between people and the spiritual and natural worlds. *Ho'oponopono* was developed for this purpose; that is, not only to preserve harmonious interpersonal relationships within the family, but also to maintain intimate relations with the spiritual forces and natural world as well.[9]

Usually this process of *ho'oponopono* took place within a family which was called together in a meeting where, "everyone of us searched his heart for hard feelings against one another. Before God and with His help, we forgave and were forgiven, thrashing out every grudge, peeve or resentment among us."[10]

The volume just quoted, *Look to the Source*, is part of a program "to provide factual information that reaches back to unwritten history and legend to clarify Hawaiian concepts." A part of the Queen Lili'uokalani Children's Center, it seeks to preserve the original Hawaiian culture, which included "insuring harmonious interdependence within the *'ohana* (family) through regular family therapy (*ho'oponopono*)."

This program intends to preserve the pre-Christian culture (before 1820) without excluding the early Christian practices and styles of life. This preservation seems quite difficult regarding the practice of *ho'oponopono*, because it was labeled "pagan" by Christians and was discarded, according to this volume.

However, it did continue sometimes in secret but more often in "bits and pieces" and distortions. The effort to find its pure form is a great contribution to our own efforts at peacemaking, in spite of the earlier "pagan" label.

Oddly to Western views today, the process of *ho'oponopono* sounds very religious, even in its pre-Christian form. This process is summarized in the eight steps that disputing family members take under the firm leadership of an elder, or *kahuna*: "Prayer, discussion, arbitration, contrition, restitution, forgiveness and releasing, and thorough looking into layers of action and feelings called 'mahiki.'"[11]

Other important ingredients were traditionally involved: silence (*ho'omalu*) could be called by the leaders to cool down tempers and press for greater depth and honesty during a *ho'oponopono* process. Prayers were used throughout the *ho'oponopono*, as the spiritual dimension was always involved. God or gods were never absent from this healing process. Physical sickness was not separated into a different medical compartment either, but rather could be seen as a result of a long-smoldering dispute that needed *ho'oponopono* to bring about physical as well as spiritual healing.

Perhaps the greatest difference from our standard Western processes of conflict resolution is the *mahiki*. This involved getting down to the many and deeper levels of a dispute between people so that a complete and spiritual resolution could be found.

One example was a dispute between a daughter-in-law and mother-in-law conducted by a great-aunt. The daughter-in-law was half Haole (Caucasian) and half Hawaiian. The mother-in-law was Hawaiian and wanted to teach her son's wife the old ways. This daughter-in-law was modern and resisted the old ways. It took eight years for the son/husband to get both to come to have a *ho'oponopono*. These differences were allowed to emerge over a long, sometimes emotional process. Eventually the relationship was reestablished, so that the two women "get along pretty well," according to the son and husband.

When such a process is used to get deeper and deeper into the many layers of a conflict, naturally one gets to the issues of personal guilt and forgiveness as well as a concrete plan for restitution. If, for example, one party has taken something from the other, a concrete repayment is worked out, together with the prayer and spiritual attention to ancestral gods. So there is no separation, as we make in Western societies, between the practical area of restitution and the spiritual. Also the private, interpersonal, and family spheres are all together in a *ho'oponopono*, as well as in all of daily life.

The earliest form of *ho'oponopono* were followed by ritual offering of animal sacrifices to the gods, a ceremonial ocean bath, and a feast (*'aha'aina*). Unfortunately, the *ho'oponopono* is rarely used today, although it is not completely lost. When I asked my host, who had taught me about talk story and had given me this book, *Look at the Source*, if he had ever experienced a *ho'oponopono*, he said he had. Such a healing process happened only a few years ago in his family, involving a dispute between his two sisters.

Certainly there are many learnings for Western people to gain from this *ho'oponopono*. The first is the need to avoid assuming that the Western view of dividing the spiritual, practical, and family dimensions of life is the best way to organize life. It is one way, and it is a way that has advantages and disadvantages. But the long histories of warfare in Western societies leading up to the current capability to destroy the whole earth should make us pause to look again at other more holistic worldviews of indigenous peoples like Hawaiians, even as we are realistic about conflict in all human beings.

For it is tempting to romanticize pre-Christian Hawaii. It was not a peaceable kingdom. War after war raged there too until King Kamehameha conquered all his opponents in the eighteenth century. Still their battles do not compare with the violence in the West. Much can be learned from Hawaiians.

I will mention two more distinctive elements in the *hoʼoponopono*. Except for Quaker practices, and among American Indians, silence is rarely used in Western methods of conflict resolution. We think we are too busy. This should be rethought. Also Westerners have often limited prayer to a brief "call to order" use, even during church meetings. We could well use more of prayer in our conflict management sessions.

Finally, we might acknowledge that complete spiritual forgiving (releasing) and restitution is a long-term goal (if not an immediately realistic expectation) of our usual conflict resolution sessions. Such complete cleansing symbolized in ocean bathing and ritual feasting is rarely practical for people today. But as a long-term goal it sets our sights on ideals that guide our halting steps to learn how to live more peacefully.

My own first step was to realize how limited my Western education was because it drew such strict boundaries separating aspects of life and gave highest value to objectivity, fact, and control. The rest of life was considered soft, mythical, and subjective. Story was unwelcome in the pursuit of propositional and verifiable "truth," even in my field of theology. I thought a conflict was solved when, after a battle, one reached a "meeting of the minds." In Hawaii I learned that the meeting of the hearts is important too—indeed, and fortunately, stories from the heart are a precondition to even communicating, not to mention resolving conflict, with Hawaiian people.

Part Two

The Practice of Resolving Conflict with Justice and Peace

Introduction

Part Two is essential to learning conflict resolution as anything more than an abstract theory. Practice may not make perfect, but it makes real. Practice means both using the skills and showing others how to do so. Thus, Part Two is designed as a skill-training course for those who want to learn and to teach these skills.

Assumptions

- a church context, although this course is usable elsewhere
- that the leader(s) already has some leadership skills
- that people have different levels of commitment
- that many people are afraid of conflict and even of a course on it
- that even so, people want to become effective in dealing with conflicts
- that the destructive handling of conflict is a hard-to-change habit

The Design

This course is designed for a maximum of twenty-seven hours but assumes that initially there is only a limited level of commitment to the whole course, and that resistance to conflict calls for persuasion to overcome it. Some people may commit themselves only to a one-hour sample of the course. Others may agree to three hours. Therefore, the first two sessions are interest-building sessions to help persuade participants that they have nothing to fear and a great deal to gain by staying with this course for an extended period. These additional sessions can be offered in retreat settings or in extended weekly sessions over a longer term or a quarter. The design intends to be flexible enough to fit most learning situations and time commitments.

We will begin with that one-hour introductory session for use when people have time only for a taste of conflict resolution on a Sunday morning or at a conference workshop. Be sure, however, to use that time to explain how this is only a beginning of conflict resolution skills training. Also, invite people to set aside time for a three-, five-, thirteen-, or twenty-seven-hour course, using progressively more of the sessions outlined below. For example, a three-hour course would begin with Session 1 and finish with Session 2. A five-hour course would include Unit 1, Sessions 1, 2, and 3, and so on, in units that include:

Unit 1

Basic Communication   5 hours

    Session 1: Conflicts Are Resolvable   1 hour ´
    Session 2: What Is Conflict?   2 hours
    Session 3: Communication   2 hours

Unit 2

Types of Conflict Resolution   13 hours

    (includes Unit 1),   5 hours
    Session 4: Conflict Resolution in Oneself   2 hours
    Session 5: Interpersonal Conflict Resolution   2 hours
    Session 6: Intragroup Conflict Resolution   2 hours
    Session 7: Managing Intergroup Disputes   2 hours

Unit 3

Power, Empowerment, and Getting People to the Table   19 hours

    (includes Units 1 and 2),   13 hours
    Session 8: Power in Conflict Resolution   2 hours
    Session 9: Empowerment   2 hours
    Session 10: Getting All Parties to the Table   2 hours

Unit 4

Process Steps in Conflict Resolution   27 hours

    (includes Units 1, 2, and 3)   19 hours
    Session 11: Introduction   2 hours
    Session 12: Expressing the Problem, Step 2   2 hours
    Session 13: Attacking the Problem, Step 3   2 hours
    Session 14: Reaching the Agreement, Step 4   2 hours

Getting Started

Getting a group together requires some serious leadership efforts and patience. Begin by proposing the course to the church education committee, social action committee, or other church board. Seek participants during the announcement time in worship and in the church newsletter. Or offer the course to a community group. Or volunteer to lead a conference workshop to introduce the longer course. It can be offered in an ecumenical setting also, or as a help to a smoldering dispute. The design is adaptable to settings other than the local church.

Allow for people's fear of conflict. You may get people only for the first one-hour session, but there they may come to understand that conflict is not to be feared and that there is hope that in an extended course they can learn how to deal with it.

Using Stories of Conflict

There are stories of conflict in each session. They can be used as case studies which the participants must work to resolve. Often participants will come up with resolutions better than those given in the text, if the leader delays the resolution given here. Sometimes participants will have their own stories of a conflict. Using their stories of conflict should be encouraged. The ones here are given to "prime the pump" for other stories to emerge.

Such stories are happening all the time, especially in churches. Using them is only a matter of looking at conflictive events with some distance and in a hopeful way. The stories of conflict here come from some of this author's experience in trying to do social action in the churches. They all happened, but the facts have been rearranged into stories for this book. They are fiction that still expresses the realities of resolving conflict.

Conflicted Old First United

In a sense, we all know abstractly how to live in harmony without destructive conflict, and can wisely advise others how they should live. But we find this hard to do ourselves in the little, everyday places like Old First United, the church in the following stories. There are lots of fights at Old First. To say that Old First United is united in more than name is to be casual with the truth. The truth is the members fight over everything—the budget, the organ, the parking lot, the leaky roof, the curriculum, social action. But their favorite fight is over the minister, the Rev. Buford Beasley. Of course, you can't see the fights on the surface. On the surface it is a friendly church. The warfare is subtle. They fight under the blanket of friendliness. They fight dirty because they don't know the skills of nonviolent struggle and conflict resolution. So there is wonderful material right at home at Old First Church for stories of conflict and its resolution on which to practice. That is probably true in your church, family, or work situation too.

Basic Communication

Unit 1 is an introduction to communication skills that are a basic requirement for preventing and resolving destructive conflicts. Although many people already have some of these skills, they are so essential and so easy to forget to use in conflictive situations that no conflict resolution course can take them for granted. So don't skip this part. It contains three sessions:

Session 1: Conflicts Are Resolvable
Session 2: What Is Conflict?
Session 3: Communication

Conflicts Are Resolvable

The Flag in the Church

The Conflict

Old First United had never had flags in its sanctuary, even during the wars. As far as anyone knew, this absence of flags was not because of a theological or political doctrine. When Frank Simmons asked the minister, Mr. Beasley, at the council meeting why we did not have the American flag in the sanctuary, Beasley said it just never occurred to anybody to put one there.

Frank thought it was about time we showed a little more respect for the flag and that we should put one up front, like other churches. Beulah

PURPOSES	SESSION PLAN OUTLINE	60 min.
• To reduce fear of conflict by showing how conflicts can be resolved	**Beginning**	
	Share names.	10 min.
	Give images of conflict.	5 min.
• To interest those present in a longer course on conflict resolution	Read story.	5 min.
	Continuing	
	Explain how conflict is normal.	10 min.
	Name goal.	5 min.
SCRIPTURE	Present characteristics of conflict.	10 min.
Matthew 18:15	Read story resolution.	5 min.
"Go and point out."	**Ending**	5 min.

PREPARATION

- Find a conflict in your own experience that was successfully handled or use the story "The Flag in the Church."
- Prepare to tell the story you have selected.
- Make newsprint charts of conflict characteristics.
- Collect supplies, newsprint, easel, marker, name tags. (This will be assumed in each session.)
- Set up room with circle of chairs.

Schuman fired back, "Over my dead body, Frank. The church is an international body, not a veteran's club."

"If we left it up to you, Beulah," Frank replied, "you'd probably hold a service of flag-burning. What's wrong with honoring the war dead and showing how we cherish the freedom to worship?"

Beulah came back, "Give me a break, Frank. If I was into burning, you'd be first on the list. But I don't come to church to worship patriotism. As far as I know, God is not a citizen of any nation."

Beasley interrupted with, "Oh, hold on you two. This item is not on the agenda of the council meeting. We can put it on next time. Let's get back to the agenda. Who's going to recruit church school teachers?"

THE SESSION PLAN

BEGINNING

Share names. Greet people and give each a name tag to fill out and wear.

Give images of conflict. Have people introduce themselves and give one word that comes to mind when they hear of conflict. Write these words in a left-hand column on the newsprint as they are spoken. Point out how we normally think of conflict in negative, destructive terms taken from images of warfare and violence. If positive terms are mentioned, build on them and challenge participants to add additional, constructive terms. Write those on the newsprint in a right-hand, parallel column opposite the negative terms.

Read story. Read the conflict part of the story presented above. Do not give the resolution yet. Ask participants to discuss possible resolutions.

CONTINUING

Explain how conflict is normal. Point out how we become stronger by dealing with conflict and how life, growth, excitement, and learning all involve conflict. Every story, drama, novel, movie, relationship, and learning experience has conflict as a necessary ingredient. Nature is full of conflict, from heat waves to snowstorms. Life *is* conflict. There is no way to avoid conflict. The Bible is full of conflict and assumes that conflict is part of life. Our only option is to decide how we will deal with conflict. There are constructive and destructive ways to handle conflict.

Name goal. The goal of this course is to *learn skills for constructively dealing with conflict.* Write this goal on the newsprint. Ask participants if they understand and agree to this goal. Point out that skills in conflict resolution involve simple, daily conflicts as well as complex conflicts among groups. There are many levels of conflict, and extensive practice is required to develop skills for constructive resolution. This is only an introduction.

Present characteristics of conflict. Uncover the left side of the prepared newsprint chart. When a fight starts, the following often happens:

Issues are viewed with:*

Personal antagonism	instead of	as problems to solve;
Focus on last insult	instead of	root causes;
Indirect communication	instead of	direct communication;
Polarization	instead of	multiple solutions;
Extremism	instead of	moderation;
Multiple issues	instead of	specific ssues.

Keep the right column covered for a while and discuss the left column. Explain how fights usually involve these six elements. Explain how a destructive conflict, as illustrated in the story, is different from a contest that has rules which are honored. In destructive conflicts, the rules have broken down; in a contest, rules are strictly honored. Ask participants if they can think of other characteristics of a fight. Add them to the newsprint.

Then reveal the right-hand column, as characteristics of a constructive conflict. Explain and compare each column. Ask for questions and comments. Then point out how this course is a training course in moving destructive conflicts (fights) in the left column to constructive conflicts (problems to solve) in the right column.

Read story resolution.

Resolution

At the next council meeting the first agenda item was Frank's motion "to purchase an American flag and dedicate it to a place in the sanctuary on the next Sunday nearest Flag Day." Beulah was ready to fight it to the end. But Beasley had done some homework too.

He suggested that rather than having an all-out battle, both of them express, not their hardened positions, but their interests or needs in this matter.

Frank said, "I want to show respect for our freedom to worship in this great land."

Beulah said, "I come to church to worship God, not a country or a flag."

Beasley asked that they all brainstorm ideas by which both interests could be served. They did, and came up with these ideas:

- Put a flag in the narthex, not in the sanctuary
- Have a sermon series on the freedom to worship
- Offer a Bible study course on church and state
- Research what other churches do about flags

*Adapted from John Paul Lederach, Mennonite Conciliation Service.

Beulah said, "Hey, Frank, you always like to delay my action ideas 'for further study.' Why don't we do that with your flag?"

Frank said, "Only if we study this deliberately and decide on it by Flag Day." They did study and later decided to buy both an American flag and a Christian flag and place them both in the church school.

By expressing their interests or needs rather than hardened positions or their do-or-die solutions, they were able to move from polarized positions to multiple and acceptable solutions.

ENDING

Assignment If people agree to continue the course, assign the reading of chapter 1 of this book and explain the procedure of the course. Assign the participants to be alert for conflicts that they experience or observe before the next session. Each should be prepared to share one at the next session. (If this is the first hour of a continuing course, with no time between sessions, have people recall a conflict to share now.)

Scripture Read Matthew 18:15. Point out how Jesus calls us to direct communication, person-to-person.

Prayer God of peace, help us to know that your peace brings us into conflict with the world and that to be at ease with the world brings us into conflict with you. Give us your peace and the courage and hope to deal constructively with conflicts in our world while we find our peace in you. Amen.

Session 2

What Is Conflict?

The Styrofoam Cup Conflict

The Conflict

The hospitality committee, Lois and Warren Beal, had just cut a real bargain by purchasing ten cartons of Styrofoam cups for the church coffee hour and potluck dinners. The volume purchase reduced the price by one third, and they were proud of the deal even though it meant that they had to store most of the huge cartons in their garage as there was no room for them at the church.

About that time the youth group returned from camp where they had learned about how polluting and nonbiodegradable polystyrene cups are. Burgess Schuman, Beulah's daughter, quickly recruited a four-person army to rid the church of foam cups. Forthwith, at coffee hour they demonstrated the evils of foam by wearing the cups as caps on their heads and picketing

PURPOSES	SESSION PLAN OUTLINE	120 min.
• To define conflict and conflict intensity	**Beginning**	
	Make introductions.	10 min.
• To begin practicing skills of conflict resolution	Read story.	5 min.
	Continuing	
	Role-play.	20 min.
SCRIPTURE	Define conflict.	10 min.
	Present conflict levels chart.	30 min.
Matthew 18:15–16	*Break*	10 min.
"Take one or two others."	Make reports.	20 min.
	Read story resolution.	5 min.
	Ending	10 min.

PREPARATION
- Reread chapters 2 and 3.
- Duplicate the conflict levels chart (in chapter 1). Read and prepare to tell the story.
- Make a newsprint list of some rules of conflict resolution.

the coffee urn, daring thirsty, coffee-craving adults to cross their picket line.

When Lois and Warren saw this spectacle, they became very distraught. Lois began to cry as Warren, with his arm around her shoulders, asked, "What's so evil about little white cups? We have twenty-five thousand of them in our garage." They left immediately and sent word back that they were leaving the church and going over to the church across the street where they were wanted. What can be done about this conflict?

THE SESSION PLAN

BEGINNING

Make introductions. Make sure everyone knows each other. Use name tags again if necessary.

Read story. Read aloud or tell the story of the foam cup conflict without the resolution.

CONTINUING

Role-play. Divide the participants into three equal-size groups. One will be the "youth," one the "hospitality committee," and a third "witnesses" or "mediators." Ask each group to meet separately and discuss their side of the issue of foam cups at church. Have the mediator group organize a mediation of representatives from each side. Tell them that they simply need to give each side uninterrupted time to tell their side of the issue to the other side. Hold the mediation for ten minutes. Then end the mediation even if it is incomplete.

Define conflict. Analyze the conflict in a group discussion by asking participants to define conflict. Record definitions on the newsprint. Add other definitions, such as:

- *con*, together + *fligere*, strike = strike together
- "two pieces of matter trying to occupy the same space at the same time"
- goals clashing
  (See chapter 3 for more definitions.)

Apply these definitions to the foam cup story, where the goals of the youth and the goals of the Beals clash. Ask participants to illustrate some characteristics of conflict from session 1 using this story.

Present conflict levels chart. Now present the prepared chart on conflict levels for fifteen minutes. (Copy from chapter 3.) Ask participants to study the chart in pairs and prepare an example of conflict levels using a conflict story they brought to the session, one they remember from another church, or the foam cup story. If they disagree with points in the chart, feel free to make changes. After a few minutes of discussion, excuse pairs for a ten-minute break.

Break

    Make reports. Ask one person from each pair to illustrate conflict levels from a conflict story before the whole group for a total of fifteen minutes. Point out how conflict resolution is a process of moving the levels from war and fights, to a challenge, to problem-solving.

    Read story resolution.

Resolution

Buford Beasley talked to the youth group and explained the problem that Lois and Warren had with the cups. The group felt that maybe they had overdone it, but still held to the principle of converting the church—that is, converting the church from foam to paper or washable cups. Burgess volunteered to visit Lois and Warren and discuss the matter.

    She did and told them she was sorry about their stockpile of foam. Warren said he did not care what kind of cups the church used, but he did not want to keep a garage full of them for eternity.

    Burgess suggested that the youth group might raise some money to buy them out or trade them in for paper. Lois agreed, "Just so we don't have to haul them around anymore." During the next few weeks the youth group raised $72.18, enough to cover the loss on a trade-in of ten cartons of foam for two cartons of paper cups. The next Sunday they arranged a celebration after church for Lois and Warren. They came back to be honored as the first paper cup users at Old First United, the town's first polystyrene-free zone.

ENDING

Assignment	Assign reading of chapter 2 and document stories of conflict for the next session.
Scripture	Read Matthew 18:15–16. Note how witnesses or mediators help move a conflict to a higher level.
Prayer	God of Creation, we believe we were meant by you to live in shalom and to find harmony as well as fairness among us. Help us to find those ways of shalom in our church, our lives, and our world. Amen.

RULES OF CONFLICT RESOLUTION

1. Know your feelings and fears.
2. Express your needs and interests.
3. See conflict as a problem to solve, not a war to win or lose.
4. Respect people.
5. Avoid polarizing or positioning.
6. Claim the church's peacemaking role.
7. Get all disputing parties to the table.
8. Accept conflict as normal.

Session 3

Communication

Clovis Opens His Mouth

The Conflict

The annual meeting of the regional church conference focused on homelessness. Reverend and the church's lay delegate, Clovis Calhoun, drove many miles to fulfill this obligation to the "wider church." It was Clovis' first contact with other church organizations. He was always puzzled at phrases like "local church" because there wasn't anything else in his church world but the church local. The delegates listened attentively to the speakers, all of whom were white men dedicated to serving the homeless and getting the church involved in the issue of homelessness.

Clovis came with his answer to the problem, which was, "Tell the homeless

PURPOSES	SESSION PLAN OUTLINE	120 min.
• To work on communication skills	**Beginning**	
	Explain communication.	10 min.
• To show how communication leads to destructive or to constructive conflict	Read story.	5 min.
	Continuing	
	Role-play story resolution.	20 min.
	Debrief.	10 min.
	Explain good listening.	10 min.
SCRIPTURE	Model good listening.	10 min.
Matthew 18:15–17	Practice in twos.	15 min.
"Tell it to the (whole) church."	*Break*	10 min.
	Present conflict cycle.	10 min.
	Read story resolution.	5 min.
	Discuss.	5 min.
	Ending	10 min.

PREPARATION
- Read and study Session 3.
- Make newsprint of listening skills, paraphrase definition and conflict cycle.
- Practice paraphrasing.

to get a job and pay the rent like I do." He was shocked to learn from the speakers that some homeless people do have jobs but can't afford even minimal rent, that many homeless people are children and the mentally disturbed, and that affordable housing, not just a temporary shelter, is necessary.

So when the plenary session broke up into small work groups assigned to come up with some ideas for what the churches could do, Clovis kept his mouth shut and listened (for a while). He learned even more.

Brenda Walker, a person of color in the small group, complained that the speakers' panel consisted solely of white males. This seemed unfair, because a large portion of homeless are people of color. She suggested that the small groups protest this to the whole conference when they reconvened, but added that it probably would not be heard. "This white male patronizing has gone on for years. Words don't get anywhere, only action like walking out would have any effect."

Then Clovis got excited because he felt he had a good idea. Beasley cringed, fearing that Clovis might better just listen in this volatile context. So he whispered to him, "Better hold it, Clovis." Well, it is not that easy to reign in an idea that will save the world. So Clovis got the floor from the convener, but did not keep it long. He said, "I think we should tell the conference to hold a special convention where the only speakers are you colored folks."

A stunned silence froze over the room. All eyes diverted to the floor. The convener of the small group dropped her felt marker and decided to retie her shoelaces. Beasley could hear the loud scraping of the laces being twisted around. Clovis was mystified. What had he said to cause this silence? He did not say, "Be quiet." He only let out his great idea.

Finally, he learned. Brenda rose to tell him. "That is exactly my point. This whole church is completely insensitive to us." She walked out and slammed the door.

How can the conference deal with this conflict?

THE SESSION PLAN

BEGINNING
Explain communication. Point out that most of us are "hard of hearing" even if our ears pick up sounds OK. We listen selectively in order to manage our lives. But we get into trouble and hurt other people when we don't hear what is important to them. Then we speak and act in ways that invalidate other people—even whole groups of people—whose experience we find hard to hear. Poor communication is the beginning of destructive conflict and good communication is a way to ensure constructive conflict. In order to communicate well good hearing is required, and that requires deliberate practice.

Read story. Read aloud or tell the story conflict.

CONTINUING

Role-play story resolution. Divide the participants into groups of three. One person in each group plays "Clovis," one "Brenda," and one the mediator. Assign the groups the task of resolving the conflict in the story. The mediator should help "Brenda" and "Clovis" speak one at a time and should summarize what each says when they are through talking.

Debrief. Call the groups back together and share what happened. First, the "Brendas," then the "Clovises," and then the mediators can report. Help the discussion to focus on how people do and don't listen to one another. Do not expect them to have communicated ideally. This role play helps people experience how valuable it is to learn good listening skills. The skills training comes next.

Explain good listening. Explain on newsprint the difference between what good listening is and what it is not:

Good listening is not:
1. Merely waiting to respond
2. Condemnation of content or how it is delivered
3. Clearly making your own case

Good listening is:
1. Hearing words and feelings
2. Objective reception of both
3. Ability to restate other's content and feelings

Model good listening. Ask for a volunteer to model with you, the leader, an example of good listening. Have the volunteer express his or her feelings about the course so far, or about how the volunteer normally responds to conflicts. Then practice good listening in your eye contact and positive response. Reverse the telling and listening roles with the volunteer.

Practice in twos. Ask participants to divide into groups of two and practice the same listening dialogues that you have just modeled with the volunteer, on the same topic: on the course so far, or on their normal response to conflict.

While participants are still in pairs, explain paraphrasing with this definition on newsprint: *Paraphrasing is responding to speakers' words with a brief summary of their words and the feelings behind those words.* The paraphrase must be stated to the satisfaction of the presenter so the presenter believes he or she has been heard and understood.

Ask the pairs to practice paraphrasing. One person states a concern about how a church usually handles conflict, giving an example. The other listens, then paraphrases the concern to the first person's satisfaction.

Break

Present conflict cycle. Explain, using newsprint, that conflicts that are constructive stay at the level of problems or mysteries to be solved or at least contests or games within rules. A destructive conflict may begin as a challenge or a contest, but it spirals out of control into a win/lose attack/counterattack without rules, except perhaps the "rule" that "might makes right." Graphically, a destructive conflict cycle looks like this. Show this graph to the group.

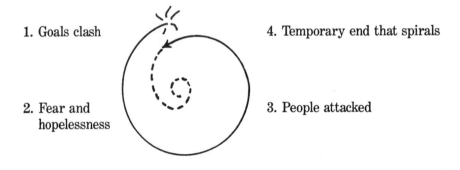

1. Goals clash

2. Fear and
   hopelessness

4. Temporary end that spirals

3. People attacked

Explain that our goal is not to avoid conflict or to win battles. Rather, when goals clash we learn to deal with the fear and hopelessness so that we then attack problems, not people. In a word, our goal is to move fights (conflicts without rules) to contests or problems or challenges (conflicts with rules).

Read story resolution.

Resolution

The small group sat helpless, wondering what to do about the conflict between Clovis and Brenda. Clovis felt his popularity had not risen with his great idea. The convener finally said to Clovis, "Well, I'm sure you did not know your use of the words 'colored folks' is perceived as a racial slur that was going to offend Brenda."

Clovis replied, "I sure didn't. I'd be glad to apologize if it would help. I meant no harm." The convener left the room to find Brenda, then arranged for Clovis' apology. She also took the idea of a convention that included homeless people of different colors to the plenary session. It was affirmed, and a subcommittee of the outreach commission was set up to get it done. Clovis volunteered to serve on the committee as a silent partner.

Discuss. Briefly discuss what the convener of the small group did right.

ENDING

Assignment   Assign reading of chapter 3.

Scripture   Read Matthew 18:15–17. Show how "taking an issue to the whole church" may mean doing it through our usual committee structures, in the "local" and the "wider" church, and that how we communicate and listen in every exchange is critically important.

Prayer   God of infinite patience, forgive us for not hearing you in the cries of our sisters and brothers. We get so busy listening to our own beat, getting our own lives in order, that we miss your Word in our midst. Open our ears to hear and our eyes to see your love and justice in our daily lives. Amen.

UNIT 2

Types of Conflict Resolution

There are different types of conflict and of conflict resolution, depending on the number of people involved. We will deal with four types in Unit Two: personal, interpersonal, intragroup, and intergroup. There are similarities in how these conflicts are resolved. But there are differences also. In real life they are all connected. A group conflict, for example, certainly involves us in personal conflict dynamics.

However, it is helpful in learning the skills of conflict resolution to separate the types. Unit Two assumes that persons have mastered the communication skills in Unit One but are always helped by continued practice to reinforce those skills. Now we will apply them to each type of conflict in four sessions.

Session 4: Conflict Resolution in Oneself
Session 5: Interpersonal Conflict Resolution
Session 6: Intragroup Conflict Resolution
Session 7: Managing Intergroup Disputes

Session 4

Conflict Resolution in Oneself

The Reverend Buford Beasley, Sexist

The Conflict

At Old First United they have not taken a position on the doctrine of God's omnipresence because they have such a wide variety of theologies. But one thing they know of omnipresence. Fighting among the believers is omnipresent at the church. They fight all the time. They even fight over words like "repentance." If they ever got down to real repentance, they would not agree on what it means. Frank Simmons says it only means "accepting Jesus as Lord and Savior." But Beulah Schuman says repentance costs more than that. She says, "Repentance means getting as far away as you can from big bankers, who should repent and forgive all Third World debt that the big bankers instigated in the first place." Buford Beasley, a liberal theologian, says repentance means a little of both.

One fight occurred that inspired repentance even in the pastor. It was over Reverend Beasley's calling on church members. He is always behind in his calling. On his first day at Old First he was 350 calls in debt. By now, if you could put a dollar figure on his calling debt, it would match the federal

PURPOSE	SESSION PLAN OUTLINE	120 min.
• To focus on repentance in personal conflict resolution	**Beginning**	
	Explain repentance.	10 min.
	Read scripture.	5 min.
• To make clear the biblical source of conflict resolution	**Continuing**	
	List Jacob's acts of repentance.	25 min.
	Recall one's own changes.	20 min.
	Break	10 min.
SCRIPTURE	Read story conflict.	5 min.
Genesis 32:3—34:4	Role-play.	25 min.
"Deliver me, please, from the hand of my brother."	Debrief.	10 min.
	Read story resolution.	5 min.
	Ending	5 min.
PREPARATION		
• Study chapter 2.		
• Be ready with a personal example of how you have changed.		

budget deficit. But when Beulah Schuman pinned him to the narthex wall before worship one Sunday for not visiting her niece in the hospital, Reverend Beasley knew he was in trouble. She got into her confrontation and added a few more complaints to her list—how he was neglecting social action in general and inclusive language in particular. Beulah's attack was so upsetting to him that he began the service of worship with the benediction and ended it with the call to worship. How could he deal with her charges of sexism and negligence in social action and calling?

THE SESSION PLAN

BEGINNING

Explain repentance. Explain how the overarching vision throughout the Bible is shalom, translated as "peace" in English, but including justice and the general well-being of human beings and of all creation in Hebrew. Shalom is what we seek in conflict resolution. That is, a real peace in which all people are treated fairly.

Another idea appears throughout the Bible as a necessary beginning point on the way to shalom. We must change the way we see things, including conflict. Our natural way to see conflict is as a threat. But conflict does not have to threaten us and cause us to act funny—hiding like turtles or beating our chests like apes. No, we have to change the way we see conflict—viewing it not as a threat, but as a chance to seek shalom.

This change of view is radical. It means changing ourselves or, rather, being changed. The word for such change in the Bible is "repentance."

Read scripture. Read aloud Genesis 32:3—34:4.

CONTINUING

List Jacob's acts of repentance. Ask participants to name all the things Jacob went through to repent, such as, "pray for help, offer gifts." As these are named, list them on newsprint. There should be ten or more.

Point out how reconciliation of a conflict with our brothers and sisters also means wrestling with God. Discuss the radical nature of real repentance.

Recall one's own changes. Ask participants individually to recall a time when they changed, repented from something, and to list some things that happened. Give an example from your experience; for example, "I once thought [white, black, yellow, red, or brown] people were unreliable. But I got to know some of them and I realized my views were wrong. I changed."

Ask participants to work privately on the recall for five minutes, then to share only what they feel comfortable sharing with one other person for ten minutes.

Ask for brief and voluntary response in the full group for five minutes.

Break

Read story. Read the story "The Reverend Buford Beasley, Sexist"

Role-play. Act out a conflict over inclusive language, using the communication skills learned in the last session. In separate groups of three, resolve a conflict in which pastor A does not use inclusive language. Groups of three work together at the same time. B wants to suggest that A, the pastor, change and use inclusive language in the church services. C is a mediator, who mostly observes but occasionally helps A and B to use good communication skills and paraphrasing.

Debrief. Allow A's, then B's, then C's to tell how well they used their skills and what resolutions they reached.

Read story resolution.

Resolution

Beulah's charges rang through Buford Beasley's head all during the service. When he finally got through it, he made his way to the parsonage for a strong drink and some serious thinking. After finishing his tall glass of Gatorade, he sat down and thought about Beulah's charges. He did what we all do under attack. It's not that easy to repent and say you're sorry. Whatever the Bible says about repentance:

- There are always extenuating circumstances in our daily lives. He was so tired from driving nine hundred miles to the Conference office, he forgot all about Beulah's niece. But it was not intentional.
- We repent for other people first. "O Lord, Sovereign One, forgive Beulah Schuman. She is probably very sorry for her nasty outburst."
- We seize the victim role. "Why is she always on my case?"
- We list all our unappreciated good deeds. "Like my courageous sermon against gluttony."
- We discredit our attackers. "No doubt about it, Beulah needs professional counseling."

Finally, it occurred to Beasley that when you get into trouble, religion is supposed to help you out, maybe with prayer, and he was supposed to be religious. So he began to pray—this time for himself: "O God, deliver me from the hand of my sister, Beulah Schuman."

He sat for a long time before a voice came to him: "Beasley, pick up the phone and call Beulah's niece. Congratulate her. Ask about the baby, and say you're sorry that you did not see her in the hospital. Ask her if it's OK to visit her this week. That's not so difficult to do, is it? Beulah will find out soon enough. Even good news travels fast in your church.

"Two more things, Beasley. One, you will clean up your language, and, two, when the women's center asks for a token male volunteer, you will raise your hand and open your mouth, and you will say, 'I am eager to serve.'"

Real repentance means being radically changed. That's what happened to Jacob and to Beasley.

ENDING

Assignment Assign participants to practice paraphrasing at least once before the next session. Assign the reading of chapter 6.

Prayer Forgiving God, we like to change without changing and stay the way we will feel comfortable. But we hear your call to keep growing and changing in search of your shalom. Give us the openness to see in our conflicts words of your vision of shalom. Amen.

Session 5

Interpersonal Conflict Resolution

Forgiving LeRoy

The Conflict

Jacob's task was to repent because he had cheated Esau. But there is another condition of conflict resolution. That is Esau's side. What is Esau, or any of us who are cheated, betrayed, or hurt, supposed to do? We can forgive, as Jesus said. But forgiveness is not so easy to do. That problem tied up Old First's board of Christian education for days in one church fight. It was over what to do about LeRoy Putnam's shameful behavior in the church school nursery—called "the cradle roll." The church found it hard to forgive LeRoy. But they still wanted to forgive him, and at the same time be responsible to the cherubs too, especially the cherubs that were brought in by prospective members at Old First United. The membership problem had moved from the category of "troublesome" to "desperate." They kept

---

PURPOSE	SESSION PLAN OUTLINE	120 min.
• To learn skills of resolving conflicts on an interpersonal level	**Beginning**	10 min.
	Explain interpersonal conflict resolution.	
	Read the scripture.	
	Continuing	
SCRIPTURE	Practice confrontation in twos.	25 min.
2 Cor. 5:17–20	Practice three things exercise.	5 min.
"the ministry of	Debrief.	5 min.
reconciliation"	Reverse roles.	5 min.
	Debrief.	10 min.
	Break	10 min.
	Read story.	5 min.
	Experience fishbowl.	20 min.
	Read story resolution.	5 min.
	Have plenary discussion.	15 min.
	Ending	5 min.

PREPARATION
- Study the session plan.
- Prepare the newsprint with "three things."

thinking they had bottomed out, but the bottom kept finding new depths of profundity.

Here is an interpersonal conflict that affected the whole church. They had only one baby in the cradle roll most of the time. But finally one Sunday morning a new couple showed up with another baby. The greeters that morning were the membership committee, consisting of Flo and Bob Denton. When they spotted these hot prospects coming in the church door, they started out to recruit them to join and pledge even before they got through the narthex. Reverend Beasley had to restrain them. He whispered to Flo and Bob, "Not yet. At least let them sit down first."

They had the cradle roll waiting for the baby. It met at the same time as worship. But Shirley Burns, the chair and sole member of the board of Christian education, was having the usual recruiting problems. The best she could come up with was LeRoy Putnam, whose incompetence was matched only by his enthusiasm. They kept giving LeRoy second chances which they lost track of back before the war.

He was assigned to manage the cradle roll that Sunday. He did very well, for a while. But by the end of the service of worship he had fallen asleep holding the new couple's baby. Of course, no harm was done (to the baby), but the new couple found all three of them sound asleep in the cradle roll after the service. The parents were not happy with this arrangement, but were restrained in expressing it, unless you think that slamming the door when they left was a sign of something. Way down in their hearts, though, the congregation knew that the family was gone for good, so they all got mad at LeRoy. But it wasn't much fun to get mad at LeRoy because he never seemed to acknowledge it. So then they got mad at Shirley Burns for allowing such negligence in the church school.

Like most churches, Old First United tolerates a lot. But tolerance is different from forgiveness. The usual pattern is simply to avoid any kind of conflict unless it is staring people right in the face. And even then they are too shy to stare back at it. They would have ignored this little disaster too, except that LeRoy liked the job and wanted to keep on supervising the cradle roll. They thought that someone had to tell him that he was not qualified for the position. How could they do it? He meant well. Shouldn't they forgive him?

THE SESSION PLAN

BEGINNING

Explain interpersonal conflict resolution. Explain how trivial conflicts as well as threats of global warfare involve interpersonal communication and negotiation. Buford Beasley has to try to get along with Beulah Schuman and the U.S. President with the U.S.S.R. President, whether they like each other or not. The interpersonal level of conflict resolution is unavoidable, in small or large disputes. So learning the skills of conflict resolution on this level is essential. One aspect of interpersonal resolution is confrontation.

Read the scripture.

CONTINUING

Practice confrontation in twos. Ask participants to pair off and choose an interpersonal conflict in which one person has to tell another that he or she has messed up or must stop doing something. Use conflicts they have brought from their experience or one of the following. Examples: The pastor has started preaching too long, the treasurer keeps confusing the budget figures, a teacher uses only fundamentalist curriculum and has "altar calls" in each class, the youth advisor has a drinking problem, an usher keeps smoking in the narthex during hymns.

Practice three things exercise. Ask the pairs to role-play the encounter between the offended person (A) and the offender (B), in which A uses good communication skills learned above and tries out the following formula. Write on newsprint:

What I like about your contribution is . . .
What I'd like to improve in this matter is . . .
What I will do is . . .

Debrief. After the pairs of A's and B's have worked on one problem, debrief in the whole group with A's and B's volunteering comments.

Reverse roles and practice. Ask the A's and B's to reverse roles and practice using another problem from the above or, preferably, from their own experience.

Debrief these encounters again in plenary session.

Break

Read story. Read aloud the conflict section of the story "Forgiving LeRoy."

Experience fishbowl. Ask participants to form a fishbowl. That is, one half of the group is in a discussion circle in the middle of a larger circle made up of the other half. The inner circle discusses what to do about LeRoy. The outer circle must stay quiet until the inner circle finishes, in ten minutes. Then the outer circle forms an inner circle and repeats the discussion for ten minutes.

Read story resolution. Read aloud the resolution of the story, and hold an open discussion of the difficulties of confronting others about their behavior. List such problems on newsprint and ask persons to volunteer wording that confronts the offending behavior in a gentle but firm way. Use the formula in the "Practice three things exercise" or other wording that forgives but also speaks the truth.

Resolution

Two main approaches were discussed at a meeting on Wednesday night at Shirley Burns's house. Beulah, who made a guest appearance, wanted to tell LeRoy off good and let the chips fall. Confrontation was her style, and now Beulah was ready to give LeRoy a little of it. But Shirley had a different style and theology. She wanted to forgive LeRoy. As Jesus says, "Seventy times seven." Beulah replied, "You mean to let LeRoy keep on sleeping in the nursery? That's insane. We could be sued because of his negligence. No way."

For Beulah, LeRoy had made such a mess of every assignment that he had now passed 490 offenses and was due for an unforgiving blast of her wrath. She figured 490, or seventy times seven, was an outside limit and LeRoy was way overdue.

Beulah wanted to confront without forgiving. Shirley wanted to forgive without confronting. Both solutions were different from Jesus' way of handling conflict which is confront *and* forgive.

After hours of dead-end discussions about the problem, Reverend Beasley finally joined the meeting after visiting Beulah's niece and her new baby. He listened for a while, then suddenly solved the problem. He said, "There are ways to forgive and ways to be stupid." Then he volunteered to confront LeRoy face-to-face and tell him his fault. If he listened, then Beasley suggested he could do the job, but only with a helper to make sure that he stayed awake. Everyone agreed with this solution, but no one realized it came from Matthew 18:15.

Have plenary discussion.

ENDING

Assignment Assign persons to use the three things formula at least once before the next session.

Prayer   God of power, give us the courage we need to confront others with what we believe is true and give us the humility to realize that we don't have the truth sewn up. And keep us supplied with forgiveness. Amen.

Session 6

Intragroup Conflict Resolution

The Great Pipe Organ War

The Conflict

It will take a few generations to forget the great war over the pipe organ at Old First. There could be a war memorial erected to commemorate it, but most members would just like to erase it, once they pay off the organ debt. Surely there are learnings about resolving conflict to be mined from this great battle.

It all began when Penafore Crump was the part-time organist and choirmaster. He was a skilled musician, a high Episcopalian, at our church—a low-church Protestant congregation that was less committed to musical expertise. The hymn singing was so untutored that it kept throwing even the electric organ off key. So when Penafore announced to the trustees that he had found a marvelous deal on a pipe organ, there was a full five minutes of stunned, silent disbelief. The old electric had seemed good enough to Travis Elliot, Marsha and Ed Turner, and Beulah Schuman, trustees of Old First United.

PURPOSE	SESSION PLAN OUTLINE	120 min.
• To begin learning skills of mediation between disputing factions within an organization	**Beginning**	
	Explain intragroup conflicts.	5 min.
	Read story.	5 min.
	Continuing	
SCRIPTURE	Role-play the organ dispute.	30 min.
	Debrief.	15 min.
Ephesians 2:11–16	*Break*	10 min.
"putting to death that hostility"	Present conflict resolution cycle.	20 min.
	Read and discuss scripture.	20 min.
	Read story resolution.	5 min.
	Ending	10 min.

PREPARATION
• Study this session.
• Prepare newsprint with conflict resolution cycle.

Finally Ed said, "The timing could not be worse, Penafore. Why, we just took a year of beating from the new hymnal you introduced, which is full of hymns no one knows, sung to tunes we never heard of. Now you want a new pipe organ?"

"Well, let's hear him out," said Beulah. "It doesn't cost one old penny to listen to a new idea. Keep an open mind, Ed."

Penafore was ready. This Episcopal church, St. Throckmorton's down in Edgewater, had spent their endowment and had to close down the church. The video store that bought the building did not want the organ, and they demanded that it be out in two weeks or no deal. The priest sent to salvage the property was desperate. "He'd probably be happy if we hauled it off free just to get rid of it. We need to give him some ridiculous offer in two weeks," said Penafore. Beulah got intrigued with the idea. She could never walk past a "prices slashed" sign or a garage sale without stopping to experience the thrill of finding a real bargain. She needed at least one bargain a day to keep her going and she had not had one all day.

Penafore went on about what a really wonderful sound that pipe organ had, and for his clincher he said, "People will come from miles around to hear this fine organ. They will come back again and again until Old First United has a full house every Sunday. The collection plate will fill up once again. It's not an expenditure, it's an investment."

Now the idea of bringing in people who would let go of some money for the offering excited Travis. But Ed dug in. The more Penafore talked, the madder Ed got. Marsha wanted to get more money in, but it certainly should not go for an organ—it should go for education. Still, she said nothing until she and Ed got in the pickup to drive home after the meeting. Then she let Ed have it.

The meeting had concluded with a decision to explore the idea further with no commitment and to meet next week for "another look." Travis and Beulah also got together to promote an "open mind" campaign with the rest of the church. Ed and Marsha Turner got on the phone to the outreach committee, which had not met in a year. It had not seemed necessary for the chairman, Royce Bucannan, since they had only eighteen dollars in the budget to spend. They also called Shirley Burns, whose education committee needed money for curriculum. The sides developed quickly, polarized, and stopped talking to each other altogether. The battleground was set and the armies recruited, the weapons were readied, and the great pipe-organ battle was on.

The readiness for battle was no sudden accident at Old First. Actually, the organ was only a catalyst bringing together a long series of feuds between the two factions that gathered around Travis on the one hand and Ed and Marsha on the other. The organ only ignited a flame from the smoldering coals of persistent, unresolved conflict. All the other ingredients of a good church fight were there to be fanned to flame: personal animosity;

indirect communication; focus on the last insult; polarization; extremism; and the confusion of many issues.

Instead of framing the conflict as fruitful diversity in one body with many talents, where all could win in a rich collaboration of views to solve a problem, Old First framed the conflict as a battle to be won by the Travis' faction or the Turner faction. It began as a zero sum game of win or lose.

How could it end as a constructive conflict where everybody wins?

THE SESSION PLAN

BEGINNING

Explain intragroup conflicts. That is, look at how disputes between different factions in a group of people are different from disputes within oneself or between individuals. Intragroup disputes are much more complex because many more perspectives must be reconciled, even on one side.

Read story.

CONTINUING

Role-play the organ dispute. Divide the participants into three groups. Ask for two groups to play pro-pipe organ and con-pipe organ factions. The third group will assume the role of mediators, who must try to resolve the conflict between the warring factions. The mediator group meets to plan a strategy for resolving the dispute as the pro and con groups meet to each defeat the other side and win over the rest of the church.

Then role-play the first meeting of one of the mediators with one representative from each group. These three sit in a triangle with their groups behind them. The task is for the mediators to carry out a strategy to attain an agreement for mediating the dispute or a process for doing so.

Debrief. Discuss the role play in plenary session. Ask each group to describe its experience, with the moderator speaking last.

Break

Present conflict resolution cycle. Present this chart from chapter 6.

1. Goals clash
2. Expressions of courage, hope
3. Attack problem
4. Resolution/agreement

Compare the conflict spiral from Session 3. Ask participants to name how fear and hopelessness (#2) can be replaced with courage and hope in the midst of an intragroup conflict.

Read and discuss scripture. Read aloud Ephesians 2:13–16 and ask participants to name how Jesus helps us mediate conflicts between those who are "near" and those who are "far off."

Read story resolution. Read aloud the resolution of "The Great Pipe Organ War." Discuss how it could have been handled better.

Resolution

The pipe-organ battle raged for over a year. As it turned out, the two-week deadline was soft enough to stretch on for months, but the "practically-free-for-hauling-it-off" organ turned out to be $8,000 plus an almost infinite number of added expenditures. Meeting after meeting was held. Frank Simmons ended up adjusting the budget over ten times before they could see how to pay for it. The vote was close (51 percent to 49 percent). The "open mind" campaign faction won. They won the battle, but it's not clear who won the war, because getting the vote was easy compared to getting the organ to play. First, all the pieces were piled up in the parlor for nine months. And Ed and Marsha do not lose a fight easily. If they had to have that pipe organ in their sanctuary, then they were going to make sure that Mr. Penafore Crump never played it.

Sure enough, before the organ ever made a sound, the organist and choirmaster's salary had shrunk to an all-time low, and Penafore had heard a call to another church that appreciated his talents more than Old First. Penafore Crump did not get to play his organ, but he got another job (with another pipe organ) that pays a living wage, and he is much happier there.

As it has turned out, the church is not yet overflowing with new members and new money, even with a pipe organ. But in the midst of the effort to make the pile of pipes work, Ed and Marsha joined in with Travis and Beulah to help put it all together. Without knowing or planning it, a very strong community was built between the factions who worked on the pipe organ. They are very proud of that work and of the renewed friendship built in the common labor. God helps us grow through conflict. The world is full of bigger conflicts awaiting our efforts to reframe them as opportunities for God's grace.

ENDING

Assignment   Assign participants to bring a large-group (intergroup) dispute that they have experienced to the next session.

Prayer   God of the church, we forget how to make peace even in your church. Give us hope to overcome our cynicism about resolving disputes, and give us the patience to stay at the hard work it takes to make peace in the church and in the world. Amen.

Session 7

Managing Intergroup Disputes

Dispute in the Wider Church

The Conflict

Mildred Morse had been active in the "wider church," which was the term she used to refer to any church activity beyond Old First United. Buford Beasley had other names for the associations, judicatories, conferences, and synods. He called them all "circuses" dreamed up by bureaucrats who over-loaded his desk with endless questionnaires and undermined his ego with nosy questions about membership growth and giving campaigns.

A special meeting of the wider church was called, and Mildred was ready to go and, as Beasley put it, "get some more wild ideas to inflict on me." Beasley was also asked to attend. He agreed, not because he wanted to, but rather because at the time he just could not think of a good excuse to say no fast enough.

Both of them were asked to be on a panel to mediate a dispute between a group that sought to cut all funds and staff of the wider church unless they ended all political action and returned to the Bible by Tuesday. This group called

PURPOSE	SESSION PLAN OUTLINE	120 min.
• To begin learning the skills of large, intergroup conflict management	**Beginning**	
	Explain intergroup conflict.	10 min.
	Continuing	
	Role-play the caucus and hearing.	30 min.
	Debrief.	15 min.
SCRIPTURE	Read the story.	5 min.
Colossians 1:19–22	*Break*	10 min.
"to reconcile . . . all things"	Advise the panel.	35 min.
	Read the story resolution.	5 min.
	Ending	10 min.

PREPARATION
- Reread chapter 6.
- Recall a large-group/intergroup conflict if you can, and prepare to share.

itself The Bible First Fellowship (BFF). It was against feminism, disarmament, communism, and social action. It was for traditional values, a strong military, anticommunism, patriotism, evangelism, and Bible study.

It had gotten support from a number of churches in the denomination and was now strong enough to challenge the "bureaucrats" to a showdown. Its members had been at work for years, publishing a newsletter and speaking at churches to get their ideas across. Now they were ready to turn the church around. Beulah Schuman was ready to turn them into mincemeat. Beasley wished he hadn't gotten involved.

Opposing the Bible First Fellowship was an unorganized assortment of liberals, minority groups, feminists, and some of the staff of the wider church organization. Most church members in the area just wished this dispute would go away.

The focus of this long-smoldering dispute was the annual meeting of the wider churches, where BFF planned to stop all funding for social action. This would mean the end of a number of staff jobs and a radical change of the church's support for minority programs. But the BFF claimed that if it failed, twenty-five churches would withdraw from the denomination.

Mildred and Beasley were asked to try to mediate the issue before the final vote was taken to the annual meeting in a month. They were part of a panel of five church members assigned to take as much time as necessary to deal with the problem. All kinds of rumors were in the air. Demonstrations and walkouts were threatened. Both sides were due to be out in force.

Mildred and Beasley drove to the scheduled meeting place, the Prince of Peace Congregation. They tried to get organized. They were committed to doing an effective job in spite of their personal opinions. An outside consultant on conflict management would be available if called on. They had the morning to get organized before the disputants arrived in the afternoon. How should they proceed?

THE SESSION PLAN

BEGINNING

Explain intergroup conflict. Point out that managing large-group disputes is both similar to and different from resolving interpersonal and intragroup conflicts. The process during the mediation session is the same. But, because many more people are involved, many more interests must be managed. This is done by prehearing caucuses of the disputing groups. The caucuses (the Friends Suburban Project prefers to call them "separate meetings to avoid political overtones") is the place where each side gets organized with a clear written statement of what its people want and an affirmation about who will negotiate for them. The caucus enables the mediator to manage the process better because the written statements and single representative spokesperson mean others have no need to disrupt. They own the process and help it work because they are being heard.

CONTINUING

Role-play the caucus and hearing. Ask volunteers to present an inter-group dispute from their experience. If it lends itself to role play, you can organize that and practice it by dividing participants into three groups: pro, con, and conflict management panel. Or use the conflict story with the same three groups. Assign one group to play the "conservatives," one the "liberals," and one the dispute management panel. The conservatives have threatened to withdraw from the denomination to form a new church. They are "fed up with all the liberal social action that ignores spirituality and evangelism." The "liberals" want even more social action. They want the conservatives to stay but not to water down social action.

Assign the panel to lead each side in a separate caucus. There each side will list in writing exactly what they want and elect their spokesperson. The panel can split up to do this, but panel members are free to meet to check signals.

The caucus rules: *no interruptions; all get to speak; people who are absent do not have a voice.*

Role-play a conflict management hearing. The panel is in charge and runs the process. It will lead the process seeking to manage the dispute.

Debrief the role play.

Read the story.

Break

Advise the panel. Ask participants to discuss in groups of three what advice they would give to Beasley and to Mildred, who have not been on a conflict management panel before. In plenary session ask for the "advice," then write it on newsprint.

Read the story resolution.

The Resolution

Mildred and Reverend Beasley and the other panel members agreed to seek the consultant's help as they gathered at Prince of Peace Congregation. The consultant from the Dispute Resolution Center told them that a mediator's job is not to make the decisions but to help the disputants to make their cases in an orderly and representative way and to reach an agreement both sides can accept. The help comes through a mediation process, he said.

"This process helps both sides to be heard. Often when a dispute is fully expressed, some solutions appear. Our first job as mediators is to help sides to organize their cases so that all people are heard and support the process. Since this is a large-group dispute, we must give special attention to helping both sides to make sure all people are in on the process. I suggest that both sides caucus when they arrive. We can split up and meet with each group."

"Won't that divide them farther?" asked Mildred.

"No, the point is to help them get what they want out on newsprint and for the spokespersons to emerge from each group who will be the natural leaders, those who really represent the parties. Then the eventual agreement will be followed because people have had their say through a true representative."

This training of mediators continued until noon. After lunch, when the disputants arrived, two panelists met with each group, and one shuttled back and forth with the consultant. Confidentiality was assured. Those on each side developed a list of what they wanted, and spokespersons were elected. The mediation hearing process was explained to each side. Care was taken to invite all present to get their views out on the newsprint. Only the people present had a voice. The spokespersons would have plenty of time to explain from the newsprint what they wanted, without interruption. Then both sides would attempt to work out resolutions and an agreement. The panel would be in charge and prevent interruptions. If things got out-of-hand, they would end the hearing. But if anyone on either side thought the spokesperson was not representing that side, another caucus could be called at any time.

As it turned out, the BFF, like the liberals, were not of one voice or as united as first thought. The caucus process took all afternoon. Finally, after supper and a prayer service, the hearing itself began. To sum up the mediation hearing, BFF's list included more Bible study, more money for evangelism, a voice on funding decisions, and more say in hiring staff. The liberals' list included more funding and staff for social action and more voice for women and minorities on funding and staff decisions.

The hearing took all evening, but the essence of an agreement was worked out, with details left to a small group of leaders from each group. The liberals accepted the idea for more Bible study and evangelism, and the funding and hiring decisions would be monitored by a new steering committee proposed for vote at the annual meeting. (When that time came, it passed unanimously.) The dispute was resolved.

On the trip home, Beasley and Mildred were too tired to talk, let alone to argue.

ENDING

Assignment Assign chapter 4.

Scripture Read Colossians 1:19–22.

Prayer God of history, we know you are alive with us and we know you expect us to do your work of peacemaking in the world. Be present with us as we try to learn how to do it so that others may know your presence through us. Amen.

UNIT 3

Power, Empowerment, and Getting People to the Table

We have worked on communication skills in Unit 1 and applied them to four levels of conflict in Unit 2. Now it is essential to go deeper into a common barrier to conflict resolution. That is, a barrier that prevents people from getting to the table to work out solutions to problems.

This barrier to conflict resolution is an imbalance, or perceived imbalance, of power between the disputing parties. When one party feels powerless in a dispute, it is wise not to try to negotiate a resolution under those conditions because it will probably lose. But powerlessness can be overcome by empowerment. Once a weak party is empowered, both parties may come to the negotiating table hopeful of a just resolution. Now we will deal with power, empowerment, and how to get people to the table, in three sessions:

> **Session 8: Power in Conflict Resolution**
> **Session 9: Empowerment**
> **Session 10: Getting All People to the Table**

Power in Conflict Resolution

Beasley Versus Hernandez et al.

The Conflict

Beasley was fed up. The church just wasn't getting clean. Carlos came in, rushed around with a dust mop, and disappeared. This had gone on almost since Beulah Schuman suggested that they give a job to Carlos Hernandez, who was a refugee from El Salvador. She said, "It is our duty to do *something* to help relieve the horrible mess that our Government is making down there. If our taxes can fund death squads to kill, our offerings can pay a refugee to work."

At that time Beasley was more worried about dirty floors than U.S. foreign policy. So, for different reasons, Carlos was hired. But he never lived up to Beasley's standard of keeping the church clean. Also, Beasley rarely could reach Carlos when he wanted to tell him what to do. When he did talk to Carlos, there was a language problem, as Beasley spoke no Spanish.

PURPOSE	SESSION PLAN OUTLINE	120 min.
• To practice conflict resolution skills	**Beginning**	
	Explain power.	5 min.
• To become aware of power issues in conflict resolution	Read the story.	5 min.
	Continuing	
	Define power.	10 min.
	Share, in triads.	30 min.
SCRIPTURE	*Break*	10 min.
	Explain levels of power.	10 min.
Psalm 113:7–8	Draw the power pie.	15 min.
"[God] raises the poor from the dust."	Model a role-play.	20 min.
	Read the story resolution.	5 min.
	Ending	10 min.

PREPARATION
• Read chapter 4.
• Prepare power definitions and charts on newsprint.

Carlos spoke very little English. Beasley found dust in the corners, cigarette butts on the sidewalk, and lingering aromas in the bathroom.

The final offense was a tissue on the altar before Communion service one Sunday morning. Then and there Beasley decided to fire Carlos instantly and keep his last paycheck. After all, he thought as he cleaned the altar, the church pays Carlos to clean the church. The church is filthy, so he does not deserve a job or to be paid for not doing it. It is only responsible stewardship. It's the judgment side of the gospel. It's tough love. So that settles it. Don't get soft. He's fired, and no more pay.

After cleaning up, Beasley began the service. The Old Testament lesson was Psalm 113, part of which said,

> "[God] raises the poor from the dust,
> and lifts the needy from the ash heap,
> to make them sit with princes."

Beasley calmed down a bit by the end of the service, not so much because of scriptural influence as because he realized that he had better take the matter up with the building and grounds committee, which was Beulah, with Mildred Morse as chair. Beulah had said once, "I do not find impulsive power plays by the clergy amusing." Beasley realized that if he fired Carlos, he'd have both Mildred and Beulah to answer to. The very thought sent icy chills down his spine and gave him a shivering cold flash. But he was determined.

During the coffee hour he took Beulah and Mildred on a church tour to see the sites of "filth and squalor." They said nothing until Beasley finished the guided tour and told them his decision to fire Carlos and keep his last paycheck. Beulah's face grew stony and white, and her hand formed itself into a pointed weapon against Beasley's chest as she asserted, "Beasley, if you fire him, pack your bags too. Carlos stays, and that's that."

How can this dispute be settled with justice and peace?

THE SESSION PLAN

BEGINNING

Explain power. Conflict resolution requires more than good communication. Often two conflicting parties cannot even get to a position of beginning communication of any value because one party is (or is thought to be) so much more powerful than the other party. This is often the case with an abusing and abused spouse, a consumer and a corporation, or a superpower and a client state. When the powerless try to negotiate with the powerful, they often lose because the powerful set the terms and conditions for a settlement, and the powerless do not have the power to deal effectively in those conditions or to get what they want. So it is essential to deal with the matter of power in a course on conflict resolution.

Read the story.

CONTINUING

Define power. Write this sentence on newsprint: "Power is the ability to influence outcomes." Ask each participant individually to write down answers to these questions:

- Who has the most power in the story, and why?
- Who has the least power in this story? Why?
- What kinds of power does each person have?
  (Beasley's power, for example: the authority, with the committee's consent, to hire and fire)

Share in triads. Now ask participants to share their answers in groups of three and to suggest ways to go about resolving the conflict that accounts for the power arrangements. Call the group back together to share their proposed resolutions.

Break

Explain levels of power. Draw on newsprint and explain the levels of the power pyramid (from chapter 4):

Outcome
Process
Social esteem
Self-esteem
Existential/religious

Ask participants to name aspects of each level of power suggested in the story, in an open discussion. Record these illustrations next to the levels of power; for example, Beulah's self-esteem, Mildred's authority (process power) as committee chair.

Draw the power pie. Explain the zero sum and infinite sum game from chapter 4.

Model a role-play. Ask for two volunteers to role-play a negotiation between Beasley and Carlos. One person plays Carlos and one plays Beasley, and the rest of the participants play the mediation panel. Tell the panel to try to negotiate a solution to the problem by talking directly with each other using the communication skills and paraphrasing that were practiced in Session 3.

Read the story resolution. Discuss the uses of power in this resolution.

The Resolution (attempted)

Mildred intervened in the standoff between Beasley and Beulah. She said, "Hold on a minute. Aren't we leaving out an important part of this problem?

I suggest we talk to Carlos and see if he knows what we want cleaned and hear what he has to say." By now Beasley was relieved to avoid more confrontations with Beulah. They agreed.

She set up a meeting and Carlos came, late. He did not say much, only that his wife had been in the hospital and he would try harder to clean better. He said he needed the job badly. But when Beasley asked him about not being reachable, Carlos just clammed up.

Mildred asked him if he could say it better in Spanish. He said he could and that he just couldn't understand English so well. Mildred suggested that they end the meeting now until they could deal with the language issue. They agreed. She told Carlos to call her tomorrow to see if they could work something out. Carlos said he was sorry to make so much trouble and that he needed the job.

ENDING

Scripture Read Psalm 113:7–8. Point out how God gives support to the poor.

Prayer God of the poor, most of us are rich in many things but often poor in your Spirit. Empower us with your Spirit to keep working for justice and peace and finding ways to bring nonviolent resolutions to our conflicts. Amen.

Session 9

Empowerment

Carlos' Power

The Conflict

Mildred, Beulah, and Beasley sat silently in the pastor's study after Carlos left. They were all discouraged. Beasley saw no hope in getting through to Carlos and just wanted to get it over with and to hire another cleaning person. Beulah was let down because she wanted to help Carlos, but somehow Carlos had to come forward with some hope that the job would get done. The church did need better cleaning, she had to admit to herself, though she did not expect to admit that to Beasley. As far as Beasley was concerned, Beulah was insisting that Carlos' job with the church was nonnegotiable.

Mildred's immediate interest was in keeping Beulah and Beasley from fighting over the matter and she kept searching for a better way to name the problems. Finally she said, "We can't get anywhere until we can communicate better with Carlos."

Beasley said, "The church can't wait for him to pass an English course."

Beulah responded, "You could study Spanish, you know, Beasley. The

---

PURPOSE
- To understand how power imbalances can preclude conflict resolution
- To learn how power can be balanced with empowerment

SCRIPTURE

Isaiah 40:28–31
"[God] gives power to the faint."

PREPARATION:
- Reread chapter 5.
- Prepare chart on empowerment from chapter 5.

SESSION PLAN OUTLINE   **120 min.**

Beginning
Explain empowerment.   10 min.
Read the story.   5 min.
Continuing
Examine power in the story.   15 min.
Brainstorm Carlos' potential power.   15 min.
Role-play.   25 min.
   Break   10 min.
Explain the empowerment chart.   15 min.
Read the story resolution, discuss.   15 min.
Ending   10 min.

English language didn't fall out of heaven. Why don't you take a study leave in Central America? You'd understand better some of the misery your taxes are buying there and learn Spanish too!"

Mildred intervened with, "Let's get back to Carlos and the cleaning. One issue is the language barrier. What other issues do you see?"

Beasley: "He doesn't seem to know what being clean is, and he is unreliable, even in Spanish."

Mildred summarized: "I see three problems: language, defining what we want to have cleaned, and accessibility. Beulah, does Carlos have any relatives in the area?"

"Sure, that's why he came here. His uncle helped him get started in the cleaning business, and he called the churches to line up the jobs for Carlos."

"So his uncle speaks fluent English?" Mildred asked.

"Sure. You want him to translate for Carlos?"

"It crossed my mind," said Mildred.

"I'll call him tomorrow," said Beulah.

"OK," said Mildred, "and Reverend Beasley, will you write out exactly what you expect to have cleaned in the church?"

"In English?" he asked.

"What else?" asked Beulah.

THE SESSION PLAN

BEGINNING

Explain empowerment. Show how unbalanced power's block to conflict resolution can be overcome by balancing power, or empowerment. As there are many levels of power, there are also many levels of empowerment. A person may feel power in one context but not in another. For example, Carlos felt powerless without facility in English. But there were ways for him to gain power so he could negotiate a fair conflict resolution.

Read the story.

CONTINUING

Examine power in the story. Recruit a volunteer panel from the participants and ask them to list the power of each person in the story by referring to the levels of power in chapter 5.

Brainstorm Carlos' potential power. Ask the whole group to discuss how Carlos may be able to attain power adequate to this situation.

Role-play. The group can divide into thirds. One third is "Carlos," another third is "Beasley," and another third is the "building and grounds committee." They can discuss how each should deal with the conflict. Then individual representatives from each group play Carlos and Beasley and the committee, sit facing one another, and negotiate a solution. Others may coach each as they try to negotiate a settlement. The goal should be to use good communication skills and seriously work at a solution.

Break

Explain the empowerment chart. Draw on newsprint and explain the empowerment chart from chapter 5. Point out how the choice of action and empowerment steps depend on the level of power sought. Although all levels of power interrelate, some are needed more at one time than at another. Carlos' lack of English in this situation limited his power of group esteem. However, the process level of power (how decisions got made in the church) gave him power through Mildred and Beulah as they became his advocates.

Read story resolution, discuss. Read aloud the resolution of the story and discuss other possible endings and ways to empower Carlos.

The Resolution

Mildred arranged another meeting. And Beulah, with Carlos' permission, got his uncle to help translate. With that help, Carlos was empowered to speak more freely. He reported that his wife was still in the hospital, but she is up now. If the church would explain exactly what tasks Carlos is to do and how they are to be done, his uncle could write instructions in Spanish for him and guarantee that the job would be done right.

Beasley ventured that he was tired of having no way to reach Carlos. Carlos responded that he would get a telephone answering machine if the church would split the cost. Then, if Beasley did not like his work, he could leave word on the machine and Carlos would come back at any time to redo the job at no extra charge.

Beasley said he would write down what he wanted and give it a two-month trial period. They all agreed.

ENDING

Scripture   Read Isaiah 40:28–31. Note how God wills the empowerment of the weak.

Prayer   God of power, sometimes we feel powerless ourselves and sometimes we lose patience with powerless people. Empower us with understanding and compassion for the weak and courage to confront the strong. Amen.

Session 10

Getting All Parties to the Table

The Stewardship Campaign

The Conflict

Frank Simmons and Bill West, new cochairs of the stewardship campaign committee at Old First, were determined to get the giving off its downward slump and back up into the ballpark that the budget required. They had a theory that had crystallized into an absolute doctrine of faith: that giving was off because of all the liberal social action the church had gotten snookered into doing. They believed that all this action was not only heretical, it was worse: it drove off potential new members, with new money, who would be attracted to the church if it would just return to the true faith. The true faith calls the church to convert unbelievers to it and lets individ-

---

PURPOSE	SESSION PLAN OUTLINE	120 min.
• To learn the skills of assessing what is a resolvable conflict, what power balancing is needed, and how to get parties to the table to manage a conflict.*	**Beginning**	
	Explain getting all parties to the table.	5 min.
	Share conflict cases.	15 min.
	Continuing	
	Choose doable cases.	15 min.
	Share answers in threes.	20 min.
	Discuss in plenary.	15 min.
SCRIPTURE	***Break***	10 min.
Acts 6:1–3	Role-play.	25 min.
"The twelve called together the whole community" to settle a dispute.	Debrief.	5 min.
	Read the story resolution.	5 min.
	Ending	10 min.

PREPARATION:
- Reproduce doable cases checklist.
- Read *A Manual on Resolving Large Group Conflicts* (see Bibliography).

---

*The word "table" is used here as a metaphor for an opportunity to get people to talk together seriously. The metaphor does not work in some cultures in which people do not settle disputes around literal tables. In some cultures people sit in circles on the ground, in others they sit in a line so that there is little or no eye contact. But all need the opportunity to get together to talk seriously about a dispute, even if it is through a third party go-between. The word "table," with its limitations, is used here to mean just this opportunity and not a literal table and chairs.

uals carry out their ethics as private persons without all this noise about social action and prying into their private affairs.

Furthermore, there were some valuable things to learn from the business world about money-raising, and the men wanted to try them out forthwith in a no-nonsense campaign that picked up the bottom line and did not let it go until the giving could demand respect once more. Some risks had to be run and some new gimmicks tried out. Yes, gimmicks. It is not a bad word in the real world, where gimmicks work. The committee developed a catchy, upbeat campaign packaged to boost Old First's flagging generosity, calling for an end to social action and a beginning of spiritual action. They prepared for doubters' questions about such tasteless tactics with answers like "Do you want what works? Do you want money or nice talk?" It was going to be a new day at Old First.

That is, it was going to be a new day until they presented the campaign package to the church council where some of the social activists sat, including Beulah Schuman. Frank and Bill had not expected the response they got. Their carefully designed stewardship campaign package hardly got off the ground.

Their proposed slogan, "Trust your dollar to the man who wears the collar," received stony silence. Their rebate plan of giving a "crisp dollar bill for every one hundred pledged" drew rolls of the eyes. Their drive-through Communion plan got unbelieving smiles. Their gifts of toasters, clock radios, can openers, and a year's supply of panty hose for new pledges received snickers. Their frequent attendance awards, giving a free trip to the Holy Land for every $20,000 pledged, got laughs of disapproval. Their return to a pew rental plan went nowhere. Their idea of collecting overdue pledges by posting delinquent pledgers' photos over "Wanted for Money" signs in the narthex drew groans. And the final idea that broke up the meeting was their other slogan idea: "Tired of seeing your church dollars go to politics? Come join us and grow with 'God's party.'"

"As usual, Beulah was the first to respond to the stewardship campaign package: "I've never heard of a worse pile of pure toxic waste in all my life. I thought you guys were joking with this garbage. If you are serious, you should be locked up. I can't believe you would presume to dump such trash on the council and waste our time like this!"

Frank and Bill did not wait around very long to hear more responses. Bill just said, "Do you want money, or what? OK, some of it is corny, but it works for winners. Frank, we are wasting our time with this bunch of liberal losers. I quit. This church can die if it wants to, and these losers are trying to kill it."

Both left in a hurry. Clovis' attempt to call them back did not work. How would they ever be reconciled, and how would Old First ever get its stewardship campaign back on track? How would we get the campaign committee back to the negotiating table?

THE SESSION PLAN

BEGINNING

Explain getting all parties to the table. Show how this course intends to help make us aware of how many conflicts are going on every day around us and how we may gain courage, hope, and skill to resolve them. This initial awareness which sees a conflict and says, "Aha! That's a solvable problem, not a war to wage," is the beginning. The second step is getting the other person or persons into a situation where the conflict can be reconciled, negotiated, or managed. That is getting *them* to the table. One of the main reasons some people don't get to the table is that they feel powerless.

Remind the group that conflict resolution fits in between empowerment and coercion. That is, powerless parties have to be empowered enough to negotiate a fair resolution. For example, Carlos was empowered by having a translator and advocates. So the fight with Beasley could move up to the mediation table. But conflict resolution does not use coercion (threats or legal action). It does not try to prove right or wrong. It is not adversarial.

This session will help us to be able to assess which conflicts may be appropriate for the conflict resolution table, how to get disputants there, and what kind of empowerment is needed to give enough hope to get them to the table.

Share conflict cases. Distribute copies of the checklist on page 153. Ask the participants to share brief reports of conflicts they have experienced since the last session. Afterward analyze the process of getting the disputants into negotiation.

CONTINUING

Choose doable cases. Distribute copies of the checklist on page 153. Ask individuals to check which of the conflicts are appropriate for conflict resolution. Note that some are doable cases, others are not. Cases that are not doable are natural, given, unchangeable problems or psychological cases. Some are not yet doable because they may call for power balancing that is disruptive, so that low-powered people are empowered enough to get to the table with hope of gain. Others may require help from the police. The rest may be doable cases for conflict resolution. Check the doable cases.

Share answers in threes. In groups of three, have people share their answers to the form and explain why they checked the ones they checked and explain how they would get disputants to the table in doable cases. Also ask groups of three to discuss why some cases are not doable.

Discuss in plenary. Focus on what you can do to get negotiation started.

Break

Role-play. The task is: getting the stewardship committee to negotiate a resolution. Ask for volunteers to play Frank, Bill, Mildred, Beulah, and Beasley. The role-play begins with this sentence: "They go to meet Frank and Bill, and the following happens . . ."

Debrief. Discuss the role-play and various ways to get Frank and Bill to negotiate.

Read the story resolution.

The Resolution

Mildred Morse stepped into the conflict over the stewardship campaign. She said to Beulah, "Clearly you have strong feelings about Frank and Bill's campaign package. Let's hear from some others."

Clovis said, "Well, it was pretty silly stuff, but it did have creativity to it and I don't think they meant the package to be a final proposal. They were just testing out some ideas."

Marsha said, "Somebody ought to thank them for their efforts and suggest some constructive criticism."

Beasley volunteered to call them in a day or so, once they were cooled off. He proposed an expanded committee to rework the campaign plans, making sure the committee was more representative of the church—including some who were committed to social action.

"Forget me," Beulah responded. "Those clunkers are trying to make the church into a sideshow at the circus. I'm not into clown acts."

"OK, we know your feelings, Beulah," said Mildred. "Can we support Reverend Beasley's idea?" All but Beulah did. Clovis and Marsha agreed to help rework the plan with Frank and Bill. They did and a completely revised campaign was brought back to the council the next month. Its theme was: "A gift to the poor is a gift to God."

ENDING

Scripture   Read Acts 6:1–3. Note how the conflict over neglecting widows was solved.

Prayer   God of wisdom, help us to be peacemakers who know what to do when conflicts get out of hand. Give us the hope and courage to empower others to find just resolutions to conflicts. Amen.

Checklist

_____ 1. Your neighbor's dog barks all night long.

_____ 2. Drugs are being sold openly on your city block.

_____ 3. In the apartment upstairs, the live-in man beats the live-in woman frequently.

_____ 4. The church softball team loses every game.

_____ 5. Frances is jealous of her cousin Maude.

_____ 6. The fishing tournament called off because of rain.

_____ 7. Your kids borrow your car and empty the tank.

_____ 8. Your neighbors play music loudly all night.

_____ 9. You are depressed over the state of the world.

_____10. Your pastor does not visit enough.

_____11. Oswald has developed hay fever.

_____12. You can't sleep at night.

_____13. You're the only one who does the dishes.

_____14. Argentina is threatening to invade the Malvinas/Falklands again.

_____15. Winthrop is first in sales for five months in a row.

_____16. Nude sect predicts end of the world, won't leave mountaintop.

_____17. The church roof leaks.

_____18. Olga nags Martin.

_____19. Skinheads beat up an Asian nurse.

_____20. Your colleague tells people you came to work drunk.

UNIT 4

Process Steps
in Conflict Resolution

In the last three units we have worked on communication skills, distinguished different levels and types of conflict, and dealt with power blocks and how to overcome them. Our final unit in this skills training course takes the basic four steps of the conflict resolution process as they are used in a hearing and offers practice sessions in the details of each step. This detail practice is important because the highly emotional setting at the hearing table requires calm, firm leadership. Such leadership skills are attained by careful, step-by-step practice.

Now that you have the disputing people at the table, what exactly do you do? You use the process. Here are four sessions on the four basic steps of the process of resolving conflict:

Session 11: Beginning a Hearing, Step One
Session 12: Expressing the Problem, Step Two
Session 13: Attacking the Problem, Step Three
Session 14: Reaching Agreement, Step Four

Beginning a Hearing, Step One

The Economic Dispute

The Conflict

By now some of the saints at Old First United had gotten better at handling conflict in the church, but the big ruckus on economics really tested their skills.

When Reverend Beasley opened the package from the national office of the church, he started to file it with the other piles of mail addressed to "Church Occupant." But this one had a personally addressed cover letter that he decided to read. It seems that the denomination wanted each church to accept a position paper on faith and economics. But this paper was not the "a penny saved is a penny earned" kind of stuff. It was not "waste not, want not" lessons on thrift or inspiration on giving to foreign missions. No, it was radical stuff that questioned the unquestionable. It questioned the

PURPOSE	**SESSION PLAN OUTLINE**	**120 min.**
• To develop confidence and skill at beginning a conflict resolution hearing	**Beginning** Explain hearing. **Continuing** Read the story.	15 min. 5 min.
SCRIPTURE	Design and share a process. *Break*	30 min. 10 min.
Romans 12:9–13 "Be patient insuffering. . . . Extend hospitality."	Read the story resolution. Practice introduction in pairs. Debrief. **Ending**	5 min. 35 min. 10 min. 10 min.

PREPARATION

- Study this session.
- Prepare outline of introduction from the story resolution.
- Practice modeling introduction.
- Read C. Moore, *The Mediation Process*, pp. 153–172. Or read MCS, *When You Disagree . . .* , D2, D3. (See Bibliography.)

whole economic system and preached about how society ought to behave with its money.

What is this? Beasley thought. People get killed for being on the wrong side of economic systems. He looked over his shoulder to see if any of his conservative members might have gotten into his study and catch him reading this radical material. It was safe for now, but just in case, he wrapped the position paper in a brown paper bag.

The cover letter asked him to organize an all-day hearing at Old First for the churches in the region, to consider adopting the position paper. He groaned: Now that is just what I need, right in the middle of our stewardship drive—another troublemaking program from the bureaucrats. Here, we may not fight openly about the doctrine of the Trinity, but even the mention of economics rouses people up like beating on a hornet's nest. I could be tried for treason, racked as a communist spy, and burned at the stake for infidelity to the American way of life—and Beulah Schuman would love every minute of it.

But the letter was signed by the church president, who was hard to turn down. She also called him on the phone, during which time Beasley found himself saying yes, and then grinding his teeth for having done so.

Copies of the paper were distributed, a date was set for the hearing, and arrangements were made for fifty people, practically filling the little church hall. It took a while for the steam to build up. Gradually the conservatives in the area got organized to reject this "Marxist treachery." The liberals were slower to get revved up, but finally they got going under Beulah's coaxing. She told them, "The right-wingers are out to destroy Beasley for this. That might be a blessing, but it's for the wrong reasons. And besides, the position paper is too tame and needs more to beef it up."

In the meantime, both groups began forming into angry camps, arming their positions with arguments, hostility, and experts. The paper had been analyzed and had spun off more polarizing papers. Rumors floated about regarding right-wing or left-wing "takeovers." The Bible First Fellowship threatened a demonstration and picket line, a Klan group hinted that it might burn a cross, while others threatened to burn a flag. What should Old First United do about this conflict?

THE SESSION PLAN

BEGINNING

Explain hearing. Establish the importance of starting off a hearing carefully and practicing doing it. In a destructive conflict situation people are frightened and defensive, and often lack the courage, hope, and energy to seek alternative solutions. They have usually settled for a solution that is not working.

Your job as a conflict resolver is to model firm, calm hopefulness. You are in charge, and you must assert this authority while being gentle, patient, and impartial toward each party. Gradually, however, you will turn the authority to solve their problem over to the disputants. You control the process by stating and following the rules. By assuming this role you free them *from* the control of fear (such as the fear of being cheated by rule-breaking) and free them *for* hope that the problem can be solved so that they will gain something. Thus the energy normally used for fearful defensiveness is released to seek new solutions.

You take over from them the burden of making and keeping a just and peaceful context so that the disputants can look at their problem differently. Then the destructive warfare can be raised to the level of a constructive challenge, a problem to solve.

This is not an adversary procedure, like a legal case that seeks to prove right and wrong, blame and innocence, winners and losers. Most disputants will want such a judgment, and in their favor, of course. But you are not a judge or an advocate for either side. You are a judge and an advocate for the *process only*. If the disputants do not follow the process, you must correct them and, if necessary, end the hearing.

You are not a lawyer, but you need to go through training, something like a law school, to develop the skills of conflict resolution. We can create our own skill-learning contexts and practice doing conflict resolution skills over and over, taking the process step by step. This session will focus on the introduction to the hearing process, the first step.

CONTINUING

Read the story. Read aloud the first section of the story "The Economic Dispute."

Design and share a process. Divide the group into pairs. Assign them the task of designing a process for managing the conflict in the story. Share these designs in plenary.

Break

Read the story resolution.

The Resolution

The church council tried to prepare for the hearing and used all the tools of conflict resolution they had learned from Mildred and Beasley in the "wider church" conflict with the Bible First Fellowship.

They decided to attempt a conflict management hearing rather than a parliamentary vote. They asked Mildred if she would lead it, as she was the calmest and best-organized person around. She thought for a minute and calmly said in an organized way, "Under two conditions: One, we form a panel of four people, and, two, they take the time to practice over and over what we are going to do." Clovis, Frank, and Beulah were added to the panel, and they agreed to practice.

Mildred organized the practice into four training sessions based on the four parts of a hearing: (1) introduction, (2) expressing the problem, (3) problem solving, and (4) agreement. At the first session she outlined four more parts of the introduction:

A. Setting
- Room: informal, neutral
- Chairs arranged so that all can see one another
- Disputants can be separated by a table if any fear the others may physically harm them
- Restrooms, smoking area located where
- Writing paper, pens, newsprint, marker ready
- Tasks assigned to each panelist

B. The Opening
- The greeting—warm, serious, encouraging
- Ask names, preferred usage
- Time setting, agreement on time

C. Procedure
- Briefly outline four steps in a hearing
- Define role of panel: to manage a fair process of hearing—not to judge or to establish the "truth" or to solve the problem for people
- Role of disputants: to express your side of the problem, its effects on you, and your interests, then to join in a search for solutions
- Breaks for rests, or for caucuses, can be called by anyone at any time

D. Ground rules
- No interruptions except at agreed signal for a break or caucus
- Ask for agreement on no interruptions
- Participants write down points, to express later

Mildred asked Beulah to role-play a conservative, Frank a liberal, and Clovis the conflict manager. Each would practice the introduction. They did, and rotated the roles quickly as Beulah gagged on playing a conservative. Then they got ready to meet with the caucuses of the two groups.

Practice introduction in pairs. Present on newsprint the outline of the introduction from the story resolution.

Divide the group into pairs and assign them to take turns practicing the introduction steps with each other. They should go over each step verbally.

Debrief. Discuss in the whole group and deal with "what if" questions.

ENDING

Assignment	Outline the rest of the steps in a hearing. Assign each participant the task of seeking to resolve a dispute between two other people before the next session.
Scripture	Romans 12:12–13 Stress the value of hospitality and patience in resolving conflicts.
Prayer	God of hope, we get ourselves into conflicts that seem so hopeless that we give up and either avoid the issues or fight to defeat our "enemies." Give us hope for resolutions that turn "enemies" into coworkers, and help us to trust that you will open our eyes to see ways out of our warfare. Amen.

Expressing the Problem, Step Two

Equipping the Saints

The Conflict

The second training session of Old First United's conflict management panel was scheduled before the caucuses were to meet. The anxiety that they felt about trying to manage the groups drove Mildred, Frank, Clovis, and Beulah into high energy and promptness. Normally, if you just showed up for coffee and cookies at the end of a committee meeting, people understood and you got credit for showing up. Not on this one. Mildred started on time and brooked no baloney. Beasley stuck his head in, got assigned a greeting and a prayer at the hearing, and was excused. On to the business.

Mildred had done her homework. She explained, "Step two is getting the disputants to state their points of view without interruption. To be able to

PURPOSE	SESSION PLAN OUTLINE	120 min.
• To develop confidence and skill in leading step two, expressing the problem in a hearing on conflict management	**Beginning**	
	Explain step two.	10 min.
	Read the story.	5 min.
	Continuing	
	Present the agenda and framing.	15 min.
	Practice step two in threes.	20 min.
SCRIPTURE	Debrief in plenary.	15 min.
Ephesians 4:25–32	*Break*	10 min.
"Speak the truth."	Read the story resolution.	5 min.
	Role-play expressing interests.	20 min.
	Debrief in plenary.	10 min.
	Ending	10 min.

PREPARATION
- Study this session.
- Read C. Moore, *The Mediation Process*, pp. 172–198.
- Read MCS, *When You Disagree . . .* , D4. (See Bibliography.)

have your say without any interference is so rare in our daily lives that it goes a long way toward conflict resolution."

Frank asked, "But how do you keep the conservatives quiet when, let's say for example, the liberals start calling them names like 'fascist pigs'?"

Beulah replied, "That's easy. You just say, 'Shut up,' and do what you usually do, Frank: call them 'pinko Communists.' That won't help much, but it might make you feel better."

Mildred said, "I don't think we should encourage name-calling, but it could happen, so what do we do when that or other acting out occurs?"

THE SESSION PLAN

BEGINNING

Explain step two. Indicate that expressing the problem from the points of view of each party *without interruption* must be done in order to move the disputing parties toward defining their interests. Their interests are usually negotiable. Their points of view (positions or solutions) rarely are. Your task is to help them to name the problem (that is, the issue, the agenda), record the positions on newsprint, and lead them toward naming their interests (their needs, what they want) that underlie the problem.

Ask participants to volunteer any conflicts they have experienced and how the expressing of the problem took place.

Read the story.

CONTINUING

Present the agenda and framing. Write this list on newsprint:

- Setting the agenda
- Framing the issues
- Focusing on key problem(s)
- Hearing both sides: views, effects, interests

Practice step two in threes. Assign participants to practice setting agendas and framing the issues in groups of three. They can play three roles in this practice session: a liberal, a conservative, and a conflict manager. The suggested topic is: "A guaranteed minimum wage will be available to all." The point is not the topic, but practicing the process. Each role is played once by each of the three persons for ten minutes so that all can practice managing this portion of a conflict hearing.

Debrief in plenary.

Break
Read the story resolution.

The Resolution

The members of the conflict management panel looked to Mildred to tell them what to do if the disputants began shouting and name-calling. She said, "Your job is to stop interruptions. You can firmly remind the interrupter, 'We have agreed to a ground rule of no interruptions. Please take notes on the points you want to make. Here is some paper. Write down your points. Your turn is coming to respond to all that is said.'"

"You can reframe the conservative's name-calling by paraphrasing like this: 'You are saying that the free market benefits the whole nation,' or something like that."

Mildred continues: "Now let's move on. The overall goal of step two is to move both parties from stating their points of view of the problem through to what effects the problem has on them, that is, to the interests they want served. You do this in two stages.

"First, build an agreed-upon agenda and push both parties to find and state their interests after they have gotten out their points of view."

Clovis said, "That is getting a little thick for me."

Mildred replied, "I'll give you an example. Let's say that the conservative spokesperson says, 'This economic paper is Marxist propaganda that will lead to a communist dictatorship, with church dupes leading the way.' You, as the conflict manager, can try to get back to their interest behind this conclusion by asking, 'What specifically in the paper leads you to this conclusion?' Also, you can see if you have heard an underlying interest by testing: 'Are you interested in protecting democracy and in the church's being well informed about the effects of a government-planned economy?'"

Beulah inserted, "Wow! You sure sanitized that one."

Mildred said, "Now, you are catching on. That is the point. Sanitized or neutral language helps the disputants back off from their hardened solutions to their interests, interests that they assume will be served by their solutions and conclusions. If we can get the real interests out on the table, we can start moving to step three, solving problems that meet both parties interests."

Clovis was puzzled again. "What does this have to do with interest payments?"

"No," said Mildred. "By interests I mean people's real needs, what they really want, as distinct from the conclusions or solutions that they are fighting for. In this example, the implied interests are democracy and well-informed church members. Of course there are probably others."

Beulah said, "Well, liberals want democracy and good education too. So why all the ruckus?"

"Exactly," said Mildred.

The foursome then practiced by role-playing the two sides speaking, with each having a turn at managing the conflict. The more they practiced, the more ready they felt for the big day.

Role-play expressing interests. Ask volunteers in plenary to practice a role play focused on getting interests out on the table. Ask four volunteers to play a liberal, a conservative, and a panel of two conflict managers. The topic can be "The church should set an example of economic justice by paying all clergy the same wages."

Debrief in plenary. Examine how well role players expressed their interests.

ENDING

Scripture   Ephesians 4:25–32

Prayer   God of truth, we cannot see the whole truth, but that does not
             stop us from assuming we know the answers. Open our hearts
             to see things from others' points of view and to seek peace and
             stand for justice. Amen.

Session 13

Attacking the Problem, Step Three

Believers' Basic Training

The Conflict

The caucuses met. The Fearsome Foursome—Mildred, Clovis, Beulah, and Frank—gained some good warm-up experience from the caucuses for the hearing on economics scheduled for next Saturday at Old First. The caucus hearings had these goals: to help each side, the liberals and the conservatives, to organize their leadership and their presentations, and to agree to the rules of the process. These separate meetings actually became mini-hearings, as neither of the groups fully agreed among themselves. Each had to go through its own conflict management session in the caucuses. The panel-in-training then discussed what came out of the caucuses.

Beulah began, "Clovis, when are you going to learn to keep your mouth shut?"

Clovis responded, "Why? What did I do?"

PURPOSE	SESSION PLAN OUTLINE	120 min.
• To develop confidence and skill in leading step three, problem-solving, in a conflict management hearing	**Beginning**	
	Explain problem-solving.	10 min.
	Continuing	
	List attitudes and techniques.	10 min.
	Read the story.	5 min.
	Model problem solving.	15 min.
SCRIPTURE	Debrief.	10 min.
Matthew 5:43–47	*Break*	10 min.
"Love your enemies."	Read the story resolution.	5 min.
	Discuss problem-solving approaches.	10 min.
	Practice in threes.	30 min.
	Debrief.	5 min.
	Ending	10 min.

PREPARATION
- Study Session 13.
- Read C. Moore, *The Mediation Process*, pp. 199–217.
- Read MCS, *When You Disagree . . .*, D4. (See Bibliography.)

Beulah: "You did not have to ask that unemployed man why he didn't get a job. That is not your task on the panel."

Mildred: "Beulah is right. It is not our job as conflict managers. But we did get both groups organized, I think. If we can just keep Ms. Arndt quiet! I'm still not sure she agrees to the 'no-interruptions' rule. She has so much anger at big business.

"We actually got through step one, the introduction, and step two, expressing the problem, in the caucuses. Then we moved to electing the spokespersons. Now we need to focus on step three, attacking the problem. That will be key in the big hearing."

Clovis: "I'll be glad when this is over."

Mildred: "Don't be discouraged, Clovis; we are just getting started. If we don't succeed in getting some kind of agreement, this could split the church. But if we do, it could be the beginning of a whole new way of peace-making in the church and society. Right now, about the only way people know how to settle disputes is through violence or defeat, win or lose. We are pioneering the third way, the one Jesus tried to teach two thousand years ago. Finally, some people are catching on, and we are in the vanguard of a peacemaking army."

Clovis: "Do you really think so?"

Frank: "Can't we just get on with step three?"

Mildred: "Right. OK, step three assumes that step two got the interests of both parties out on the table or on the newsprint. Now we start to help them find common ground and, rather than attacking each other or each other's position, they attack the problem together."

Beulah: "We already have common ground. Both want to end poverty, promote democracy, and be informed."

Mildred: "*We* know that, but it's best if they state it to each other. Our goal is to shift the authority for problem-solving to them. How can we do that?"

Frank: "Well, we learned about paraphrasing. Let's paraphrase their interests and then try to get them to paraphrase each other."

Clovis: "It's not that easy. They are still labeling each other and insisting that only their own solution will work. The liberals are fighting for government-guaranteed economic rights and the conservatives insist on a market free of government guarantees, at least for the poor."

Beulah: "The conservatives don't seem to mind government guarantees for the rich, like big business bailouts, limited liability for corporations, and cutting capital gains taxes."

Frank: "*Somebody* has got to keep the liberals from taxing us to death."

Mildred: "Let's get back to how we can get both sides to work together on the problem of a church statement on economics. How can we do that?"

THE SESSION PLAN

BEGINNING

Explain problem-solving. Show how step three logically follows step two, expressing the problem by both sides. However, it may not be obvious at the hearing table exactly when the parties are ready for problem-solving. You have to sense when both parties have gotten out their statements of the problem, their views, and what effects it is having on them. Usually, each party is sure that it has found the best and only solution and that it is simply a matter of getting the other party to agree with that solution.

Our job, as leaders of the hearing process, is to help each party to see that neither party has to lose—that there are other solutions to the problem than the conflicting ones assumed by the disputing parties. Their job is to find those alternative solutions.

It is also our task to encourage, affirm, and model our hope and belief in the possibility of many other solutions, and to discourage adherence to rigidly held positions. There are a number of techniques for doing this, along with the encouraging and supportive attitude. We will practice these attitudes and techniques in this session.

CONTINUING

List attitudes and techniques. Ask participants to name words that describe the conflict manager's ideal attitude during step three of a hearing. Then list them on newsprint. Some descriptions, for example, are: positive, serious, affirming, hopeful, respectful, firm, caring, coaching, optimistic, communicates that we are making progress, a "you can do it" approach.

Ask participants to name some techniques for getting disputants into working together on solving the problem(s), such as: brainstorming, small-group work on details, solving the easier ones first, rewriting a single script, paraphrasing.

Read the story.

Model problem-solving. Ask for volunteers to model with a role play this problem-solving step in a hearing before the group. The roles are one liberal, one conservative, and two conflict management panelists. The panelists' task is to get the parties into problem-solving after the two positions are stated briefly; for example, the liberal's position (the church should support economic democracy) versus the conservative's position (the church should stick to spiritual matters and to individual ethics). Remember to practice the attitudes and techniques named earlier.

Debrief.

Break
Read the story resolution.

The Resolution

The panel worked on problem-solving in this exchange:

Mildred: Frank is right. Paraphrasing is a good idea. What else can we do to move them toward working together?

Beulah: Start with the agreed upon-areas and the easy problems.

Mildred: Yes, by starting out with some small agreements, we create momentum toward attacking the bigger ones. Frank: Get agreement on the basic principles, then deal with particulars later.

Mildred: We could do that or use the building-block approach.

Clovis: What is that?

Mildred: The building-block approach breaks up the big issues like taxes and welfare into small pieces and solves each, one at a time.

Beulah: Well, since this is a church statement and it is not as if the U.S. President and the Treasury Department were holding up the next federal budget to see what happens down in Old First United, I say we go with the broad principles and leave the details to the Feds so they will have something to do.

Mildred: OK. Now let's rehearse. Who is going to be the conflict manager first?

Clovis: Do we have to?

Beulah: Clovis, if you don't pull out of it, I'm going to forget this mediation stuff and poke you in your runny nose.

Discuss problem-solving approaches. In plenary compare the merits and demerits of the building-block versus the basic-principles approaches to problem-solving.

Practice in threes. In groups of three, practice the attitudes and techniques of problem-solving with three roles: liberal, conservative, and conflict manager. The suggested issue is: The church should leave economics and political issues to "the experts." Or use another conflict brought by a participant. Rotate the roles so that each person plays a conflict manager for ten minutes.

Debrief.

ENDING

Scripture   Matthew 5:43–47. Point out that "loving enemies" may be what conflict resolution is all about. Loving your allies is easy. The challenge is to at least listen to your "not-yet-friends."

Prayer   God of the one who taught us to love, help us to understand what loving enemies means in our daily lives and to live out this understanding, not by defeating others or surrendering to them, but by patiently working to find alternatives to destructive conflicts. Amen.

Session 14

The Agreement, Step Four

Big Day at Old First

The Conflict

Anxious excitement, like the final play-off game between the Adam Smith Capitalists and the Karl Marx Socialists, was in the air. There were no banners, streamers, or marching bands, of course, and the demonstrations did not materialize either. But it could have been the world-class final showdown for the Stanley Cup in the minds of the members at Old First. They were not used to the attention that such a major league event brings.

In the last day before the hearing on economics, Mildred had shaped up the conflict management panel. They had one final training session the night before to go over step four, reaching agreement, and had checked out the meeting spaces, the menu for a light lunch, and who was to do what. Mildred would begin with the opening, Frank would follow with procedures, and Beulah would state the ground rules. Clovis chose to be the recorder—a critical role in that the exact wording of a document was to be the concrete product of the hearing.

They set a schedule to pressure the spokespersons toward progress in

---

PURPOSE	SESSION PLAN OUTLINE	120 min.
• To develop confidence and skill in leading step four, reaching agreement in a conflict management hearing	**Beginning** Explain agreement step. **Continuing** Read the story and resolution. Present checklist. (Take no break.) All participants practice. **Ending**	2 minutes 5 minutes 3 minutes 100 minutes 10 minutes

SCRIPTURE

Matthew 5:23–26
"Come to terms quickly
with your accuser."

PREPARATION

• Study Session 14.
• Read C. Moore, *The Mediation Process*, pp. 218–261.
• Read MCS, *When You Disagree . . .*, D4. (See Bibliography.)

resolving the conflict between the liberals and the conservatives. They expected some kind of agreement by five o'clock and suggested general time periods as goals for ending steps one, two, and three. By doing this, if the parties agreed to the time schedule, they would assure progress.

They knew the general views of each party from the caucuses and had some ideas about how they might be negotiated. The ideas could be called forth if deadlines were not being met. Clovis asked, "But what if it gets to be five o'clock and both the liberals and the conservatives are miles apart and everybody is screaming at each other? What do we do then?"

The Resolution

No one responded for a while to Clovis' last question of desperation until Mildred said, "We trust in the Spirit and the process, in that order."

The people arrived on time and were ready at nine o'clock to begin with Reverend Beasley's greeting and prayer. The caucuses had helped prepare expectations, acceptance of the process, and the impartiality (or at least balance) of the panel. Mildred's opening, the explanation of the procedures and time line, as well as Beulah's stern warnings against interruptions, reinforced the leadership authority of the panel.

By noon both sides had presented their views. In essence, the conservatives called for a rejection of the whole idea of the church prying into economics or political affairs. While all religious people seek an end to poverty, it is best to leave it to charity and education and the experts who, as individuals, may help solve these economic problems. But the church should stick to spiritual matters and, if it must speak out on such issues, it should condemn godless Communism rather than attack the invisible capitalist hand that feeds the church in the market economy.

The liberals vigorously opposed this view, saying that God, morality, and justice could not be excluded from public or economic affairs. God, they said, is God over *all* of creation and, as such, seeks to convert all individuals and systems that exploit and oppress the poor and the weak. Jesus preached to the rich fool and the rich, young ruler and to the nations to turn from seeking treasures on earth to first seeking God's reign of peace and justice. He did not separate the church from the world.

After lunch, Mildred challenged both groups to seek common ground, as, for example, recognizing that both desire to be faithful to God and, by different means, to end poverty and injustice. Progress was made on how the document could be worded so that free market forces should be as free for the poor as for the rich, and how government "incentives" in the economy could help not only the rich but also the poor.

By five o'clock the two spokespersons were editing the text together, with Clovis recording the changes. They were determined, with some coaching from Reverend Beasley, to straighten out the bureaucrats who wrote the original draft. They wanted to tell them a thing or two about economics and about how to make the original position paper into a decent statement that represented the best of the two views even at the places where they could not reach a consensus. Clovis insisted on specific and clear wording which he would type up for everyone's signatures under the document's new title: "Old First United's New Economic Order." They all signed.

THE SESSION PLAN

BEGINNING

Explain agreement step. Indicate that reaching an agreement will be possible only if the parties feel that they have been treated fairly and that their interests have been taken seriously. When this is done in steps one, two, and three, then many alternative solutions, trade-offs, rearrangements, and bargains can be negotiated. Our goal in this step four is to keep the disputants on track and to enable them to come to a specific and realistic settlement in which both parties gain some of their interests and maintain all of their respect.

CONTINUING

Read the story and resolution. Do not break the story this time.

Present checklist. Here are the things to remember in the step for reaching agreement:

- —set deadlines for compliance
- —be specific
- —set up follow-through mechanisms
- —set criteria for verification
- —make panel assignments
- —put it all in writing

All participants practice. Give each participant an opportunity to lead a conflict resolution before the whole class, using the story conflict or one brought by a participant or any in the book. Volunteers can role-play two disputing parties. The person leading the hearing seeks to go through all four steps and reach an agreement. The steps can be done quickly or can require a very long time. The short length of time used here is only to enable each participant to practice a "solo flight." The time needed also depends on the number of people in the group. The maximum time, counting the feedback, is a hundred minutes.

Divide the hundred minutes equally between participants. Two people would have fifty minutes each. Ten people would have ten minutes each. If there are more than ten participants, divide into two groups. Each participant must have at least ten minutes to practice leading a conflict resolution session before other participants and to learn from it and from the feedback of the other group members. After each group of three (the mediator and two disputants) have done a role play, ask if the leader wants feedback. If so, the class can make affirmations first and then suggestions for the leader's further growth.

ENDING

Scripture   Matthew 5:23–26. Note how Jesus advises us to settle a dispute and befriend our "enemy" ("accuser") before we go to court or to worship.

Prayer   God of hope and courage, we know that there is a way to live free of violence because you have shown us this way. Now we need only courage and hope from you to follow this way. Guide us now in your steps toward a world of justice and peace. Amen.

Notes to Part One

Chapter 1

1. Hizkias Assefa, *Mediation of Civil Wars: Approaches and Strategires—The Sudan Conflict* (Boulder, Colo.: Westview Press, 1987).

2. Ibid., 142.

3. "Carter Played Pivotal Role in Hours After Polls Closed," *Washington Post*, Feb. 27, 1990.

4. Cynthia Sampson, "A Study of the International Conciliation Work of Religious Figures." Unpublished paper sponsored by the Program on Negotiation, Harvard Law School, October 1987.

Chapter 2

1. The words in quotation marks are those of Walter Brueggemann in *Genesis: A Bible Commentary for Teaching and Preaching* (Atlanta: John Knox Press, 1982), 261—273, and used by permission. The rest of the dialogue is imaginary.

2. I am indebted to the Rev. Ann Asper Wilson for the idea of this story.

Chapter 3

1. Speed Leas and Paul Kittlaus, *Church Fights* (Philadelphia: Westminster, 1977), 28.

2. Roy W. Pheuman and Margaret E. Bruehl, *Managing Conflict* (Englewood Cliffs, N.J.: Prentice-Hall, 1982), 3.

3. Renes Likert and Jane Cubson Likert, *New Ways of Managing Conflict* (New York: McGraw-Hill, 1976), 7.

4. Joyce L. Hocker and William W. Wilmot, *Interpersonal Conflict* (Dubuque, Iowa: William C. Brown, 1985), 29.

5. Adapted from John Paul Lederach, Mennonite Conciliation Service.

6. Roger Fisher and William Ury, *Getting to Yes* (Boston: Houghton Mifflin, 1981), passim.

7. This conflict cycle was inspired by, but drastically changed from, *Conflict Resolution Workshops*, Genesee Ecumenical Ministries, Rochester, N.Y., 1988. Thanks especially to Ginny Mackey. See also Norman Shawchuck, *How to Manage Conflict* (Irvine, Calif.: Spiritual Growth Resources, 1983) and Jerry Robinson and

Roy Clifford, *Managing Conflict in Community Groups*, (University of Illinois, 1974).

8. I am indebted to Speed Leas for the idea of levels of conflict. See his book *Moving Your Church Through Conflict* (Washington, D.C., Alban Institute, 1985). This excellent book develops the concept of levels of conflict in the church setting. I have built on his schema (see Bibliography) and expanded it beyond the church to include everyday individual and social conflicts. Also, I emphasized the constructive, creative conflicts and developed different categories that fit my experience.

Chapter 4

1. Saul Alinsky, *Rules for Radicals* (New York: Random House, 1971), 119.

2. Mary S. Winters, "Should Family Violence Be Mediated?" unpublished paper. See also John Horner-Ibler, *ICC Link*, Fall 1986.

3. Dan W. Dodson, "Using Conflict Creatively," unpublished paper, 3–4.

4. Alinsky, op. cit., 127.

5. *Conciliation Quarterly*, Summer 1987, 10, 12.

6. Letty M. Russell, "People and the Powers" in *Princeton Seminary Bulletin*. Warfield Lectures, March 1987. See also *Household of Freedom* (Westminster Press 1987).

7. Charles R. McCollough, *Morality of Power* (New York: Pilgrim Press, 1977).

Chapter 5

1. I am indebted to Richard Killmer, director of the Presbyterian Peacemaking Program, for the idea of the list, although I have adapted his idea considerably.

2. Olga Wikerhauser, "Pride Returns to Miller Homes," in the *New York Times*, 25 December 1988.

3. Emma Lee, "Eyesores Spur Showdown," in the *Trentonian*, 21 May 1986.

4. Jim Hooker, "Property owners say they'll clean up areas," in the *Trenton Times*, 22 May 1986.

5. Letty M. Russell, *Human Liberation in a Feminist Perspective: A Theology* (Philadelphia: Westminster Press, 1977), 118–120.

6. Ibid., 170.

7. Saul Alinsky, *Rules for Radicals* (New York: Random House, 1971), 126–164.

Chapter 7

1. James Schellenberg, *The Science of Conflict* (New York: Oxford, 1982).

2. Glen Fisher, *International Negotiations: A Cross-cultural Perspective* (Chicago: International Press, 1980).

3. *Disputes and Negotiations: A Cross Cultural Perspective* (Ontario: Academic Press, Inc., 1979).

4. Ibid., 234.

5. *Mediation of Civil Wars: Approaches and Strategies—The Sudan Conflict* (Boulder, Colo: Westview Press 1987).

6. Ibid., 203.

7. John P. Adams, *At the Heart of the Whirlwind* (New York: Harper & Row, 1976).

8. See *Conciliation Quarterly Newsletter*, Summer 1989, Winter 1990.

9. E. Victoria Shook, in *Ho'oponopono*: A discussion guide for two videotapes. University of Hawaii, 1983, 14. See also her recent book by the same title which gives an extensive study of this process.

10. From *Nana I Kekumu: Look to the Source*, Vol. I, by Mary Kawena Pukui, E. W. Haertig, M.D., and Catherine A. Lee (Honolulu: Hui Hanai, 1972), 61.

11. Ibid., 70.

Annotated Bibliography

The field of conflict study is so broad that it often bewilders newcomers. In some conflict resolution programs and books, conflict means international warfare and peace study. In others it refers to family disputes or labor-management or community justice struggles or business negotiations or church fights. The vast expanse of conflict resources needs sorting out. Here is a sampling of some useful resources sorted into seven categories. It is clearly not an exhaustive list. It should be seen, rather, as an annotated summary of resources that this author finds helpful.*

This bibliography is not organized alphabetically but deductively, from general conflict studies to particular church disputes. The reader may thereby test resources in the broad field of conflict study in order to supplement a focus on church conflicts related to social issues, the special focus of this book.

This sampling begins with general studies of conflict, moves to international peace, then to organizational conflict in business and labor, to community justice, then to the church, first in mission then in internal conflict, and finally to conflict resolution in church-related curricula, and how to teach it.

By reviewing this extended sampling of selected books the reader can gain at least two things: (1) the broader context into which this book fits in the larger field and (2) enough detail of the resources so that the reader can have the information needed to decide on how to further pursue his or her own special interests.

---

*Note: In preparing this list the author recognizes that books listed may not be in print, especially the resources listed under "Curricula." Interested readers may be able to find many books in libraries.

General Books

Getting to Yes: Negotiating Agreement Without Giving In Roger Fisher and William Ury. Boston: Houghton Mifflin, 1981.

This upbeat, how-to book is a good place to begin learning conflict resolution. It is a practical and easy to read book that covers all kinds of negotiations from bartering with an antique dealer to the Camp David peace treaty. It recognizes the need for memorable dos and donts in a tense conflict situation, where it is natural to either fight or take flight. The authors call this fight or flight behavior "hard" or "soft" bargaining. But they offer a third way to bargain or negotiate. They call it "principled" negotiating, which is both soft and hard. It is soft on people and hard on problems.

The first "don't" is "don't bargain over positions." Rather, "do" focus on the interests or needs of the other person. It is their own self-interest that led them to assume the position they hold. Disputants probably will have more in common with the other's interests than with the other's position.

The second "do" is "separate people from the problem." Show respect. Don't get trapped in irrelevant personal animosities. Save your hardness for the problem and stay soft on the person.

The third "do" is to "invent options for personal gain." Rather than fight over entrenched positions, assume that creative problem-solving will come up with solutions that neither party has yet thought about.

The fourth "do" of principled negotiating is "insist on using objective criteria." This means that you seek agreement on impartial procedures or goals or pricing standards that serve as stable, objective standards for agreement to be reached and implemented. So "yield to principle, not to pressure." As simple as these four principles sound, they are not easy to follow in many ongoing relationships. In a more recent book Roger Fisher teamed up with another writer to deal with ways to build and keep good working relationships. That book is called *Getting Together*.

Getting Together: Building a Relationship That Gets to Yes Roger Fisher and Scott Brown. Boston: Houghton Mifflin, 1988.

Fisher and Brown lay out six principles on how to work with people we disagree with and to maintain good relationships by being "unconditionally constructive." To achieve our substantive goals, we need effective working relationships, relationships that have a high degree of rationality (balanced with emotion), understanding (their point of view), communication (listening and consulting), reliability (even if the people are not trustworthy), persuasiveness (not coercion), and acceptance (take them seriously). That is about it in a nutshell. These six principles are spelled out with many details and illustrations and charts. But they are not complicated. In fact, one may ask why they bothered to put this in a book as "a lot—perhaps most—is just organized common sense" (p.173). The answer is that we still do not follow these principles even if we know them already.

The Science of Conflict James A. Schellenberg. New York: Oxford University Press, 1982.

This scholarly overview of the history of conflict is a good balance to the practical guides by Fisher et al. The author, a professor of sociology at Indiana State University, presents a big picture of conflict and peace studies that spans the globe and history. He concludes, "Dealing with the issue of world order by a new generation of peace researchers may well be the most important activity to be pursued on earth in the final years of the 20th century" (p. 259).

This is Schellenberg's last sentence. The preceding 258 pages include a broad review of conflict studies from Plato to modern game theory, from Machiavelli's *Prince* to Rawls's *A Theory of Justice*. This breadth is intentional, for Schellenberg is raising the question of whether or not conflict study is a science. He recognizes that it is not generally regarded as such. At least it is not a pure science that is free of normative values. Rather, the study of conflict is an "elusive intertwining of empirical facts and human values" (p.8). After more or less settling that issue with that conclusion, Schellenberg goes on to lay out the perspectives on conflict of Darwin (biology), Adam Smith (social psychology), and Marx (sociology).

These thinkers give general world views into which conflict fits, but the presentations of three pioneers in conflict study as such are more to the point: Lewis Richardson, *The Causes of War and the Conditions of Peace*, a mathematical analysis of war and peace, 1935; Crane Brinton, *Anatomy of Revolution*, 1938; and Quincy Wright, *A Study of War*, 1942. A feeling for these classic works is most helpful, even in summary form, to aid one's grasp of the vastness of this field of study. These works are updated by Schellenberg's summaries of more recent studies of the causes of war and the strategies of warfare. One especially helpful insight is his correction of the popular notion that poor, deprived countries go to war more often than others. A careful analysis of the history of war proves the contrary, that it is the rich and powerful nations that start wars more often than the poor do.

In the final section of this book the author analyzes different kinds of conflict resolution and types of bargaining. He illustrates a wide variety of types of resolution, using the history of how conflicts over the locations of county seats in the United States were settled. He concludes with hope for the peaceful resolution of international conflicts through reason, with conflict seen as normal and peace as not the absence of conflict but the central aspect of conflict.

Interpersonal Conflict Joyce L. Hocker and William W. Wilmot. Dubuque, Iowa: William C. Brown, 1985.

This is another general book that is both practical and theoretical. The authors in this team teach at the University of Montana in the field of communications. Although they limit the scope of their study of conflict to the interpersonal level, that limitation appears to be scholarly modesty. Their rich overview of the nature, styles, power, goals, and tactics of conflict relates to group disputes as well as to interpersonal conflicts. These elements of conflict are examined in the first half of the book and are called "conflict components." The second half of the book deals with "conflict intervention." Intervention refers to what one can do to overcome "dysfunctional perspectives on conflict" with the use of conflict assessment, self-regulation, and different types of third-party intervention.

This is a textbook for college students. Each component and intervention is richly illustrated with cases of concrete disputes that give the reader interesting images on which to hang the ideas. Being a college text, many of the cases are from student life, such as disputes between roommates. They can be generalized, however, beyond this school setting.

The authors demystify some common images of conflict as war, explosions, mess, trial, for example. They try to substitute the image of conflict as a bargaining table where "two positive interests are connected by a promise." Bargaining is contrasted with the common, coercive method of settling conflict through warfare. "The chronic use of the military metaphor severely limits creative problem-solving."

The book is full of other wise sayings that are built on the assumption that "conflict is natural and inherent and can be regulated." It should be seen as "a problem to be solved rather than a battle to win." And "personalities don't conflict, behaviors that people do conflict."

The book's survey of conflict styles, power analysis, and techniques for self-regulation and third-party intervention are helpfully presented. The book makes the case well that "conflict reduction and peace keeping have emerged in this age as necessities for survival." The authors show how we can start to learn these survival skills.

Disputes and Negotiations: A Cross Cultural Perspective P. H. Gulliver. Ontario, Canada: Academic Press, 1979.

In a general introduction to conflict study, one question quickly arises: What about cultures other than white and North American? Do these theories and processes of conflict apply to cultures that are not white or North American? This book helps answer these questions. Gulliver makes the case "that patterns of interactive behavior in negotiations are essentially similar despite marked differences in interests, ideas, rules and assumptions among negotiations in different societies." The author is an anthropologist who worked in Africa and studied conflict resolution patterns among African people and compared them to those in North America. There are similarities in the conflict resolution processes. He also found better relations and more shared values among the African people than in the North American sample. The obvious conclusion is that North Americans can learn from African conflict resolution.

Beyond that, the book is a scholarly effort at fine definitions of conflict terminology and technical points worthy of a scholarly piece. However, the thesis stated above and the details that distinguish negotiation from adjudication and the developmental and cyclical models make the reader aware of the complexity and final limitations of theory about disputes. The point is well made that real-life cases are all different but that we can nevertheless generalize and learn from them to apply to other cases.

The main value of this study is to keep us aware that not only do other cultures share with us similar patterns of conflict resolution, we can learn to do it better by cross-cultural comparison. Another value of this study is the validation of the use of empirical case studies as compared to abstract theory, as in game theory and bargaining models.

The Mediation Process Christopher W. Moore. San Francisco: Jossey Bass, 1987.

Moore works at the Center for Dispute Resolution in Denver and is a mediator, arbitrator, and member of the American Arbitration Association. This book is a detailed study of the process of mediation, which can apply to a wide range of disputes. It is a textbook on the procedural steps of dispute resolution, and it gives more specifics than a beginning reader may want. But it is very helpful to the serious student of conflict resolution as it spends over three hundred pages on four steps of the mediation process: (1) understanding dispute resolution and mediation, (2) laying the groundwork for effective mediation, (3) conducting mediation, and (4) reaching a settlement.

A case study of a dispute between two medical doctors gives the book a concrete illustration of the dispute resolution process. The reader may wish for more such cases to enliven the text. But after one has attempted to mediate a dispute and then wonders, What do I do now? the book serves as a valuable reference for answers. For example, in the book *Getting to Yes*, Fisher and Ury tell us to bargain with our interests, not with our positions. Moore goes much farther and tells us how to find these hidden interests, why they are hidden, and the difference between direct and indirect interests.

Where other books define what conflict is and why it is important to deal with it effectively, Moore's book is all about the *process* of mediating conflict. It is a valuable reference book for those who practice mediation.

International Peace

The Politics of Nonviolent Action Gene Sharp. Boston: Porter Sargent, 1973. The hard-cover book is 903 pages; the paperback version is divided into three volumes.

Is it possible to settle international disputes nonviolently in the real world? Does nonviolence really work? Sharp has dedicated his life to proving that a fair look at history and the hard facts, like the number of war casualties, proves beyond a doubt that it works and is far more practical than violent warfare.

Argument one: "Gandhi succeeded only because Britain was basically civilized."

Answer: Torture, murder, collective retaliation, and public executions were all used on Gandhi's followers. They failed because his nonviolence had a "jujitsu" effect, which threw British violent action off balance, making it ineffective against those who were courageous, disciplined, and united enough. The cycle of violence-counterviolence is broken. Violence is only prepared for violence. Therefore, disciplined nonviolence has a chance against it.

Argument two: Nonviolence could not have worked against the Nazis.

Answer: But it did work in many instances; e.g., Norway (teacher's strike), France (the final solution was thwarted there), and even in Berlin as late as 1943 (six thousand non-Jews hit the streets to protest the arrest of their Jewish spouses; they were released in two days).

Sharp also answers many other misconceptions about nonviolent action. It is not passive. It does not take longer than violent solutions. It is not done only by saints and pacifists. It is not more Eastern than Western. It does not assume its opponent is nonviolent, nor is its use limited to the oppressed with a just cause. In fact, governments use nonviolent tactics all the time. Basic civic rights are expressed nonviolently.

At this point of civic participation Sharp limits his study. He writes for the grievance group that is left out of the basic processes of civic involvement. Also Sharp is emphatic about avoiding any religious or ideological requirements for nonviolent action. He seeks rather to prove that it works in spite of any ideology or faith stance. He clearly would rather be included in government discussions of national security than in discussions in the basements of churches. This self-limitation has the advantage of avoiding the usual easy dismissals of nonviolence as a utopian notion of religious do-gooders. But is also limits Sharp from having a clear basis for judging between just and unjust uses of nonviolent acts. For example, a government might unjustly ration food to punish its people. It is a nonviolent act, but it may be unjust. By what criteria does one say it is wrong?

However, within these limits the book is a formidable collection of well-organized structural analyses and usually ignored historical details, convincing arguments, and exhaustive references about the successes of nonviolent action. Further proof of Sharp's case is that it would take many more volumes to document the additional instances of successful nonviolent actions in Eastern Europe in 1989. Even though Sharp clearly rejects the need for visionary and normative thinking common to the church, his encyclopedic survey is most helpful to support people in the church who must confront those who doubt that international peace can be attained through nonviolent conflict resolution.

The Conquest of War: Alternative Strategies for Global Security
Harry B. Hollins, Averill L. Powers, Mark Sommer. Boulder, Colo.: Westview Press, 1989.

This book intends to show how the "abolition of war" is possible, even though "war is still taken by most people to be 'inevitable,' a permanent affliction like some incurable social disease" (p. 7). The abolition of war is possible just as the abolition of slavery and of the divine right of kings was possible, in spite of all the powerful entrenched forces and economic powers opposing it.

The authors, who are related to the World Policy Institute and the Alternative Defense Project, seek this goal by linking visionary principles with pragmatism, avoiding the "chronically vague" visions of the peace movement on the one hand and the "assiduous pursuit of the achievable compromise" of the arms-control experts on the other (p.6).

Although slavery did not require us to invent a replacement for it, warfare does. For "in its place must be established a wide range of alternative means for playing out those conflicts now carried out by warfare." These alternatives are analyzed in the book's three sections.

The first section is an examination of the wide range of global security systems that are alternatives to the current balance-of-terror policy. These systems are: the United Nations structures for peacekeeping, peacemaking, and peace-building, a world federation (the Clark-Sohn plan), minimum deterrence, qualitative disarmament, nonprovocative defense, civilian-based defense, and strategic defense. This list of security systems is a clear and helpful spectrum of the range of the options available by which we can pursue global security.

Part two deals with three vital elements to peace- keeping: verification, economic conversion away from a military economy, and international law. The last topic is presented in a special essay on international law in peace-keeping by Roger Fisher.

Part three pulls together the authors' own proposal for a Common Security System that builds on the strengths of each system analyzed in part one. Here they try to strike a balance between strategic defense which requires the least change from the current balance-of-terror policy, and the World Federation (Clark-Sohn plan), which stands little chance of acceptance as it requires so much change, namely, having nations give up some of their sovereignty. They seek a synthesis of the various policies which they call a "Common Security System." This system would build on a considerably reinforced United Nations, substitute verification for weapons, and gradually employ aspects of the other systems, including civilian-based defense.

This is a very rational and realistic approach which should make sense to rational world leaders. But given the largely nonviolent civilian revolution in most of Eastern Europe, we now have a much stronger case than they make for civilian-based defense and even civilian-based offense.

Conflict Regulation Paul Wehr. Boulder, Colo.: Westview Press, 1979.

This book seeks to interconnect some of the material scattered throughout numerous academic disciplines on conflict analysis, conflict resolution, and justice theory. Wehr, a professor of sociology and director of the Environmental Conciliation Project at the University of Colorado, notes a serious gap in our learning.

> Historians . . . normally devote chapters to the fighting stages of war and paragraphs to the termination process. There has also been a noticeable lack of scholarly interest in nonviolent resistance to tyranny, aggression and conscription for war. (p. xv)

Wehr intends to address this gap in the study of how wars are terminated and how tyranny is nonviolently resisted. He aims the study at teachers and students of peace studies and mixes reflection with action ideas and theory with practical exercises. Wehr begins by laying out a wide spectrum of theories of the origins of conflict in societies. Different theories of the origin of conflict claim that conflict is innate and structural to human societies, or that it is an aberration from a natural order, or that it is only a functional aspect of society, or that is it the result of incompatible national interests, or of poor communication. Or, finally, the origin of social conflict is that it is a natural process common to all societies, with predictable dynamics which are amenable to constructive regulation. Wehr believes in the last theory of the origin of conflict and that view suggests the direction of this study.

He lays out propositions that define the dynamics of conflict and violence and presents a helpful tool for analyzing conflict, called "mapping." Then Wehr does a similar analysis of the methods and techniques of conflict resolution, including legal deterrence, bargaining and negotiating, and third-party models of regulation.

While the analysis of conflict helps clarify the broad phenomenon of conflict in societies, the case studies that follow this analysis help a great deal to illustrate the analysis. Those case studies are of Gandhi in India, the Norwegian resistance to the Nazis, and a nonviolent action against the nuclear weapons facility at Rocky Flats in Colorado, along with a number of other actions around environmental conflicts in the western United States.

The book is an ambitious attempt to cover a very broad area of conflict regulation. It succeeds in its attempt to be a primer for students of peace studies and to encourage further study. It is helpful for readers of this book in the clear way it lays out the options in understanding what conflict in society is. Also the case studies helpfully enliven the theoretical analysis. For those who are not academically oriented, however, the book may be less useful.

Terrorism and Hostage Negotiations Abraham H. Miller. Boulder, Colo.: Westview Press, 1980.

Terrorism is an apparent exception to the usual types of warfare and thus of conflict resolution. But this helpful book shows how some of the same principles apply even in terrorist situations. It is a timely book because terrorism has become a frequent problem in recent years and requires the attention of all concerned with peacemaking. Abraham Miller makes an important contribution to conflict resolution and to the goal of saving lives in this particular form of conflict.

Miller, professor of political science at the University of Cincinnati, worked with the National Institute of Law Enforcement and Criminal Justice, U.S. Department of Justice. Thus he speaks from the perspective of the police who seek to save lives in situations of political (as opposed to state) terrorism. The basic assumption of the six essays in the book is that by understanding modern terrorism, liberal democracies can learn how to cope with its methods.

Miller seeks to give a levelheaded, nonromantic view of the dynamics and problems of terrorism and hostage-taking. He plays down the "romantic" approach of SWAT teams' storming a hostage situation and policies of non-negotiation. Although there may be last-resort exceptions, Miller says these are usually unworkable. In one illustration, the police ended up shooting at each other. Miller bases his views on four critical understandings:

1. The terrorist's goal is political power by means of the manipulation of political symbols to control the public agenda.
2. Terrorism is theater. Such acts are media events, the stepchild of technology and weapons.
3. Terrorism and hostage-taking are not zero plus games of win/lose. They are negotiable situations.
4. Terrorists are rarely suicidal, as few as 2 percent. Since they want to live, negotiations with them are possible.

The goal of saving lives can be attained more easily if one assumes these understandings and also feeds in other factors like transference, exhaustion, and timing ("throw away the clock"). If these understandings seem obvious, they are apparently not so obvious to the press, who pay too much attention to terrorism and thus assist the terrorists' goal of manipulating political symbols. If the press give terrorists too much attention, Miller believes that governments give them too little. Hence, governments are too eager to jump to nonnegotiation policies, risking lives that could be saved with a realistic understanding of the dynamics of terrorism.

This book is especially helpful in affirming that some basic tenets of conflict resolution apply even in these extreme situations. Both the police and the terrorists are human beings who can reach negotiable solutions.

Alternatives to War Keith Suter. Sydney, Australia: Women's International League for Peace and Freedom, 1986.

This book makes a strong argument for the development of citizen conflict resolution capabilities as a complement to disarmament. Suter, who heads an agency that he founded in Australia called the Trinity Peace Research Institute, argues that we cannot expect a nation to disarm generally. Nations must know that there are secure means of protecting their interests. Hence, there must be developed a system of conflict resolution that parallels steps in disarmament. The separation of disarmament and conflict resolution is, for Suter, one of the "major tragedies of contemporary history."

He presents this point effectively by using case studies of the failed Falkland Islands (Malvinas) war and the successful resolution of conflicts such as the Gibraltar and Hong Kong settlements by England and the early Panama Canal treaty settlement of the United States. The Falkland war cost England 255 lives. Argentina lost 712 soldiers. All the war attained was a status quo.

Yet while this and other wars fill news headlines, peace settlements like those mentioned above do not. Thus very few people know about them or others, like the settlements of the Beagle Canal dispute between Chile and Argentina that was settled by the Vatican. Suter calls for a mobilization of public opinion to counter the war bias of the media.

The rest of the book gives a description of the United Nations and the nongovernmental processes of resolving conflicts. It lists organizations and efforts of a growing number of conflict resolution centers.

Suter, who previously served as General Secretary of the Uniting Church of Australia's Commission on Social Responsibility, has pulled together three vital links that connect and empower the church's peacemaking mission: the church's moral voice, disarmament, and conflict resolution processes.

Organizations, Business, and Labor

Fundamentals of Negotiating Gerald I. Nierenberg. New York: Harper & Row, 1987.

This book is a good transition from general and international peace-oriented books. Such conflicts may not be one's daily concern, but organizational and work situations do involve most people in conflict every day. It could have been listed in the general category, as *Getting to Yes* was listed. Like that book, *Fundamentals of Negotiating* is a how-to guide. It is listed here, under the business category, because it has more of a how-to-succeed-in-business focus.

The writer is a lawyer and also the author of *How to Read a Person Like a Book*. He takes a broad view of negotiating and includes interactions on three levels: interpersonal, interorganizational, and international. It is a well-written and well-organized book, and it includes helpful illustrations of its basic theme: "The underlying philosophy of negotiating success is: everybody wins." Everybody wins because everybody's needs are met. It is as simple as that.

But it is complex too. Nierenberg lays out a complex three-dimensional matrix chart, which he calls the "need theory of negotiating." Seven needs (a la Maslow's need theory) are arranged in a matrix with the three levels of interaction listed above. This chart could mystify readers at first, but it is well illustrated in the appendix.

The style of the book is an upbeat, how-to-win approach based on figuring out what your opposition wants in a negotiation. You can win if you let your opponent win too by having his or her needs met. The author suggests many techniques, such as reading body language and asking key questions. There are also many helpful observations like the distinction between negotiating and playing a game or fighting a war. The goal of negotiating is not a dead competitor or even a beaten one as in a game or a war. Rather your opponent should win too. Negotiating has few rules, games have many. Negotiating does not end like a game. It goes on. Games do not. The main distinction between negotiating and games or war is that they are win/lose. Negotiating is win/win. This is a readable and helpful book if one is not put off by the feel of manipulation for success.

New Ways of Managing Conflict Rensis Likert and Jane Cubson Likert. New York: McGraw-Hill, 1976.

The title of this book may confuse the reader at first, because the book is less about conflict managing as such and more about how to run an organization. But how an organization is run sets the context for how conflicts are resolved. The goal of managing an organization in this approach is to move from a hierarchical, authoritative approach (called system 0) to an interactive influence approach (called system 4). Systems 1 through 3 are intermediate steps between the two management systems. Each is progressively less authoritarian and more interactive up to the ideal in system 4. That is, all persons in the organization are encouraged to speak up and to interact with others and thereby to influence the decisions made and also to resolve the conflicts in the organization. The authors get to managing conflicts by changing the whole management structure from a hierarchy to a democracy.

They base this approach on extensive and well-documented social science research. It is a thorough effort to pull together many studies into a coherent system (4) that uses this knowledge of human behavior in groups to guide leaders of organizations toward this system, which they say is more productive of higher quality products.

This interactive influence system is needed because here all persons take responsibility for the goals of the organization. They protect one another's worth and dignity and view their differences as creative diversity. Such a perspective is vital to solving problems and resolving conflicts. They seek to transform hierarchical power to group power by moving the power from a zero sum game to a power arrangement that benefits all in the organization.

Conflict is dealt with as a positive and necessary aspect of organizational life, if all members are involved in the interaction and influence the decisions. System 4 is built on the basic human need to achieve and feel worthwhile rather than on the human need for reward and aversion to punishment that are in turn based on fear and threat (systems 0-2).

It is a sobering thought to take this thesis to its apparently logical conclusion: that is, the need to change a whole system from hierarchy to institutional democracy in order to turn conflict from destructive conflict to creative change. The Likerts do not say this, but it seems to follow from their thesis. This book is a valuable contribution to resolving conflicts in organizations.

Managing Conflict: A Complete Process Centered Handbook Roy W. Pneuman and Margaret E. Bruehl. Englewood Cliffs, N.J.: Prentice Hall, 1982.

Pnueman and Bruehl have a highly refined and organized guide to managing conflict by managers and supervisors in organizations. The guide is for well-controlled organizations and directed only at their managers. The central goal is the organization's well-being as distinct from the good of the personnel. Whereas most books on conflict deal with the negotiating procedures themselves, this book focuses on the process that leads up to the negotiation. Negotiating comes after one goes through eight or nine prior steps.

The reason for this focus on the process leading up to negotiation is that the authors promote self-awareness and critical reconception of the conflict by the managers they are training with this handbook. They seek to guide the learner to change how the conflict is perceived. To do this, they propose tools such as Strategic Issue Analysis (SIA) and Evaluative Choice Analysis (ECA). These procedures are done step by step before parties meet to negotiate a conflict.

The manager/supervisor orientation of this book contrasts sharply with the Likert book, and tends to be rigid and hierarchical. Thus we have an ancient conflict named: Who comes first, the person or the institution? Many minor conflicts center around this big one. These last two studies state well each side of the debate. Those who side with the individual employee will prefer the Likerts' approach. Managers who want a tight ship and a highly structured process of conflict resolution may prefer Pnueman and Bruehl.

When, however, both democratization and control fail in negotiation, a third-party mediator or arbitrator may be needed between management and labor. A good introductory book to understand arbitration is this one by Robert Coulson.

Labor Arbitration: What You Need to Know Robert Coulson. New York: American Arbitration Association. 2d ed., 1978.

This practical reference manual is written by a president of the American Arbitration Association (AAA). It is a handy guide for the arbitrator, who can use it to refer to rules of arbitration, a glossary of "jargon," the code of ethics for arbitration, and many more easy-to-read pieces in the appendix which take up over half of the 168 pages of the book. The U.S. Arbitration Act and a bibliography are included also.

The first half of the book is four short chapters which introduce the labor arbitration process to people who are not familiar with it and who may discover that they "have a labor grievance." These chapters tell how to select a labor arbitrator, how to prepare for an arbitration hearing, and also about arbitration in the public sector. This manual gives a clear, simple picture of what arbitration is all about.

It is a process in which an impartial judgment of a trained, professional arbitrator assigned by the AAA is sought by disputing parties, avoiding a judicial process. This book shows how to do it and how the AAA seeks to assure professional standards. Coulson also puts labor arbitration in a larger context:

> Arbitration is more than a mechanism for coping with existing problems; it is a moral force, encouraging a spirit of cooperation which makes it possible for companies and unions to resolve problems without the agony of an adversary process. This book is dedicated to the proposition that the highest calling of mankind is the task of bringing peace and understanding to the human condition.

Those who approach conflict resolution from a moral or religious perspective could hardly fault such ideals.

Community Justice

Roundtable Justice: Case Studies in Conflict Resolution Reports to the Ford Foundation. Robert B. Goldman, editor. Boulder, Colo.: Westview Press, 1980.

The editor of this book is a program officer of the Ford Foundation who has collected and edited the seven case studies of community conflict resolutions. These cases give valuable examples of how disputes can be settled outside the judicial system. They show how complex, tedious, and long-lasting community disputes can be. The reports about these conflicts are far from tedious, however, as one is taken step by step through each case to its resolution. The variety of the cases also gives the reader a sense of the broad scope of community disputes that can be successfully dealt with outside the judicial system.

1. The dispute between the Mohawk Indians, who took over a location at Moss Lake by armed force, and the New York State authorities took three years to settle. The Mohawks demanded return of tribal lands and were ready to fight New York State police to get it. A mediator was called in, who carefully negotiated an interim settlement which granted the Mohawks trust of lands in a different location and hunting rights in another tract. There were "no big winners, no big losers," but lives were saved.

2. A grievance procedure was worked out in the California Youth Authority in which young wards of the state can settle disputes they have with the authorities without threat to the overall administration of the prison system.

3. An environmental dispute over uses of the Snoqualmie River was finally settled after a long battle. One learning is that fear—the fear that something worse will happen—motivates settlement.

4. In Forest Hills, New York, three twenty-four-story low-income apartment buildings were to be built. The neighbors protested. A young lawyer, Mario Cuomo, mediated a compromise that reduced the building heights to twelve stories.

5. In St. Louis a tenant strike in public housing units went on for two years, led by a minister, Buck Jones. Finally a teamster organizer, Harold Gibbons, helped negotiate an agreement.

6. In Atlanta the public schools had delayed integration for fourteen years, until black and white community leaders worked out an agreement.

7. In Dayton, Ohio, the Community Relations Service of the U.S. Justice Department, founded by the Civil Rights Act of 1964, sent mediators who succeeded in settling the desegregation dispute there.

In this book Westview Press and the Ford Foundation have helped begin to correct the dearth of research on dispute settlements, which rarely make headlines but provide rich learning for how conflict resolution can happen in the real world of community life.

A Manual for Resolving Large Group Conflicts The Community Boards Program, Inc., 149 Ninth Street, San Francisco, CA 94103, 1986.

This manual is representative of other practical and helpful pieces produced by Community Boards, a community or neighborhood justice center for dispute resolution. Other step by step guides can be ordered from this address.

Community Boards is an organization that mediates neighborhood disputes and trains mediators, as well as publishing useful, hands-on materials such as this. Its basic philosophy is expressed by Raymond Shonholtz in a widely circulated article published in *Mediation Quarterly*, #5, 1984. Here Shonholtz defines the gap between neighborhood harmony and law enforcement. For the law, conflict is seen as an aberration from the norm, or law, and must be avoided, contained, or suppressed. Even in traditional mental health models, conflict is viewed as deviance, acting out, and a social illness. By contrast, Community Boards views conflict not as an exception but as the norm, a normal part of individual growth and community life. When one accepts the value and importance of conflict, then disputants have an opportunity to improve and change their situation.

Community Boards emerged and developed out this assumption of the positive and normal reality of conflict and the great need in communities to settle disagreements without resort to violence, suppression, or the court system. In most neighborhoods, but especially the poor, the courts do not serve to help settle conflicts, but only to suppress what can be a source for community growth and harmony.

This manual grows out of this philosophy and out of the practical experience of the Boards' members. It defines a large-group dispute as a case that "involves multiple, identifiable and responsible parties, multiple issues, a history of conflict . . . between the sides." Such a case may be between landlords and tenants, youth and police, or two groups struggling over the use of a park.

Community Boards does not accept for mediation disputes that do not have responsible leaders or that are already tangled in the courts or government agencies, or from groups seeking a stage for publicity or a means to organize a following. The process for resolving large-group conflicts is similar to that of small-group procedures. That is, a hearing usually has four steps: telling each side's story, talking to each other, working with new understandings, and reaching agreements.

However, large-group conflicts are usually much more complex and involve many more people. In order to allow for this difference, Community Boards holds prehearing caucuses with each party to firm up each group's leadership and to clarify its case. Then when the mediation hearing happens there is a minimum of confusion about who is rightly speaking for whom and what rightly represents the positions that can be negotiated into an agreement.

The Manual gives a number of checklists and levelheaded advice on what to do and what to avoid in mediating a large-group dispute. Like other publications from Community Boards, this piece is a vital contribution to conflict resolution that arose from neighborhood grass roots.

Taking Charge/Managing Conflict Joseph B. Stulberg. Lexington, Mass.: Lexington Books, 1987.

The author is a professional mediator and professor of management at Baruch College. His mediation experience comes through in this book as he explains with great authority what to do and what never to do when one tries to mediate a dispute. He has gotten the mediation process down—even to sets of acronyms, as if to remind himself and his readers what to do next in a mediation.

For example, the mediator can assess the right entry point to a dispute by remembering the word PRIORTO. This acronym stands for Parties, Resources, Issues, Options, Rules, Time constraints, and Outcomes. By remembering this one word, the mediator can have a mental checklist by which to enter the process of mediation.

The second code word is COMMIT. It stands for Commitment of parties to mediation, Organizational resources, Mediation is appropriate, Matters are ripe for discussion, Incentive exists, Talents of mediator exist.

The third acronym is BADGER. This stands for Begin the discussion, Accumulate information, Develop the agenda and strategy, Generate movement, Escape to separate sessions, and Resolve the dispute.

If the reader is put off by this clever use of acronyms, he or she can still benefit from the experience of the author, for there are many more pieces of helpful advice in the book. For example, take Stulberg's definition of a mediator's job and qualifications. The job is simple: "Get parties to agree to terms that resolve the dispute." The qualifications are demanding: the mediator must be neutral, impartial, objective, intelligent, flexible, articulate, forceful, persuasive, empathetic, a good listener, imaginative, respected, skeptical, honest, patient, persevering, and have a sense of humor and access to resources.

Another example of the author's experience is his answer to the question of whether one should COMMIT to mediate a dispute between unequal parties. His answer is, "It depends." It depends on a complex analysis of factors that are a great deal more obvious than the usual stereotypes of the powerful and the powerless. Nevertheless, if it becomes clear that one party is determining the outcome, the mediator is advised to withdraw quietly from the dispute lest she or he be party to a sham justification of the power imbalance. Wise words from a professional.

Church in Mission

At the Heart of the Whirlwind John P. Adams. New York: Harper & Row, 1976.

This personal account of mediating social conflicts by a social activist covers his involvement from the Milwaukee fair-housing marches of 1967 to the Wounded Knee confrontation of 1973. In between are Adams' first-hand accounts of the church's presence through him in these conflicts: Gary, Indiana (election disturbances); Jackson, Mississippi (racial bombing); Memphis, Tennessee (King assassination); Washington, D.C. (Poor People's

Campaign); New York (Black Manifesto); Kent State and Jackson State (killing of students); and Miami (national party conventions disturbance).

In these conflicts, Adams represented the United Methodist Church and the National Council of Churches of Christ as a mediator, communicator, and liaison between warring groups. Looking back over his experience in the disputes, Adams sees the role of the church to be one of brokering and facilitating. The church should perform not only in a "national disaster" but also in a "social disaster." He says, "I became convinced that in our society the church does not need to be a protest movement in and of itself . . . but support those who present their grievances." "Sometimes all that is required is to be present and to be identified as 'impartial observers' to prevent useless confrontation."

Some will question his view that the church need not always be an activist or an advocate. But he makes a strong case for the role of mediation in which the "truth-giver" and "reality tester" helps defuse the "object—dehumanization" which is the psychological condition that prepares one to be able to kill. The go-between can build the trust of both sides and can prevent explosions of violence by doing many things, from simply observing to actually writing the terms of negotiation.

Adams vividly describes how the church can perform this special role to prevent violence but also help the oppressed to be heard. He rejects the easy way out suggested by slogans like "I am more aware than I can bear," or quotations from Jesus like "I am the way," which is distorted into "I am the way out." Rather, the church has a unique go-between role to play. Sometimes that role may be to play scapegoat so that two warring groups can begin to talk to each other.

Adams comes off as a tireless worker, especially when he represented the NCCC at Wounded Knee, where he traveled time and again through a raging battlefield in order to save lives threatened by the government and vigilante responses to the Indian takeover of a trading post.

The book is a reminder of the nonstop frenzied, sleepless nights and restless days in the sixties. It also reminds us that we still "have to fight for non-violence." It is a hard battle, and one that is often misunderstood by the press and by both sides in a dispute. But the case is well made for the church's role as a mediator.

Repairing the Breach: Ministering in Community Conflict Ronald S. Kraybill. Scottdale, Pa.: Herald Press, 1981.

Kraybill is the former director of the Mennonite Conciliation Service in Akron, Pennsylvania. He has written a book for church people from a Mennonite perspective, but one that is useful to others who are committed to peacemaking. It begins with a Bible study, showing how the Bible calls for human reconciliation throughout. He goes on to show how the early church as a pacifist church sought the same goal as the center of the

Christian life. Then he argues that conflict ministries are at the heart of the church's life and mission today as well.

But the focus is not on dealing with the church's internal conflicts. Rather the mission is directed out of the church. It is a mission of mediation or peacemaking between groups, between individuals, and within groups. Half of the book deals with group conflicts in which the different roles of ministering are spelled out and well illustrated with actual conflict cases of group conflicts. These roles are: observer, legitimizer, advocate, resource expander, and mediator.

The section on conflict between individuals gives practical skills, techniques, and procedures for settling disputes between people. Included here is a clever list of eight ways to turn disagreements into feuds. They are attitudes and actions to avoid, but are all too common in the usual way we deal with conflict. (1) Fear conflict, (2) be vague, (3) assume you know all the facts, (4) give the burden of reconciliation to your opponent, (5) grab any evidence that supports your side, (6) judge your opponent's motives, (7) go for a win/lose outcome, (8) pass the buck of decision-making to others.

The mediation procedure has a four-step process that is especially helpful: Introduction, Storytelling, Problem-solving, and Reaching agreement. The book concludes with a description of a number of successful mediation programs and an annotated list of resources and organizations. This 95-page resource is written out of Kraybill's extensive experience in conflict mediation and out of a deep spiritual commitment to empowering the church to do its peacemaking role in the world. It is a special combination of practical techniques, vivid illustrations, and an earnest dedication to reconciliation as the way of Christ.

Peacemaking: The Journey from Fear to Love Ronice E. Branding. St. Louis: CBP Press, 1987.

Ronice Branding describes her life as a "rather ordinary middle-class, suburban existence" (p.54). She is a mother of four, yet she has found time to be a peacemaker and to use her "ordinary" life experience to connect peacemaking to the experience of other "regular" churchgoers. She assumes that we in the church would also be peacemakers if we were not blocked from being peacemakers. The main block is fear.

Her opening words are "We are a people living in a siege of fear." She makes her case well that fear rules us spiritually, in our personal relations, and in our social order, where we worship at fear's altar "sanctified by weapons and fortified walls" (p.15).

Even though the Bible repeatedly assures us to "fear not," we faithlessly count on vast security systems, from padlocks to star wars in order to appease our fear. Our spiritual being is directly connected to our physical doing, so we must start by dismantling the "vast web of fear that spins out from spiritual poverty . . . to unjust systems and nuclear weapons" (p.41).

Branding's goal is to begin where "the regular churchgoers" are in their faith, coax them beyond this fear into love and deeds of justice in solidarity with the poor. How? She covers every base: education, lifestyle change, community service, for example, as well as seeking to change the conditions that lead to war and poverty, through voting, advocacy, community organizing, networking, public protest, prayer, and resistance.

The last third of the book is dedicated to patient, practical ways of peacemaking in congregations. Recognizing that there is much resistance, even hostility, to peacemaking, Branding persistently seeks out the common ground of Christian faith between activists and patriots with whom she seeks "to lessen fear by restoring true security" (p. 116). This task includes respecting differences, meeting people where they are, patience, confidence, vision, empowerment, and learning the skills of conflict resolution. These all add up to a very down-to-earth but well-written journey of an "ordinary" Christian who is moving from fear to love.

Church: Internal Conflict

Generation to Generation: Family Process in Church and Synagogue
Edwin H. Friedman. New York: Guilford Press, 1985.

The way we deal with conflicts in churches and synagogues and in families depends on our overall perspective or model of how they work. Friedman seeks in this book to replace the individual counseling model with a model of the whole family system in which the individual, family, and church/synagogue are seen as a whole system rather than as isolated parts. The author is a rabbi and therapist who believes that a systemic, family approach to relationships in congregations helps pastoral counselors and religious leaders to explain and to deal better with the conflicts in counseling in all these systems.

The book lays out in a rich and complex way what effective functioning means on all three levels from a systems perspective. It avoids treating individual pathology. Since conflicts result from the whole system, treatment and conflict resolution require one to deal with the whole system rather than individual personalities.

Five concepts are basic: the identified patient, homeostasis, differentiation of self, the extended family field, and emotional triangles. Instead of focusing on individual problems, a mediator looks at the whole family or church system of relationships, coaching persons to seek differentiation throughout the relationship that can be a problem because it is "stuck together." People who are self-differentiated can then "be together" rather than being stuck together.

They will always seek homeostasis, that is, a balance of organizational principles to preserve the relationship. An emotional triangle is an unproductive attempt to balance a relationship by attacking a third person or thing. However, such triangles need to be untangled in counseling by includ-

ing the whole extended family. The book takes family systems theory into
the whole congregation by way of the clergy, who must learn to think in
systems terms. For example, when a house plumbing system breaks down
it is not just a single leaking pipe. That individual leaking pipe (the identified patient) is not the problem. It is the whole system that is broken and
the whole system must be repaired.

This detailed and wise book is a critical resource for conflict resolution
because it introduces systems thinking and action into conflict in families
and congregations. It goes so far as to excuse the individual, identified
patient even if that person is acting out in bizarre ways. The clergy do not
treat that individual but rather coach other family or related persons to separate themselves (get unstuck) and give paradoxical feedback to the "identified patient" that breaks the conflictive cycles in the system.

Excusing that person who acts out will be hard work for people who for
centuries have thought in individual terms of sin and salvation. If Friedman
states his case too strongly, it is a good corrective nonetheless, for all the
"pipes" are members of the same body and are connected to each other.
Disputes must be solved in the whole system or they will break down again
in other places.

Church Fights: Managing Conflict in the Local Church Speed Leas
and Paul Kittlaus. Philadelphia: Westminster Press, 1977.

Church Fights is a miniclassic in the field of church personal and interpersonal conflict resolution. It sets the terms for the discussion and limits
the battlefields for what really is a managable conflict. The most helpful part
of the book is the authors' way of framing a church fight so that we are dealing with a fight that can be resolved. For example, they distinguish between
personal and interpersonal conflicts on the one hand and "substantial" conflicts on the other. The first two are conflicts within an individual and
between individuals and are not, as such, church fights. They are dealt with
in therapy and counseling, not with the conflict resolution process laid out
in this book. It is not bad feelings or anger that makes a conflict, but rather
behavior that blocks another person from meeting his or her needs.

Leas and Kittlaus spend a number of chapters making such distinctions
before they actually present the conflict resolution process. And this is helpful because their process works on real, "substantial" church fights, not on
such "nonconflicts" as the fear of impending doom, a situation where one
party has walked out or withdrawn from others or where there is simply
a lack of planning. There must be at least two forces trying to occupy the
same space at the same time—the authors' definition of conflict. There must
be at least two sides that are willing to do battle. If one side pouts in the
corner, there is no substantial conflict.

So they have limited the field considerably to what really is a church fight.
It must be a substantial church fight. There is more precise definition yet.

The authors distinguish between collaborative and noncollaborative strategies. Noncollaborative strategies are ways disputants behave, such as avoidance and repression, that result in costs much greater than cost of conflict faced and dealt with. Still we do not really have a conflict unless at least two parties will collaborate enough to "do battle."

Finally, we have winnowed out a lot of confusion in the church to a real substantive conflict in which two or more people will openly fight. Another distinction is made earlier by the authors. That is whether or not a third party will be called in to help manage the conflict. They like to use the term "referee"—a disinterested party who insists on the disputants following the rules of the process. A contract is let, data is gathered, substantive issues are defined, a second collaborative contract is drawn up. Then a process similar to other mediation procedures is employed: define problems, set objectives, brainstorm solutions, select solutions, develop strategies, and implement and evaluate them.

This process may seem cut-and-dried as I have presented it. Indeed, there is a two-page graphic chart that lays it all out in the back of the book. But the book does not read this way. It is full of wise observations, such as, the more conflict, the more stable an organization, or properly managed conflict is conflict continually managed.

By limiting church fights to substantive, collaborative, contracted negotiation, usually with a referee, the authors have given us a very rational scheme by which to manage conflict in the local church. However, such rational schemes are not highly valued in some cultures (see chapter 7). To employ the conflict resolution process only on "substantive" conflicts is to risk a value judgment on other conflicts, such as interpersonal conflicts. Do the authors mean to say that the latter conflicts are not substantive? It might be less risky to say that the authors are limiting their process to conflicts that can be solved by their process. That may seem redundant, but it avoids the feeling that they are dismissing all but substantive conflicts. We do have to deal with all conflicts whether or not they are personal, interpersonal, or fit this rational process.

Moving Your Church Through Conflict Speed B. Leas. Washington, D.C.: Alban Institute, 1985.

Leas begins with this description: "This is a how-to book. The reader will find some theory, but not much" (p.7). He writes as a conflict management consultant with fourteen years' experience in "how to" help local churches to work through conflict. He is a no-nonsense guide who knows all about the fears and realities of fights in the church and our usual efforts to squelch conflict, to tolerate cranks, and to rush to fire the pastor.

His alternative is a rational process whose application depends on which of five levels a conflict has come to. The ultimate goal of this process is reconciliation. But since that is more in God's hands than ours, we aim toward the subgoals of fear reduction, clear decisions, opportunity for all to decide, and learning conflict management skills, guidelines, and issues.

In order to do this, Leas lays out a helpful analysis of the levels of conflict. The first level sees conflict as a *problem to solve*, where reason and collaboration allow members to find common solutions. The second level sees conflict as a *disagreement*, where the issues become more serious. Members may begin to distance themselves from each other, act cautiously, and seek self-protection. The third is a *contest*, where self-protection is replaced with the goal of winning, factions develop, and distortions of language and issues begin. The fourth is conflict in a *fight/flight* pattern, where winning turns to hurting or doing away with the opponent. Ideology replaces reason. On the fifth level the conflict is *intractable*. It has "run amok." People seek to destroy each other. They have lost even enough control to stop fighting.

Leas then takes the reader through conflict on each level and examines what we should do to reduce fear and move to problem-solving and clear decision-making. Each level is approached differently. On level one we can move directly to defining the problem, gather data, and seek and choose solutions. At level two we must reduce fear, build trust, and empower members with communication skills before we get to problem-solving. At three, people may not have patience for skills training, but still need help identifying their interests and deciding how decisions are to be made. At four, a neutral, outside consultant is essential as local leaders have, by now, taken sides and cannot manage the conflict. But it is important to go by the book of established rules in the church to reduce the fear of chaos. At level five, outside authorities are needed to keep the warring parties apart.

Leas gives more good advice in special conflict situations and in a case study of a conflicted church. This is an excellent book from the real world of a conflict management consultant who has seen it all. His idea of distinguishing levels of conflict works well and can be applied to conflicts beyond the local church, but he avoids this as well as theory and theology. As he says, "This is a how-to book."

When Good People Quarrel: Studies in Conflict Resolution Robert S. Kreider and Rachel Walter Goossen. Scottdale, Pa.: Herald Press, 1989.

"That's fine theory, but what about real-life conflicts?" This book is the answer to this question which is often put to authors who write only about the theory of conflict resolution. It is a case study book, with almost 176 pages of cases of conflicts in families, churches, schools, and communities. Almost all of them are related to the Mennonite Church. Only the last few pages have conflict theory, and here it is up to the reader to apply the theory to all the cases. The cases and the theory are kept separate.

The conflicts are not resolved in the book. So the reader must try to figure out how to resolve them with or without the brief lists of theories of conflict resolution. Instead the authors say: "This volume invites the reader to find ways of resolving the little wars among and around us" (p.16). However, the cases are useful in real conflicts and can be used to practice resolution. Kreider is an active Mennonite leader who just retired as professor of peace studies from the Kansas Institute of Peace and Conflict Resolution. All the book says about Ms. Goossen is that she wrote another book with him.

This resource book of cases also has many Bible stories of conflicts and questions for discussion throughout. This book is a helpful collection of cases.

The Contentious Community: Constructive Conflict in the Church
John M. Miller. Philadelphia: Westminster Press, 1978.

This short book is structured around six chapters and six polarities within the local church that cause conflict and contention. But such contention is normal. If Christians could accept it, "they would discover that it augments, rather than threatens, the community of Christ."

The polarities that get us into fights are: Idealism versus realism. This is not only a source of conflict, it is a part of us all. Even Jesus was both idealistic and realistic. Both the idealism of youth and the realism of adults are valued, but not the cynicism of either.

Hard- versus soft-core Christianity: Both are necessary. Hard on sin, soft on sinners. Like a pineapple, "there can be no sweet outer ring without a pulpy hard inner core" (p. 50).

The fortress versus the front line: Should the church be a tender fortress on the defensive or a tough army on the offensive? It has been both in history. The first five hundred years were an advancing front line, then a thousand years in a defensive fortress of the Middle Ages. Then it returned to the front line in the world. The division now is between fortress mainline suburb and front line urban and militant conservatives. We must choose. Either choice is war.

The "arrived" versus the "arriving" polarity as a source of church conflict is about members who know they are saved and those who wonder or think they may be on the way. Even though it is a subjective judgment, the church must decide who can and who cannot be members, leaders, teachers of the faith. It's a tough choice, requiring, like marriage, great toleration.

God's democracy versus God's bureaucracy is about church politics. This polarity is about how decisions are made and carried out. Three forms of church government—episcopal, congregational, and presbyterian—are spelled out. Many conflicts are inherent in these political decisions.

"The spotless bride versus the arbiter of society" polarity lays out church abstinence or involvement in society and opts for a middle ground between purity from or identity with society.

This book appears to be a series of sermons full of clever, even cute, sayings, some quite distracting (like "owwwwww-eeeeeee!" p. 31). But it deals realistically with these polar sources of church fights. The author concludes

with the confident hope that "God will not leave himself without witness."
The church has and will survive its battles.

**When the Saints Come Storming In: What the Bible Says About
Friction in the Fellowship and How to Resolve It** Leslie B. Flynn.
Wheaton, Ill.: Victor Books, 1988.

Leslie Flynn is the Pastor of Grace Conservative Baptist Church,
Nanuet, New York. As "holy wars" of TV evangelists made headlines in
1987, Flynn sought to look at "great church fights" (the book's original title)
in the Bible, particularly in Acts and Paul's epistles, to show how churches
can "turn their internal skirmishes into training grounds for victory"
(Preface, pp. 8-9). This readable book, written from a fundamentalist perspective, begins by saying, "Through the centuries the church of Jesus
Christ instead of majoring in communion, has often muddled in contention."
Yet, though such conflicts are inevitable, they can be destructive or "they
can be a constructive force for uniting the body of Christ." Flynn uses a
sermonic style with many illustrations and graphic images to make his
point: Like two porcupines in the cold woods, we in church need but keep
needling each other. "Fortunately we have the ultimate healer of all church
rifts who is the God of peace."

How does God heal our conflicts? Flynn wisely goes to the Bible for the
answer. The church's first recorded dispute was the slighting of widows of
Grecian Jews. "It faced the problem squarely and charitably, so that out
of trouble came triumph." He points out how Hellenic Jews were appointed
to serve the widows—a conciliatory gesture. Flynn also packs the book with
catchy phrases, like "problems should be brought up, not bottled up."

Other "great church fights" that are expounded on are: Peter's rebuke
by Paul (Galatians 2) for returning to dietary laws; circumcision and the
Jerusalem Council (Acts 14—15:1-2); Paul and Barnabas over including
John Mark in the missionary team (Acts 15:36-41); Paul and the Corinthian
factions (1 Corinthians 1).

Each of the battles is resolved one way or another, and Flynn draws learnings from how they managed conflicts to help us do so in the church today.
We can solve our church conflicts: by facing conflict, not avoiding it; by seeing and listening to all sides; by being firm and courageous in our beliefs
as Paul was in his rebuke of Peter; by parting company; and by exhorting
each other to see each faction as complementing each other.

Flynn also expounds on the famous Matthew 18 passage, the three-step
conflict resolution process: confront the offender, take friends, take it to the
whole church, but not to the courts (1 Cor. 5:6), finally banish from the
church "in order to bless."

He deals with "potshots" and firing of ministers and with strong and
weak Christians. The conflict between Euodia and Syntyche in Philippians
4 is patronizingly titled "Ladies Get Your Act Together." Third John 9–10

is a case of conflict around an autocratic boss and the need to serve each other in the church in a spirit of humility.

Flynn's illustrations of battle are often taken from the fundamentalist church leaders: Bill Bright, Tony Campolo, Harold Ockenga, Carl McIntyre. Their conflicts are compared to those of Paul and Barnabas and Peter and Paul. This may not impress nonfundamentalists, but there is a certain humanity to it, even if the reader does not share Flynn's admiration or biblical comparisons.

The strength of this book and the correction to liberal opponents is Flynn's strong reference to the Bible. We can learn from that and from his lively, readable style. His assumptions about fundamentalist absolutes, converting Jews, patronizing women, and cute phrases are hard to take. But the book is a useful Bible study, even though this writer disagrees with much of it.

Resolving Church Conflicts: A Case Study Approach for Local Congregations G. Douglas Lewis. New York: Harper & Row, 1981.

The best part of this book is the clear, well-composed, and simple theological foundation that it gives for conflict resolution in the Christian church. While other books have developed more detailed foci on conflict processes (for example, *Church Fights*) or on the psychology of conflict (e.g. *Generation to Generation*), this work is a helpful, general combination of (1) Christian theology, (2) process, and (3) case studies on church fights.

1. The theological overview of church conflict includes, for example, Lewis' answer to a common belief about conflict in the church: "If we could be better Christians and love one another, we wouldn't have all this conflict." Lewis counters this with a vivid scriptural analysis of Matthew 5:43–48 about loving your enemies and becoming, like God, all-inclusive (*teleios*), rather than depending on the usual translation of becoming "perfect" like God. This means that we are called to affirm all persons, not only those who are like us. In fact, we need our "enemies" so that we can grow toward all-inclusiveness. They help us grow by challenging our intentions and limitations.

Jesus himself was so challenged internally by the temptations of the devil and externally by his disciples on the meaning of his Messiahship. He was able to define his role as Messiah as distinct from a magician or a political savior. But he had severe conflicts in doing so.

Also in the church, the internal and external conflicts are not only inevitable, they are necessary and good because they help us grow toward full inclusiveness.

2. The process principles offered by Lewis for resolving church conflicts are useful:

(a) Help others feel better about themselves. This gives a personal power base, not necessarily a better power position.

(b) Strive for effective communication.

(c) Examine and filter assumptions.

(d) Identify goals, finding what is wanted rather than judging why.

(e) Identify the primary issue rather than being a "solutionizer."

(f) Develop alternatives for goal achievement rather than relying on the common approach: "There is only one way, and it won't work."

(g) Institutionalize conflict management processes.

3. The case studies that Lewis presents are very recognizable conflicts in the church. Such cases are used in the first part of the book to illustrate the theoretical points there. In the second part of the book the cases are posed for the reader to solve. This is a challenging way to demand that the reader use the theory to resolve the conflicts posed in the cases.

Creative Conflict in Religious Education and Church Administration
Donald E. Bossart. Birmingham, Ala.: Religious Education Press, 1980.

Donald Bossart has made a substantial and scholarly contribution to the field of conflict study in the church. This could be said about part one of the book, on basic principles. But he has added part two, on utilizing conflict in church education, and part three, on specific procedural suggestions. There is plenty here to absorb.

The scholarly contribution is found in his summaries of a vast number of writers in many fields. In fact, the book reads like a doctoral dissertation, rewritten for the public. This may not be the case, but the reader is quickly assured that Bossart has done his homework, as he quotes source after source, from Kurt Levin to UNESCO documents. Yet he does make his own contribution as well.

Two key themes stand out in part one, where Bossart defines conflict sociologically, psychologically, and theologically. One theme is constructive or creative conflict, as opposed to destructive conflict. He compares creative conflict resolution to creative thinking. Conflict prevents stagnation, arouses motivation to solve problems, stimulates curiosity and interest. But to be creative, conflict must be dealt with consciously and with a sense of power and self-worth.

Self-worth is the second major theme. Bossart makes a strong case for self-worth in conflict resolution. He says that it is the "tap root" and "central factor in the dynamics of power and conflict." "A positive sense of self-worth creates a constructive power base for behavior which enables a person to influence his/her behavior as well as that of others in pursuit of basic goals." He compares negative and positive self-worth. The former makes a negative projection, reacts defensively in win/lose processes, then becomes destructive conflict.

Positive self-worth projects positive value on others and seeks win/win solutions. That is constructive conflict. Self worth frees one's energy for healthy collaboration rather than wasting energy on internal conflicts. Thus, conflict can empower people if they are unified by a sense of positive self-worth. Then they use conflict and diversity collaboratively. In a chapter on conflict in church growth, Bossart suggests a key to growth is utilizing diversity.

In part two he focuses on Christian education. After a summary of development theorists, he poses a process that deliberately uses conflict in instruction. It is a four-step process summarized as: orientation, conflict, emergence, and reinforcement. Conflict can be structured to enhance self-acceptance and reconciliation. This connects us back to Bossart's theme of self-worth as central to creative conflict resolution.

In part three he applies all this to specific procedures in the congregation and in religious education programs. He summarizes Kittlaus and Leas (*Church Fights*) and applies that process to churchwide conflicts. He gives a weekend learning lab for youth based on the four-step process listed above.

This is a truly comprehensive study. It can get heavy for those eager to get to developing skills in conflict resolution. But it is excellent as a background summary for hearty readers.

Curricula

When You Disagree. . . . Mennonite Conciliation Service. 21 South 12th Street, Akron, Pa. 17510, 1987.

The Role Play Book: Thirty-two Hypothetical Situations for the Practice of Interpersonal Peacemaking Skills Ron Mock, editor. Mennonite Conciliation Service, 21 South 12th Street, Akron, Pa. 17510, 1988.

The first piece is an excellent basic course in conflict resolution. It is a looseleaf notebook with six cassette tapes in the binder and eight sections, including self-management, communication and group skills, mediation, group intervention, and role plays. Included are worksheets and other aids used in the MCS training course.

The first three sections deal with general framing of conflict, how to be aware of one's own style, and communication skills. The "foreign language of caring" is an excellent reminder that we often learn to speak in competitive ways that provoke rather than resolve conflict.

The fourth section deals with four stages of the mediation process as named by MCS: introduction, storytelling, problem-solving, and agreement. Section five, on group skills, covers basic group dynamics and how we usually handle conflict in congregations—that is, the bad habits we should lose and good ones we should practice. One good habit is inviting disagreement as contrasted to avoiding it or spiritualizing it, as if good Christians never disagreed. A piece on power and powerlessness makes the valuable point that the powerlessness of unfulfilled hopes is normal and inevitable, but the powerlessness of invalidation is not normal or inevitable and can be changed.

The dominant learning method in this form of mediation is role-playing.

A number of role plays are included in this basic course, but there is always a use for more role plays of sample conflicts. They are provided by the *Role Play Book*.

This is a collection of well-tested role plays used in mediation training, mostly in a Mennonite context. They are categorized under general, interpersonal, family, congregational, workplace, neighborhood, and victim-offender conflicts. The appendix contains a sample script of a mediation and an explanation of the role play as a learning tool.

The role plays are easy-to-use, but the users have to mediate their own resolutions, as none are given. Nor are there theories about conflict. This is only a supplement to the basic training manual, *When You Disagree. . . .*

Managing Intercultural Negotiations: Guidelines for Trainers and Negotiators Pierre Casse and Surinder Deol. Sietar International. Washington, D.C.: 1985.

The authors of this training manual are themselves intercultural: Casse is a Belgian sociologist and Deol is an Indian and a training officer for the World Bank. They use a "Zen approach" that points to negotiating but encourages the trainee to search for the answer. They admit their "style may seem strange, quotations esoteric and exercises ambiguous." But this is all intentional, as a way of encouraging creativity and nurturing curiosity. We negotiate all the time (we have no choice, it is life), but we can improve it, especially intercultural negotiation. Our survival may depend on it. There are ambiguous points here and many disconnected gaps. But the manual is well ordered and quite readable.

The authors define negotiations as "the process by which at least two parties with different cultural values, beliefs, needs, and viewpoints try to reach agreement on a matter of mutual interest." They refer to Carl Jung's psychology often, for example, his four temperaments, which they call a psychic compass as adapted by Ira Progoff. The authors relate these to four negotiating styles and develop a long (ten-to-twelve hour) experience of self-assessment and exercises that help participants to master their own preferred style or to change to another style.

There are ten sessions (or chapters), which vary in time from three hours to one day. The self-assessment form and worksheet is a common tool in most chapters. Each session has aims, objectives, a process of three or so learning exercises, and a conceptual framework that includes three or four "inputs" or theory from various experts, including themselves.

The self-assessment worksheets are valuable learning tools in that participants chart their own learning needs and growth. Small-group experiences and plenary sessions are used well, along with case exercises. For example, you believe that a long-handled broom could help a Third World village. How do you negotiate it? Small groups are given time to work out plans, strategies, and so on.

The book is a rich collection of educational learning experiences, charts, and summaries of other writers.

Dealing with Conflict in the Congregation Presbyterian Peacemaking Program. DDS 919-85-767.

This seventeen-page piece has four good one-hour study sessions to introduce conflict resolution in a congregation. It begins with a "think piece" overview of how a church can deal with conflict, and gives eleven working principles. The introduction tells how the early church, in Acts 15, dealt with conflict. Session 1 builds on the Bible study which says faith (past), hope (future), and love (present) are essential for conflict resolution. Session 2 has us list the benefits of conflict and create a positive and a negative resolution of three conflict stories. Session 3 lays out the five styles of managing conflict and their advantages and disadvantages. Session 4 practices negotiation of a conflict over a new church building program. Ten suggestions are listed for how best to negotiate.

The piece ends with an annotated bibliography. This is a well-organized and good introductory learning tool for beginners.

Conflict Management: A Curriculum for Peacemaking Elizabeth Loescher. Cornerstone: A Center for Justice and Peace, 940 Emerson Street, Denver, CO 80218, 1983.

This classroom set of seventeen lesson plans is meant for children, to supplement "basic" course work. It is written for public or private classrooms. No religious material is involved. But rather than being a "frill" course, it intends to be a substitute for constant disciplining. It helps students be responsible for their own conflicts (to their own problems). It is a basic course in conflict management and touches on these basics with clever learning experiences: seeing that there are many sides to truth, brainstorming, conflict survey, "I" messages, communication skills, listening.

The most interesting learning experiences include the telling of "Jack and the Beanstalk" from the Giant's point of view. Then Jack and the Giant solve their problem. The Conflict Survey is useful, as is the Robot, which tries to teach us that we aren't Robots but are responsible. The material shifts gears at lesson 14 to global education dealing with hunger and global problem-solving. It ends with a Consensus Model of Conflict Reduction, which gives a good two-page summary of a helpful process.

This is a useful piece for children and youth, with some helpful ideas for adults. But in either case, a creative teacher who can invent imaginative uses of this material is required.

Mediator's Handbook: Peacemaking in Your Neighborhood Jennifer Beer, editor and chief writer. Also Eileen Stief, Charles Walker. Friends Suburban Project, Box 462, Concordville, Pa 19331, 1984.

This sixty-four-page booklet is, as it says, a handbook, as opposed to a theoretical piece, curriculum, or essay. It is a practical guide for a mediator of community, neighborhood, or family disputes. It intends "to prepare those who are participating in the FSP training program." But it is useful beyond that, as it offers criteria for evaluation of mediation skills and procedures for determining the quality of one's skills.

There is considerable advice about what to do and not to do as a mediator and how to do the right thing. But this is advice from the front lines and not from the ivory tower. It is good advice. For example, under the "Exchange" section (that is, when disputants have told their stories and are now going back and forth), it says, "Although airing feelings helps the mediation process, the mediators are present to guide people toward specific agreements about changing behavior, not to provide catharsis or therapy." Or, "The purpose of mediation is to reach agreement, not to determine the 'facts,' the 'truth,' etc." So the mediator is not a counselor or a judge. Rather, mediation is a unique skill, and it requires training to attain the skills laid out in this handbook.

The outline of the handbook follows the steps in a mediation from Preparation, Opening, Uninterrupted Time, The Exchange, Building and Writing the Agreement, to Closing the Mediation. An introduction, an explanation of the role play and the participatory training design precede this main body of material. An evaluation and appendixes and bibliography follow it.

This is a valuable piece in that it comes from real experience of mediation training. The reader, therefore, respects the dos and don'ts. It is not a step by step training manual telling the leader what to do, like some from Community Boards. Nor is it religiously based, even though FSP is sponsored by Philadelphia Yearly Meeting. It's a handy handbook for mediators to refer to when they are in training and get stuck.

Conflict Resolution Workshop: For All God's People Conciliation Task Force. Judicial Process Commission, Genesee Ecumenical Ministries, 121 North Fitzhugh St., Rochester, NY 14614, 1988.

This is a notebook/manual for a "basic workshop on interpersonal skills to be used in preventing and resolving conflicts." It contains background readings, peacemaking models and a curriculum design with handouts. The design can fit into a three-hour, six-hour, or twelve-hour session. These sessions are called introductory, basic, and full workshops respectively. Likewise, the manual has three parts: learning about conflict, gaining skills, and putting conflict resolution skills to work.

The manual grew out of a criminal justice project and victim-offender reconciliation programs in upstate New York. It is used in "alternative-to-violence" training programs in schools, community groups, and congregations. It is oriented to the Christian faith, but hopes to be used by other faiths.

Simplicity is the word that best describes this piece. The steps in the workshop designs are all clearly laid out and illustrated. It is an easy-to-follow, basic introduction that touches on conflict styles, owning one's feelings, assertiveness training, and listening skills. Then it applies a six-step conflict resolution process to issues in congregations and communities. The experienced leader will recognize many of the exercises and readings from other well-known sources. The creative edge of this manual is the simple way it lays these sources out. This facilitates getting these skills out to the churches and community groups in a simple format to start people on the road to peacemaking and resolving conflict.